The Man Who Murdered My Mother

A Daughter's Journey of Seeking Justice

Tina Ann Healey

Black Rose Writing | Texas

2019 by Tina Ann Healey
All rights reserved. No part of this book may be reproduced, stored in a retrieval system or transmitted in any form or by any means without the prior written permission of the publishers, except by a reviewer who may quote brief passages in a review to be printed in a newspaper, magazine or journal.

The author grants the final approval for this literary material.

Second printing

Some names and identifying details have been changed to protect the privacy of individuals.

ISBN: 978-1-68433-288-5
PUBLISHED BY BLACK ROSE WRITING
www.blackrosewriting.com

Printed in the United States of America
Suggested Retail Price (SRP) $20.95

The Man Who Murdered My Mother is printed in Book Antiqua
Author Photo courtesy of Jean Schweiger

In Loving Memory of Donna Litchfield

The Man Who Murdered My Mother

Contents

Acknowledgment
Introduction
Chapter One   1
Chapter Two   13
Chapter Three   28
Interlude   *48*
Chapter Four   49
Chapter Five   54
Chapter Six   76
Chapter Seven   87
Interlude   *92*
Chapter Eight   93
Chapter Nine   104
Chapter Ten   117
Conclusion   125
The Star Thrower Story   128
Contact Information for Victims and Survivors   129
    of Domestic Violence and Sexual Assault
Bonus Material Part I   135
Bonus Material Part II   151

Acknowledgements

When asked who helped bring this book to life, many names came to mind. They may not be the names expected by some, but when you spend time alone with your thoughts and piles of papers, you appreciate life a little differently.

I'd first like to thank my editor, Brunella Costagliola from Kevin Anderson & Associates. You have truly exceeded my expectations and brought my work to life. You took what seemed to be an impossible situation and allowed me to accomplish what I have been trying to do for years.

To my father, who supported me through this long journey.

To my Aunt Diane, my mom's sister, for providing me with photos and information.

To Valerie, my mom's best friend and my guardian angel. Without you, there is a good chance I would not be here today.

For all of those who talked things over, read, wrote, offered comments, and allowed me to quote their remarks.

In the spirit of what kept me grounded, kept me writing, kept me inspired and kept me company all hours of the day and night and through all seasons, I want to thank all of the people who shut the door in my face. Without them, I may not have come as far as I have and continued to travel on this path. It has made me into the person I am today.

I would like to thank Joseph Bell, Esq. and David Shivas, Esq. from Bell, Shivas & Fasalo, P.C. Thank you for being intrigued enough to take my case, and for all your hard work.

With Love,
Tina

Introduction

Belleville, New Jersey
15 July 1976
Herald News.
Bail Denied Suspect in Belleville Murder
Stephen Moore, 26, was ordered held without bail Thursday, charged with the Wednesday stabbing murder of his girlfriend, a young Belleville woman. Moore was arraigned during a brief session in Belleville Municipal court before Judge Salvatore Intintola, in connection with the murder of Donna Litchfield [sic], 24,. Five hours after Mrs. Litchfield's body was found Wednesday afternoon in the full bathtub of her Brighton Avenue apartment, Moore was arrested in Surf City, near Atlantic City. The mother of a two-year-old daughter, Mrs. Litchfield [sic] was separated from her husband, said Anthony Mautone, the assistant Essex County prosecutor in charge of homicide.

Although Mautone declined to discuss a motive for the murder, early police reports said the victim tried to break off her relationship with Moore. A friend of the victim was in the apartment when Moore arrived Wednesday afternoon and began arguing with Mrs. Litchfield [sic], Mautone said.

The friend, whose identity is being withheld, left the apartment to call police, returning at the closing moments of the fatal attack, Mautone said. "She's just about an eyewitness". Absent her seeing him inflict the stab wounds, there could not be a better witness. Moore, dressed in blue jeans and a plaid shirt, made no statement during his arraignment except to curtly acknowledge the charge. The suspect's last known address was on Grove Street in Bloomfield, police said, but he was all along the West Coast over the past seven weeks. Indications are that he called the victim from San Diego and Oregon. Police found Mrs. Litchfield's [sic] fully-clothed body Wednesday bearing "at least a dozen stab wounds, including a gaping slash wound to the throat". According to Belleville police, Mrs. Litchfield [sic] had moved into the Brighton Avenue apartment about a year ago.

* * *

I was born on a day in June of 1974 and given the name Tina Ann Litchfield. When I was two years old, my mother, Donna Litchfield, was brutally murdered by her then-boyfriend, Stephen Moore. I was in the house when it happened. I don't remember that day. I don't remember my mother. I don't remember her loving embrace or her gentle kiss. I don't remember the lullabies she used to sing to me or her calming cooing. I don't remember her reassuring smile or her sweet smell. I don't remember how my name sounded when she called me, or what her last words were to me. All I *do* remember is that I have always felt like there was a huge void inside of me for having my mother taken from me at such a young age — a void that nobody and nothing will ever be able to fill.

My mother was only 24 years old when she was taken away from me. Now, almost twice her age and with two children of my own, I find myself wondering what her life would have been, had she been allowed to live it. I remember being her age; the world still seemed so big and full of possibilities. Those carefree days of youth that smelled of the Atlantic Ocean, made of walks down the Boardwalk, ice creams and funnel cakes at the pier, and Long Beach Island views promising to take your breath away at sunset — did she have enough time to experience all of that?

Throughout the years, I have spent many sleepless nights wondering about her. Would she be proud of me? Would she be happy to know that, even if I have carefully placed it in that famous "someday" drawer where so many dreams go to sleep, I still plan on taking that *National Geographic* cruise course so that I can become one of their photographers? Would she think I'm a good mother? Would she teach my daughter how to bake? Would she remind my son to put on a helmet when riding his dirt bike? Would she think I looked beautiful in my prom dress? Would she have come to my softball games when I was in high school? Would she have been happy to see me cheerlead? And what about when I had my heart broken by my first boy crush — would she have been sweet with me and told me not to worry? Would she have reassured me that nothing was ever going to hurt me after I fell and scraped my knee for the first time? Would she have let me believe in the Tooth Fairy when I lost my first tooth? Would she have cried tears of joy watching me walk down the aisle on my wedding day? Would she have spoiled my children like only a grandmother can?

These are questions that I will never be able to answer. Stephen Moore took that away from me. You see, it's not that he just took her life. He took *my* life as well, the life I had the right to live with my mother. I was supposed to have several photos with her; I was supposed to be grounded by her when I missed curfew; I was supposed to have her help me choose my wedding gown; I was supposed to see her joy when holding her first grandchild, and then her second one; I was supposed to take care of her when she reached old age. But none of that happened. What *did* happen was written in the newspapers and heard on the news:

24 November 1976.
Slayer Found Sane and Guilty
Rejecting a defense of insanity, a Superior Court jury yesterday convicted Stephen Moore of Belleville in the stabbing murder of his 24-year-old girlfriend. The judge immediately imposed a life sentence.

The jury deliberated nearly six hours at Essex County Courthouse before convicting Moore, 26, of the murder of Mrs. Donna Lee Litchfield of 19 Brighton Avenue, Belleville. Mrs. Litchfield, mother of a young daughter, was separated and awaiting a final divorce decree.

The victim died July 14 of loss of blood in her bathtub after receiving 69 cuts and stab wounds, most of them superficial, the Assistant Essex County Medical Examiner testified.

Moore never took the stand, and the defense was based solely on the claim of insanity. Judge Ralph Fusco immediately imposed a sentence of life in prison, and Moore, who mumbled and ranted throughout the trial, was led quietly from the courtroom.

Psychiatrists for both the State and defense testified Moore was a "paranoid schizophrenic."

Assistant Prosecutor Dennis Mautone, however, in summation, emphasized the facts in the case proved Moore was sane under the legal test in New Jersey: that he knew "the nature and quality of his acts."

Mautone argued Moore planned the crime by taking the murder weapon from a gas station owned by friends and taking $1,300 from his Montclair bank account to finance the getaway. Moore was about to head west when arrested in the Surf City gas station owned by Mr. Rodney C. Odell, Mautone said. Odell and his wife Jean appeared as defense witnesses and testified about Moore's mental deterioration over a seven- month period prior to the murder.

On the day before the killing, Mrs. Litchfield told Moore she did not wish to continue their relationship, another witness testified.

Yes, Stephen Moore was found guilty by a judge who rejected the defense of insanity and sentenced him to life in prison. Justice had been served. He was going to forever pay for taking my mother's life, for leaving her parents without a daughter, and for leaving me an orphan. So why am I writing this book, if we have a solved case with a convicted murderer? Because Stephen Moore escaped the maximum-security prison he had been sent to, was on the run for 5 years, and then, while in California, turned himself in at a minimum-security prison.

That's not all. His first sentence was overturned, and he was released from prison on a count of "Not-guilty by reason of insanity." You read that right. Another judge found him to be mentally insane and had him transferred to Marlboro Psychiatric, a mental institution. Later on, he was released from that facility and has spent the past few years in a private mental institution in Pennsylvania.

The day I learned about these changes in his sentence, I felt like my mother had been brutally killed for the second time—and this time, there was no hope for justice, because justice had been murdered right alongside her. How was it possible that he was able to walk away from this murder? "Not-guilty by reason of insanity." I kept staring at it. *"Not-guilty by reason of insanity."* The more I read it, the more haunting those words became to me. **"Not-guilty by reason of insanity".** I could hear them echo in my head. My temples were throbbing. My eyes burned. My teeth were clenching so hard I felt stabbing pain in my jaw. How could this be? Yes, he was insane—but not *mentally* insane, like they said. He was *criminally* insane.

That same day, I made the decision that I would spend the rest of my life trying to prevent such horrible things happening to other victims. My main goal in life now is to change this law in New Jersey that would allow another criminal to walk away like Stephen Moore. I want to turn it from "not-guilty by reason of insanity" to "*guilty* by reason of insanity". I want to make you, the reader, aware of how much injustice has been done to my mother, to her parents, to her sibling, to her friends, to anybody who loved her, and especially to me.

During my journey of seeking justice, I have reached out to virtually anybody and everybody, from lawyers, prosecutors, and judges to my state governor and even the White House. I have had more doors slammed in my face than I can count. I have encountered many difficulties in gathering official documents. Yet, I kept going; I kept making those phone calls. I kept sending those e-mails. And I always will. Nothing and nobody will stop me from making Donna's Law, "*Guilty* by Reason of Insanity," a reality.

So many people in my life have asked me why I am doing this. Why am I fighting so hard for what seems to be a lost cause? Why don't I just try to pretend like it never happened? Why don't I simply brush it under the rug and keep going about my life? Why don't I go see a psychologist instead of seeking justice? Why am I even bothering writing a book about this subject?

To them all, and to you, I answer with a simple question: Would you ever stop seeking justice if your own mother had been brutally murdered?

No. Neither will I.

Tina Ann Healey

My Mother and I

Chapter One

The month of June 1952 had been one of the hottest on record in recent years. A prolonged and extensive heat wave had hit two-thirds of the eastern states, and temperatures had reached well over 100 degrees Fahrenheit. It was so hot that a man walking down Martin Street in Bloomfield, New Jersey, was using his straw Panama hat as a portable fan, waving it back and forth near his face, while whistling notes from Rosemary Clooney's famous song, "Botch-a-Me," which was all the rage back then. Anywhere you went, you could hear people sing along as they listened to the radio: "Bah-bah, botch-a-me, bambino/Bah-bah-bo, bo, boca piccolino…"

On the last day of this excruciatingly hot month, Leo Markiewich, owner of the Sunoco gas station on the corner of Martin Street and Broughton Avenue, was celebrating with some close friends outside his home, passing Clear Havana cigars around to celebrate the birth of his first daughter, Donna Lee. He and his wife, Mary, had always wanted to have a big family. Family members had gathered there to congratulate Leo and wish his newborn daughter "многая літа" — "Mnohaja lita," which means "many summers" in Ukrainian, the language spoken by Leo and Mary (along with English, of course.)

Donna Lee was a healthy baby, weighing almost eight pounds. Although it was hard to tell from a distance, she had a full head of blonde, almost white, hair. Her eyes were an intense blue color, and as soon as her father saw her, his eyes became filled with tears of joy. While Mary got her well-deserved rest, Leo held his baby tight, softly kissing her forehead. Then he sat down on a rocking chair placed in the corner of the bedroom and, staring at his tiny little miracle, silently hoped for many more to come.

Leo had to wait seven more years to hold another newborn in his arms. Mary had several miscarriages through the years, which had devastated the couple. However, in 1958, she got pregnant again, and this time it seemed to be a successful pregnancy. Mary and Leo were thrilled. They didn't want Donna to be an only child and feel lonely; they knew she longed for a sibling. As her due date approached, Mary started experiencing severe complications that put her own life at risk. When her doctor told her that it could be a matter of whether to save her own life or the baby's, Mary did not blink once before saying, "Save my baby; don't worry about me." Fortunately, their second daughter, Diane, joined the family in January 1959, and Mary was very happy to hold her tight.

* * *

Donna was absolutely elated to be a big sister, and she took her role very seriously. She would help with Diane every chance she got, and as any good big sister would, she made it a point to learn how to change diapers and prepare bottles for feeding time. Sometimes her mother would even allow her to feed the baby. Like a proper little woman, Donna would sit on the rocking chair, her knees pressed together, elbows tight to the side, forearms stretched out, ready to welcome her little sister. She would spend hours staring at her baby sister peacefully sleeping in her bassinet, making sure to keep quiet just like her mother had told her to.

Donna and Diane

As time went by, Donna took great pride in watching her little sister grow up. They spent a lot of time together. Diane mirrored everything her big sister did: If Donna was brushing her hair, Diane wanted to do the same, no matter how clumsy she was while trying to use a hairbrush three times bigger than her little hand. At the funny yet sweet sight of Diane struggling with balancing and correctly maneuvering the hairbrush, Donna would gently take it from her, step behind her, and softly brush Diane's luscious blonde hair as the two sisters smiled at each other's reflections in the tall, narrow mirror in front of them.

Every evening as the sun set, Donna would show Diane how to properly kneel down on the floor by their bed, put both hands together, slightly bow down, and pray. Diane, who didn't know all the words to the prayers, would mimic sounds made by Donna who, seven years her senior, knew quite a few prayers. Diane always smiled when Donna, upon concluding her prayers, would ask God to always protect her little sister and all her loved ones. To Diane's eyes, Donna was nothing short of a miracle, the best big sister anybody could ever have.

Growing up on Martin Street was wonderful. It was such a great place to live. Everybody knew each other. It was a different time, really; the men still believed in politely taking their hats off when passing a lady on the sidewalk, with a subtle and gentle bow accompanied by a cordial "Good day!" When meeting a neighbor doing yard work, or just spending time outside enjoying a cold one, they would always stop by to inquire about the family and exchange opinions on the latest happenings in the world. Somehow, however, while discussing the latest on the Korean War or Eisenhower becoming President, their conversations always managed to switch focus onto Marilyn Monroe. *Those* conversations could go on and on until it was time for them to go catch up with the other husbands and fathers at the White Eagles or the Old Canal Inn and grab a few drinks.

The women took great pride in taking care of their homes and raising their children. However, when weekend evenings came, they were as ready as ever to get all dolled up, choose their finest dress, and meet with other wives and mothers to go play bingo. In reality, it was just an excuse to get together, dish some gossip about the women who couldn't make it that night, and dream of being married to Elvis Presley and traveling the world with him.

Those were times when children were free to go play in the streets, pretending to be the new soccer star or attend the most fashionable pretend tea party in the whole county. Many dollies were invited to those parties, and some of them probably hadn't seen the light of day in quite some time, judging by how dusty they were. Little girls magically transformed into princesses of far-away lands, while boys were busy protecting them from invisible pirates with their sticks-turned-swords. The sun going down and the street lights turning on were the only two signs for all the neighborhood kids to go back home, as dinner was about to be served.

* * *

Donna and Diane spent years as make-believe princesses, and they were always flattered when a neighborhood kid would bravely defend them against pretend eye-patched, wooden-legged criminals who sailed the seas and used words like "Ahoy!" How utterly impolite of them! The two sisters enjoyed walking down the street to Pulaski Park, where they used to spend hours. Donna would carefully push Diane on the swings, and the two of them would play hopscotch. They would then roll down the big hill by the park and laugh out loud when reaching the bottom.

During summertime, they loved going in the front yard and watching all the lightning bugs. What an amazing experience it was! One time, Donna challenged Diane to see how many they'd be able to catch. Diane rushed upstairs and grabbed two small glass jars from the kitchen cabinet. That night, while they both ran through the yard, laughing and giggling freely as only children can, they both were able to catch many lightning bugs, which they proudly showed to their friends who had been watching in awe. Best night ever for the Markiewich girls!

Every summer afternoon, at 4:00 p.m. sharp, the bell that all children in the neighborhood were waiting for happily rang to announce that the ice cream truck had finally arrived. At the irresistible and enchanting sound, Donna and Diane, along with all their friends, would rush to get their favorite ice cream flavors. Joe Mangioni, the ice cream truck guy, was an Italian man in his fifties. With a protruding belly that gave away clear signs of what a great cook his wife must have been, he had the thickest Jersey accent in the whole state. As sweet and charming as can be, he was always delighted to see Mary's daughters.

"Eh, *ciao bell*a! Whatcha doin'?"

"Good afternoon, Mr. Mangioni. May we please have ice cream?" Donna asked, ever so politely.

"Well, ah 'course! My pleasure, girls." Mr. Mangioni seemed to be completely oblivious to the fact that, had the girls not been from Jersey, they probably wouldn't have understood a word he was saying.

"Lemme guess: Cookies and cream for Donna and chocolate for little Diane, am I right?"

The girls smiled. He got it right every time. How was he able to do that?

"Here you go, little ladies." He added, offering them their one-scoop cups of ice cream.

Donna reached in her pocket to collect the coins so she could pay for her treat, but Mr. Mangioni stopped her before she had the chance.

"Nah, this gelato is on me, little ladies." He smiled.

"Well, that is so generous of you, Mr. Mangioni," Donna replied.

"Thank you," Diane added with that cute, adorable high-pitched voice little girls have.

"Ah, forget about it." He waved his hand back and forth as if trying to shoo a fly away. Then, before moving on to his other eager, tiny customers, he added, "Tell your mama Maria I said hello."

The rest of these afternoons were spent laughing, playing, listening to music, dancing, and running freely in the park. All the kids in the neighborhood would meet there. Among them, there was Tom Litchfield, a well-developed young man with long dark hair and green eyes. He was better known as Cookie, given his profound love for the sweet treat. Despite his best efforts to change the nickname, it stuck with him all through his school years and even into adulthood. Cookie and Donna were good friends. He was pretty cool, and kind of cute for a boy. His house was like a magnet for all the children who lived on Martin Street. Located up the hill of the same street as Donna's house, it offered all sorts of fun activities, from pool tables to dart boards. Peter and Audrey Litchfield, Tom's parents, had purchased the house in 1955 for the amazing price of $8,000. They took great care of it, as one could tell simply by looking at their front lawn, which was always the nicest one in the neighborhood. Peter took great pride in his lawn, as well as in the hard work that his entire family—including Tom and his older brother Pete—put in.

Tom and Donna used to spend a lot of time together because they both attended the same elementary school. In fact, during fifth grade, they were picked to be in a play together. Donna played the queen, and Tom was chosen to be the king. Given the prestige of both roles, all the other kids were pretty jealous of the power couple, and they tried to alleviate the wound by telling themselves that they had been picked for the parts only because they were the tallest kids in class. Truth was, they were both equally talented, and made a very good-looking couple. Tom, with his big red and white cape and crown, was the emblem of a great king. Donna was a beautiful sight for a queen, wearing a golden cape and sparkly crown.

For both Markiewich girls, the best part of summer evenings was when their mother called them up early so they could help her get dinner ready. They loved cooking with her, and Mary was always happy to share her Ukrainian culture with her daughters. Although Mary's main concern was to make sure that both Donna and Diane were raised to be American, so that they could feel at home and at ease around their peers, she still wanted to remind them of their Eastern European heritage. One way of doing so was by teaching her daughters how to cook delicious Ukrainian food, something that her own mother had taught her when she was just about Diane's age.

"What's for dinner tonight, mama?" Donna asked.

"Your favorite, my darlings."

"Pierogi?" Diane asked, jumping up and down at how happy she was.

Mary smiled while getting all the ingredients ready.

As usual, Donna was in charge of measuring and handling all dry ingredients, while Diane was tasked with mixing the wet ones. Even though she was still a bit clumsy and prone to making a mess all over the counter, Diane was improving tremendously—something both Donna and Mary were proud of. Once all the ingredients were blended together, Mary proceeded to roll the dough on a flat, floured surface, making sure not to stretch it too much to prevent it from breaking. Then, the fun part began: Donna and Diane alternated cutting the dough into circles, while Mary took care of placing a spoonful of cheese and potato-mash filling into the center of each circle. Diane lightly brushed some water on the edges of each circle, which Donna folded, creating the traditional dumpling shape. After boiling them, Donna rushed into the living room, where Leo was listening to the radio.

"Daddy, dinner is ready!" she shouted with great pride.

Growing up, Donna and Diane learned all about the importance of family. Mary and Leo strived to set a great example for both young women to follow one day. Even though certain standards might be considered a bit obsolete nowadays, Mary was happy to show her girls what being a good wife and mother was all about. "A wife's domain is the kitchen," she used to say. She was an exceptional cook. Even though, according to Leo, she could never go wrong with a meat-and-potato kind of dinner, Mary loved surprising him with lots of new and traditional recipes. At lunchtime, she and her daughters would go to the Sunoco station where Leo worked and bring him something warm to eat. That was surely one of Donna's favorite moments. She appreciated the serene look on her father's face when he saw his three ladies crossing the street carrying food so good he could smell it from afar.

"Did you add your secret ingredient, sweetheart?" Leo asked Donna in a whisper.

"You bet, Daddy," Donna replied with a warm smile, placing her right hand on her heart to symbolize love.

"Then I'm sure it'll be delicious!" Leo said, kissing her forehead.

Although Donna did not attend kindergarten, since Mary was a stay-at-home mom, she did go to Franklin Elementary School. Donna loved going to school. She was a very good student, and she took a particular interest in science.

Donna while attending Franklin Elementary

Every morning, Mary would walk with Donna the five minutes it took get from their house to Franklin Elementary. Even if it was not that bad of a walk, sometimes they would cut through Pulaski Park, stopping by Hilltop Bakery and get a little treat on the way. Opening the bakery door, Donna was overcome by the delicious smell of freshly baked bread and doughnuts.

"Good morning, ladies," the baker greeted them.

"Good morning!" they replied cheerfully.

"Donna, your warm jelly doughnut is waiting for you on the counter." The baker winked at her, pointing at a small brown paper bag sitting not too far from her.

Happy as can be, Donna and Mary left the bakery with full bellies and smiles on their faces.

After school, Donna loved attending dance classes at Miss Roseanna's. It was a very popular dance school, and virtually every kid who lived in Bloomfield went there. Donna was very talented, especially in tap and jazz. At the end of every season, Miss Roseanna organized a recital, for which her students had been preparing months in advance. Parents would attend proudly, ready to see their children showcase their potential. Donna loved getting all dressed up for the recital, and also because this was the only occasion her mother allowed her to apply some makeup.

"You are naturally gorgeous, my darling." Mary would remind her daughter, "You don't need a mask made of makeup to cover your beauty."

* * *

The Markiewich family holidays, whether Christmas or Easter, were always something to write home about. Every year, the girls got excited about Christmas Eve months in advance. It wouldn't be an exaggeration to say that they started planning it and looking forward to it the day after Easter. They used to follow the traditional Ukrainian Christmas Eve Supper, which featured a variety of Eastern European dishes but no meat. The dining table was filled with goodies: kutia, sauerkraut, pierogies, beets, mushrooms, *pampushki*, cinnamon sugar scuffles, and Christmas bread. It was food galore at the Markiewich household! Before dinnertime, a priest would stop by for a visit and bless the house. Knowing what a great cook Mary was, however, he would never leave without grabbing a few homemade cookies to enjoy on the road.

During Christmas Eve day, while the women were busy preparing the multi-course meal which featured as many as 13 dishes, symbolizing the apostles and Christ, the children were in charge of decorating the Christmas tree. The tree was silver with a wheel reflector. It was decorated with bright-colored ornaments and silver tinsel, and there always was a manger and little figurines of kids sledding and ice skating. When dinner was ready to be served, the women set the table using the best linens and china, as well as a sheaf of wheat tied with a ribbon. Once everybody had taken their place at the table, one of the men would stand up and recite the Mass before Christmas Eve dinner, usually from memory.

For Ukrainian people, Christmas is the most important family holiday, so it is no surprise that family members used to all come together at the Markiewich home, bringing with them lots of gifts. Even though Leo and Mary didn't have a very big house, they somehow all managed to fit around the dining table. There were cheers, laughter, and lots of stories from the good old days that always brought the most genuine smiles to their faces. Once dinner was over, the women would gather in the kitchen to wash dishes, and the men stepped outside to pour themselves drinks and talk about how stuffed they were. Beer and wine always flowed freely during the holidays and they would have a grand old time. As the ladies were busy washing dishes, you could hear them laughing and telling funny stories about their husbands. The laughter would overtake the house. You would have never guessed that any work was getting done in that kitchen with all the laughter, but it was.

Every year, after dinner had been served and dishes had been cleaned and stored away, Leo would gather all the children in the living room for story time. They would all sit down on the floor, amazed by Leo's storytelling skills.

"All right, children, it's time for the Ukrainian spider web legend," he began.

Mary would dim the lights, and after taking a moment to recall the story, Donna's father proceeded with the tale.

"Once upon a time, long ago, a gentle mother was busily cleaning the house for the most wonderful day of the year: the day on which the Christ child came to bless the house. Not a speck of dust was left. Even the spiders had been banished from their cozy corner in the ceiling to avoid the housewife's busy cleaning. They finally fled to the farthest corner of the attic.

'T'was Christmas Eve at last! The tree was decorated and waiting for the children to see it, but the poor spiders were frantic, for they could not see the tree nor be present for the Christ child's visit. But the oldest and wisest spider suggested that perhaps they could peep through the crack in the door to see Him. Silently, they crept out of their attic, down the stairs, and across the floor to wait in a crack in the threshold."

By this point, the children were mesmerized.

"Suddenly, the door opened a wee bit, and quickly, the spiders scurried into the room. They wanted to see the tree closely, since their eyes weren't accustomed to the brightness of the room. So they crept all over the tree, up and down, over every branch and twig, and saw every one of the pretty things. At last, they were satisfied of the Christmas tree's beauty.

"And then what happened, Daddy?" Donna asked.

"Alas! Everywhere they went they had left their webs, and when the little Christ child came to bless the house, He was dismayed. He loved the little spiders, for they were God's creatures too, but he knew the mother, who had trimmed the tree for the little children, wouldn't feel the same; so He touched the webs, and they all turned to sparkling, shimmering silver and gold!

There was an astonished chorus of "Ohhh" in the room, which echoed through the whole house.

"Since then, we Ukrainians add a spider among the decorations on our Christmas tree. The end."

After Leo had masterfully impressed all of them, the children gathered around the tree and began sharing stories about Santa Claus and what they were hoping to find under the tree in the morning. Santa had always been very good to the Markiewich girls. In fact, right before midnight, he would usually stop by to drop off one present, only to return later on during early morning and deliver the other gifts. Both Donna and Diane always had the nicest Christmas dresses. One year, Donna had a black and red velvet dress with a sash around the waist, and the shiniest black shoes anyone had ever seen. Diane, being much younger, could not get the same dress; however, hers was just as nice. It was red and white, and she had a pair of shiny white shoes. Donna always asked Santa to bring her dolls for Christmas. She loved her Chatty Cathy doll, as well as her Betsy Wetsy doll; but her all-time favorite was her Tiny Tears doll. She would carry it around like it was her own baby, and take it everywhere she went.

"I can't wait to become a mommy and cuddle my very own baby one day!" She was known to say over and over.

The holidays at the Markiewich household began on Christmas Eve day and did not end until the new year. On New Year's Eve, the whole family would come together once again and enjoy more delicious food made of an assortment of breads, vegetables, meats, fish, caviar, potato pancakes, pierogies, and all sorts of sweets. The house smelled so good! According to a Ukrainian belief, in order to make the forthcoming year as full and prosperous as possible, the table must burst with treats.

Therefore, most housewives would try to surprise their family members with lots of original dishes.

Once dinner was over, and bellies were full, each person at the table would make a wish for the upcoming year. Mary wished for good health for all her loved ones. Leo wished for a good economy, and for his business to keep going steady. Diane wished to grow up as fast as possible so she could do all the things her big sister was allowed to do.

"What about you, Donna? What's your wish, sweetheart?" Leo asked, holding his daughter's hand.

"I wish to be with you all forever, Daddy. I never want to leave my family."

At the sound of those words, everyone in attendance smiled.

Donna

Chapter Two

Donna was 12 years old when she began junior high. She had succeeded all through elementary school, and could not wait to go to North Junior High. Although she had been able to make many friends, she was determined to come out of her shell a bit and socialize more with her peers. On the morning of her first day of school, she found herself staring at her reflection in the mirror, carefully studying the outfit she had picked the night before. Was light blue really her color? She was not so sure anymore. The thought of having to stand up in front of her whole class and give a brief introductory speech made her palms sweat and her heart race. She really wanted to impress her classmates, but what should she say to accomplish her goal? After all, this was seventh grade, and they were all big kids now. She had to come up with something more grown up to talk about. Should she lead with the story of how she enjoyed rescuing stray cats? Nah, too childish still.

"What's the matter, my darling?" Mary interrupted her thoughts.

"Nothing, mama," she answered, looking down.

"Are you nervous about your first day of middle school?" Her mother could read Donna like an open book.

"No. Well, maybe…a little," she admitted.

"Don't be, my darling. Everybody will love you. You just need to be yourself." Mary reassured her, giving her a warm hug that always had a healing effect on her daughter's preoccupied soul. Mothers have special powers like that.

As Donna walked to her school, she was passed by a few kids her age, including Tom, who looked eager to get there before anyone else did judging by how fast he was running. This school was much bigger than her previous one, and she knew that even though she was going to study almost all the same subjects, she needed to apply herself even more to please her parents. Education was very important to them.

"Hello, my name is Donna." She began with her introductory speech.

"Hello, Donna." Everybody welcomed her in unison.

"I am twelve years old, and I have a little sister named Diane. I like listening to music, playing outside, and shopping. When I grow up, all I want to be is a mom and a wife."

All her classmates clapped their hands, and Donna was filled with a sense of acceptance, pride, and accomplishment.

At recess, she opted for stepping out in the yard. She was sitting on a wooden bench enjoying the midday sun when a girl she had seen in her class approached her.

"Donna, right?" The girl asked.

"Yes," she replied shyly.

"Hi, I'm Valerie."

"Hi Valerie, nice to meet you."

Valerie set down next to Donna, looked at her, and said,

"So, you want to go shopping this weekend?"

Donna let out spontaneous laughter that filled the air, and Valerie couldn't help but giggle as well. And just like that, a friendship was born—one that would last a lifetime.

* * *

The middle school years went by fast, and aside from the welcomed friendship with Valerie, they also brought another unexpected yet equally welcome change for Donna. Tom and Donna had become quite fond of each other, and they began dating when she was in 7th grade. Nobody on Martin Street was surprised. In fact, it seemed like the most natural step for the two of them to start dating, since they already spent so much time together and got along very well. Even their parents were very calm and accepting of how their relationship had evolved. Both families were in agreement that Tom and Donna made the perfect couple.

Those years were filled with laughter and carefree days. Donna was turning into a beautiful young woman who was very curious about the outside world, which she enjoyed exploring while getting to know herself. She and Valerie spent every second together, and Donna's parents didn't mind at all. On the contrary, they were happy she had found a best friend in Valerie, whom they loved like a third daughter. The two girls had a great time expressing their fun, outgoing personalities by changing hair color according to what season it was: dark for fall and winter, lighter for spring and summer. Mary and Leo weren't big fans of their daughter's new look, but they made sure to stand aside and let Donna be herself.

After all, these were the 1960s. Those four British lads who called themselves the Beatles had taken over the world, with their new, upbeat, optimistic sound that swept entire countries like a breath of fresh air after World War II. The decade witnessed a man walking on the moon, Martin Luther King Jr.'s march on Washington, and Andy Warhol's iconic pop art portrayal of Marilyn Monroe. You could taste and smell freedom while walking down the street. There was a promise for a better, more peaceful future, and everybody believed it.

It was a great time to be a teenager. Fashion changed a lot as well; dresses and skirts got much shorter, softies (ballerina shoes) made their entrance, and not many people frowned when seeing a lady wearing pants. Mother no longer got too upset if children came back home with dirty clothes because Father had just bought her the first automated washing machine. It was win-win for everybody.

Donna and Valerie, like any other girls their age, became inseparable from their hairspray bottles and black eyeliner à la Twiggy, the first international supermodel, and spent evenings daydreaming of being rescued by a young, handsome Sean Connery who, at the time, was also known as Bond—James Bond. In the afternoons, they kept busy scribbling in blue ink names of wannabe boyfriends in their notebooks, which were filled with red ink hearts inside and out. Every Saturday, they would catch bus Number 2 from Passaic Avenue and go to Bloomfield Center to hang out or shop. There was a record store where they would usually go to and listen to the latest releases. Some of their favorites included the Supremes song "Baby Love" and the Drifters' "Under the Boardwalk". Once they had performed their usual impromptu concert, they moved to Kresge's or Grants for French fries. Occasionally, they would take the bus to Styertowne in Clifton and shop at the five and dime, only to then reward themselves for the successful shopping spree with ice cream at Bond's, where Donna still enjoyed a one-scoop cup of cookies and cream.

Summer was definitely Donna's favorite season. She loved the freedom that those days brought, sleeping in during the mornings, spending lazy days at the beach in Seaside Heights, having pizza with friends on Broughton Avenue at Nick's Pizzeria, and staying up late past bedtime on the evenings that never seemed to want to end either given how hard they tried to hold onto the sunlight. She and Valerie would share gossip while getting their nails done or fixing their hair. It was quite impressive how there was always something new happening in such a small town.

With summer of 1966 coming to an end, Donna was very excited for what was to come. She could not wait to see what high school had in store for her. Donna and Valerie had gone shopping over the summer for a few new dresses and various other items. She decided to wear her new blue dress and new shoes, which she had prepared the night before her first day as a high schooler. She also decided that she would style her hair up, so as to properly showcase her new earrings. So many questions ran through her mind as she tried to relax in bed staring at the ceiling, with her arms folded at the back of her head! *Will I like high school?* she thought. *What will my teachers be like?* Ah…this was torture! She tossed and turned, trying to get comfortable. She knew she had to get some rest, or she'd be miserable in the morning. Finally, Morpheus held her tight in his warm and reassuring embrace, and Donna fell asleep. She knew that high school was synonymous with big changes, but she couldn't have predicted just how much her life was going to change.

* * *

As time went by, Tom and Donna only grew closer. Cookie, now being 15 years old, began working at ShopRite in the produce department. Like many other kids his age, Tom took advantage of the High School Work Release Program, meaning he would attend school for half a day and then go work from 12:30 until 9:00 p.m. This allowed him to earn a substantial amount of money for a 15-year-old boy, as he was making $100 a month. Given how close this shop was to Donna's house as well as Leo's Sunoco station, Donna would take any opportunity to go see Tom at work. She would come up with the craziest excuses to get out of the house, and almost all of them involved going to see her father to bring him something.

One afternoon, after school, Donna ran to the kitchen to ask her mother for permission to bring coffee to her father.

"Sure, my darling. I actually just made it fresh," Mary replied, handing her a warm cup of coffee.

"Thanks, Mom!" Donna said, trying not to look at her mother's face.

"Give Tom my best regards," Mary whispered, struggling not to laugh out loud at the sight of her daughter's bright-eyed and embarrassed look.

"What? Um…Mom, you don't…" Donna was having a hard time choosing her words, as well as controlling that high-pitched voice she always got whenever she was trying to hide something from her parents.

"Now go, before the coffee gets cold," Mary winked at her.

Mary smiled while she watched her daughter running out of the room. Young love was the best—so innocent, pure, full of possibilities and a bright future ahead. Watching her daughter so happy with her sweet love, Mary knew it was going to be just a matter of time before things got even more serious between the two.

After working at ShopRite for about three years, Tom was offered a better-paying job at the Shell station on Watchung Avenue. He accepted the offer, especially because part of his job involved working on cars—something he not only was very passionate about but was also very good at. Donna shared his same passion, and she actually thought he was super-cool for having over ten motorcycles in his garage. At times, they would even go cruising through Brookdale Park together. Brookdale Park was the place to be, whether you were in a car or on a motorcycle; everyone would go there, as the park went in a huge circle. It was nothing to see fifty bikes just hanging out there. Donna and Tom sure loved fast engines, and he was not the kind to shy away from showing off his motorcycle driving skills whenever she went to see him at his house.

Donna with Tom's motorcycles

Tom's parents absolutely adored Donna, and with no daughter of their own, she fit perfectly within their family, filling the void of not having another female presence in the Litchfield household. Peter, a former Army member, had proudly served his country until Tom was 5 years old. He then went on to work at Westinghouse doing wire drawing, and he was in charge of the day shift. Tom's mother, Audrey, worked at MGM Records, running a press during the night shift. She would drop Tom and Pete off at the guardhouse at Westinghouse about a half hour before Peter got off work and they would wait for him as their shifts overlapped. Then Peter would take the boys home and make dinner. His meat and potatoes were legendary, and the whole neighborhood knew that Peter made the best mashed potatoes, with not even one lump in them. Audrey was a wonderful cook as well. Whenever she was home, she always had an apron on, ready to create magic in the kitchen. Everyone would say she made the best potato salad and the best cup of coffee.

Given how much time Donna was spending with Tom, she and Valerie began seeing less of each other, although they both remained very close like sisters. Valerie would join them sometimes on their outings, especially during summertime. Tom and Donna enjoyed going to Seaside Heights, as well as the beach, where they were known for spending whole afternoons soaking up the sun. Donna was simply in love with the ocean, and she found walking down the shore to be relaxing and exciting at the same time. During spring, Tom's Uncle Bob, who lived in Rockaway, would take the two lovebirds to Lake Hopatcong to ride on his boat, an activity that everyone involved found thrilling. Then they would spend the rest of the day grilling and telling fun jokes and stories – mostly about Tom's childhood, something he found rather embarrassing.

* * *

June 30th, 1968 was a very special day for Donna, as it was her sixteenth birthday. However, she could not have predicted just how much more special this day was going to turn out. From that very morning, the day was extra- special. Mary and Diane had made a super yummy breakfast for Donna, which included chocolate chip pancakes, scrambled eggs, and freshly squeezed orange juice. Leo and Mary had planned a birthday party to be hosted at their house, and Diane had been placed in charge of decorations. After breakfast, Mary took Donna shopping to look for a brand-new dress she could wear that afternoon at her party. Donna chose a gorgeous blue dress, which accentuated her beautiful features and brought out her eyes even more. With a perfectly done up-do, her hair looked amazing as well.

All of Donna's relatives, family members, and friends had gathered at her house to celebrate her birthday. Among them was a very nervous Tom who, accompanied by his own parents, was about to make a big announcement. Just before the cake was brought out, he approached Donna and, holding her arm, led her to the center of the living room.

"What is it, Tom?" she wondered.

"I have to ask you something," he replied in a whisper.

As people made their way around the young couple, Donna felt slightly embarrassed, because she did not like being the center of attention. She liked keeping to herself, and all those eyes on her made her feel quite uncomfortable. She looked across the room and noticed that a circle had formed around them. When she turned her sight on Tom again, she was surprised to see he was down on one knee.

"Donna, these years spent together have been the most wonderful years of my life. In you, I have found a partner and a best friend. I hope that you will say yes to you becoming my wife."

A round of *aww* echoed through the otherwise silent room. Tom took a deep breath, looked at Donna in the eyes and asked,

"Donna, will you marry me?"

"Yes," a shaking Donna said with the slightest hint of voice.

At her answer, Tom got up quickly and hugged her tight. At that moment, loud applause was heard all across the house and on Martin Street. Leo and Peter congratulated each other on the happy union, while the two mothers shared a hug, formally welcoming each other into the family. It was a happy day for everybody — one that symbolized the beginning of a new life for both Donna and Tom.

* * *

After Tom's proposal, Donna went full steam ahead planning their wedding. School had almost become a second thought to her, even though she was still doing her best at keeping up grades and excelling through it with grace. Her senior year was basically spent planning the big day in homeroom. She and Valerie spent hours upon end chatting, making plans, and hashing out details. Donna and Tom had their hearts set on the date already: July 11th, 1970. This meant that right after graduation, Donna was going to become Mrs. Tom Litchfield. She couldn't wait! She was so high-strung on getting married that she actually began marking down days on the calendar. Everyone was super-excited for her; she was such a radiant bride-to-be. As time went by, she and Tom only became more inseparable. Donna had taken a job at Styretowne Bakery in Clifton and Tom would go pick her up every day after work. He would usually show up on his motorcycle, something Donna loved. She would get out of the store still wearing her little white bakery dress, and jump on the bike — and away they went.

Graduation was fast approaching, and Donna was happy to have Valerie to help plan the big day. Valerie cried the day she saw Donna try on what would eventually become her wedding gown: It was pure white color, big and fluffy, just like the one Donna used to draw when she was a child dreaming of one day becoming a beautiful bride. Although she wasn't too sold on her bridesmaid's dress, which was yellow, Valerie knew that if there was one thing you should never argue about with a bride-to-be, it was her choice of coloring when it came to her bridesmaids' gowns, so she kept her mouth shut. The photographer and the venue—the Robin Hood Inn in Clifton—had been booked months in advance, allowing a nervous Donna to sort of calm down whenever she began to feel panicky about planning for her wedding day. As for the church, they had chosen St. Valentine's in Bloomfield.

Before they knew it, the countdown had finally ended. Donna had switched her cap and gown for her wedding dress, and she looked absolutely breathtaking. Everybody thought so, especially Tom, who, as soon as he saw her walking down the aisle supported by a very emotional Leo, tried hard not to show that he was tearing up. After a wonderful Mass, the newly-married couple walked out of the church and drove away to take a few photos at gorgeous locations. Afterward, they met all their guests at the reception, where fresh flowers decorated tables that hosted hundreds of people who had come to celebrate the happy couple. For their first dance as husband and wife, Donna felt like a princess at a ball. She cried tears of joy, because that day, her biggest dream had come true: marrying the love of her life and becoming a wife. It was truly a magical day for her.

Once the reception was over, Donna and Tom left in his Corvette, and off they went to their week at Niagara Falls. She had picked their honeymoon destination, and Tom had worked hard to make sure he could fulfill her lifelong dream of seeing the falls. They stayed at a hotel nearby, allowing them to explore the area even at night when, according to Donna, everything seemed more magical and enchanting.

Donna and Tom

When their honeymoon came to an end, they went back to New Jersey and moved into a beautiful garden apartment in Little Falls. Donna took great pride in keeping her house clean and immaculate. She was very much in love with her life, as she was finally able to call herself a wife—and soon, hopefully, a mother. She took a job at the employees' kitchen at Sears in Willowbrook Mall, and she enjoyed it very much. One day, while working, Donna felt nauseous and dizzy.

"Oh, honey, you better go home and take care of that baby," Shayla, a coworker, told her.

"What baby? What do you mean?" Donna asked, perplexed.

"Honey, if there's one thing Shayla knows, it's what a pregnant woman looks like. Believe you me, I've had five children!"

At those words, Donna rushed home. Could it be that she was already pregnant? She didn't know, but she had to find out. Her heart was beating ninety miles per hour; she could barely breathe, and she had just promised herself she would never have tuna salad in her whole life ever again after seeing it in reverse—yet she couldn't wipe the biggest smile off her face. She had to tell Tom. He was going to jump up and down with joy!

Unfortunately, the newlywed couple had a short time to celebrate. Donna lost the baby. She and Tom were devastated. Donna fell into a depression after losing her child. Had she done something bad that hurt the baby? Was she ever going to be able to carry a child? She had so many questions, so many doubts. Most of all, she regretted all the daydreaming she had done about her unborn child. She even had names picked out. Her days were filled with a sense of loss. Meanwhile, Tom tried to cheer her up with motorcycle rides to Bear Mountain, where they would spend their weekends fishing, swimming, and having picnics on the grass. Soon after, Donna became pregnant again. This time, she was scared of feeling joyful, and she decided to be extra cautious. She quit her job and chose to stay home, resting as much as possible. Days went by, then weeks. Before she knew it, Donna and Tom had begun daydreaming about this baby as well. They felt this was the right time, and a baby would join the family soon. However, tragedy struck again: another miscarriage. This one hit the couple even harder. Being so young, they had no idea how to face such tragedies. They didn't know how to properly deal with their emotions, so they argued. They yelled. They fought. Donna spent most of her waking hours crying. At night, before bed, she still knelt down and prayed, just like she had taught her sister Diane many years before. She prayed hard, sobbing, asking God why she was being punished. Why was He taking her babies away? No answers.

After a while, Donna decided to no longer see about getting her job back. She was simply going to stay home for now. Fortunately for her, Valerie was there to help and support her grieving friend. You see, Valerie had become mother to a wonderful baby girl, Marlana. She had even asked Donna if she would become her daughter's godmother, and obviously, Donna was thrilled and honored. Valerie was working many hours during the day, so Donna offered to babysit Marlana, which turned out to be a blessing for Donna, who now spent her days reading stories and playing with the little girl.

Meanwhile, Tom's parents had been working hard to fix their home, as they had decided to put a second story on their house so that Tom and Donna could move back to Martin Street. When it was done, Peter let Tom know, and the newlyweds began packing. They were happy to move back to the street that had seen them as children playing in Pulaski Park for hours upon end, where their love first blossomed and they shared many happy memories together. The timing couldn't have been more perfect: Donna was expecting again. This time it felt a bit extra-special because guess what? Valerie was pregnant as well! The two best friends couldn't believe it when they shared the news with each other. Both Valerie and Donna were simply glowing with joy. The two soon-to-be-mommies spent afternoons talking about their hopes and dreams for their children, baking fresh cookies, and imagining that both their children would surely become best friends as well.

Then it happened again. Donna felt sick, and even this third pregnancy resulted in a miscarriage. This time, it was even more devastating. Donna and Tom felt a void that could not be filled. Why was this happening to them? Once again, unable to deal with the terrible loss, they began fighting. Things had gotten so bad between them that Donna wasn't sure if their marriage could ever be repaired. They both tried to keep their distance without actually saying so. Tom went to work every day, while Donna spent her time at her parents' house, mostly hanging out with Diane. She enjoyed taking her little sister shopping, a very distracting activity for both ladies. Months went by, and Valerie welcomed her second daughter, Monique. When Donna went to visit Valerie at the hospital, the two best friends had a moment together—one that turned out to be very healing for Donna.

"She's absolutely beautiful, Valerie!" Donna whispered while holding little Monique.

"Thank you," Valerie replied, still tired from giving birth.

She couldn't help but see how much Donna wished she was holding her own child. She could tell by just looking at her eyes, which still had some grieving in them.

"This is going to happen for you too, soon." Valerie tried to reassure her longtime friend.

Donna couldn't get herself to reply. She glanced at Valerie, who was resting in bed and gave her a faint smile that was meant to hide her teary eyes.

"It will," Valerie insisted. "You just have to give it time."

"Maybe God did not plan for me to become a mother," Donna barely managed to say.

"God loves you, Donna," Valerie reassured her. "He will make it happen for you and Tom."

Donna spent the rest of the day holding the precious newborn and keeping her friend company. When she went home that evening, she fell on her knees by her bedside, crying, sobbing, begging God to help her — begging God to let her become a mother. Her sobbing became so intense she could barely catch her breath. Her whole body was shaking from the pain she felt inside. That night, Donna fell asleep with puffy, red eyes and a longing desire to fulfill her most precious dream.

* * *

They say time heals all wounds, but when the wound is so big, can time really fix everything? Donna would have begged to differ. The pain caused by her three miscarriages never left her. She just learned to live with it, and so did Tom, who left early for work every morning and came back home late in the evening. Donna kept up with her wifely duties, still finding solace in keeping her house clean and tidy. Taking care of her home had always given her a sense of pride, and at times, having a neatly polished living room to look at was all the comfort she needed to make it through the day.

Her prayers had started to change. She still asked God to let her become a mother, but now she was also praying He would give her the strength to live a childless life. She was unsure if her body could take any more miscarriages. It had been a very painful process for her to go through, both emotionally and physically. However, while the physical wounds eventually healed, she had the lingering suspicion that her emotional ones never would.

A few months later, just when Donna was almost ready to give up hope in becoming pregnant and being able to take her pregnancy to full term, morning sickness came back to visit her again. As weird as it sounds, Donna was the happiest woman alive when she was hit with nausea and fatigue because that meant that she was pregnant again! This time, Donna and Tom, as excited as they obviously were about the possibility of finally becoming parents, also took extra precautions when it came to making sure Donna got plenty of rest. Both were determined to do anything in their power to fulfill their lifelong dream of welcoming a child.

Days went by, and Donna felt fine. Days slowly turned into weeks, and Donna was still doing well. Weeks turned into months, and before they knew it, they were about to approach the so-called "safe zone" of the second trimester. Previously, Donna had miscarried before her first trimester ended, so saying that she was counting down the days until she finally entered her fourth month of pregnancy would not be an exaggeration by any means. She spent most of her days praying to God to keep their baby safe. This time, it seemed God was listening. The fourth month had finally come, and Donna and Tom were overjoyed about the possibility of finally becoming Mom and Dad.

Donna was incredibly happy to watch her belly getting bigger as weeks went by. She was over the moon when she and Tom started getting the nursery ready. Her favorite thing to do was go shopping for baby clothes. She found tiny little baby socks and shoes to be irresistible. Since she didn't really care to know whether they were having a boy or a girl, as they only cared that the baby was healthy, she mostly bought gender-neutral outfits, like candid white onesies, tiny yellow shirts, and light green pants.

Those were the longest, happiest, most tiring nine months of her life, but Donna had surely enjoyed each and every minute of being pregnant. Although this was finally happening for both her and Tom, their relationship was no longer what it used to be. Something had broken between them when dealing with all those losses, something that maybe could never be repaired. They no longer spent much time together, nor did they go out together as they used to before they got married. The happy times they shared seemed to all belong in the past, and aside from their collective joy of becoming parents, they really had nothing else in common anymore.

But all these problems had to wait to be faced for the time being, because in June of 1974, Donna went into labor. Tom rushed her to St. Vincent Hospital on Elm Street in Montclair. In the afternoon, Donna delivered a healthy baby girl, weighing seven pounds and nine-and-a-half ounces. She had ash blonde hair and gorgeous blue eyes. The baby did not have one red mark on her; she was simply perfect. Tom picked her name, and he chose Tina Ann. She and her parents stayed at the hospital for four days, where she outweighed all the other newborns for the first two days of her life. Donna could not stop staring at Tina Ann. To her motherly eyes, she was the most beautiful baby girl in the whole world. Tom was absolutely in love with their new bundle of joy, and he just couldn't believe that she had such a full head of hair! Both parents knew this was the best day of their lives. Nothing could ever top this. Tina Ann had brought so much joy to their hearts—a joy they had desperately been waiting for. That baby they dreamed of, that baby they prayed for, that baby they longed to meet, was finally here. That baby was precious to them. That baby was a blessing to both Mom and Dad. That baby was me, your narrator.

Chapter Three

While Richard Nixon was likely preparing a speech to announce his intention of becoming the very first President in the history of the United States of America to resign, and the lyrics to the song "Billy Don't Be a Hero" were stuck in everybody's heads, Donna and Tom were trying to adjust to their new life as parents. After taking me home, they were overwhelmed with all the gifts they received from friends and family members, and they were sincerely surprised by how generous everybody had been to them. There was a green sweater from Jean and Larry, a pink dress set from Eileen Leary, a baby book from Mr. and Mrs. Conrad, a pink sun suit and blue bunny suit from Jean and Agnes, a savings bond from Grandma and Grandpa Litchfield, a money book from Grandma and Grandpa Markiewich, and a savings account started by Uncle Pete, my godfather. Truly, the list just went on and on.

I was baptized on July 7th, 1974 at St. Thomas Church in Bloomfield, at 3:00 p.m. All family members were in attendance, and my godparents, Uncle Pete and Aunt Diane, were very excited to be there. Father Anthony, the officiating priest, delivered a heartwarming ceremony—or he would have, had I not cried the whole time. Apparently, I only stopped whining when I was blessed with holy water. My mother looked absolutely beautiful that day.

As time went by, things between Donna and Tom did not seem to get any better. They would argue often, and they seemed to not be able to agree on anything except one: They both loved me very much. They were great parents, although I proved to be a rather challenging baby. It seems I had decided that nighttime was the best time to be awake, and I really didn't care about what my parents thought, so I made sure to keep them up all night with my lovely crying. As difficult as it was for them to properly function on very few hours of sleep, they always stood by my side, reassuring me, taking care of me, and making sure I was safe and happy. My mother spent most of her time with me while my father was at work. She loved being a mom. After all, this was something she had been waiting for her whole life. She was incredibly sweet, writing down all my baby milestones in a baby book, recording every measurement of my growth, and staring at me as I slept peacefully. She melted every time I would coo and babble and although I do not have memories of my time spent with her, I know those were some of the happiest times in my life, and she was simply the best mother a baby could ever ask for.

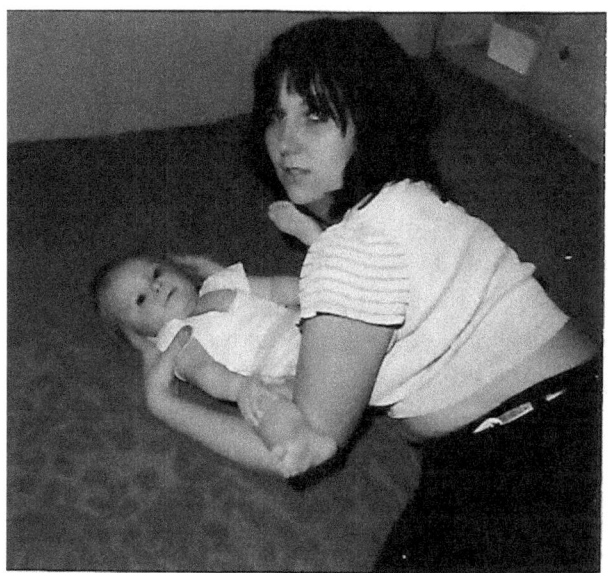

Mom and I

Donna was doing a fantastic job at raising me, and she was happily surprised when, at four months, I could sit up without back support; and at seven months I was able to hold a cup and drink all on my own, with little to no spills. One day, while I was sitting in my high chair waiting for my Mom to feed me, I decided to say my first word for the very first time.

"Mommy…"

Donna, who was standing with her back towards me while stirring my meal in the pot, quickly turned towards me. She had a spark in her eyes and the hint of a smile.

"Tina…what did you say, baby?" She asked in a whisper, as if afraid to speak too loud and scare the word out of my mouth.

"Did you just say 'Mommy'?" she asked, again almost in silence.

"Mommy," I repeated.

She carefully placed the spoon on the kitchen counter and slowly walked towards me.

"*Mommy*," I said again.

She picked me up, and with tears of joy in her eyes, she gave me a big, squeezy hug and lots of kisses filled with motherly love. To her, the sound of that word was the most precious and beautiful one. At that moment, all the grieving she had gone through during her three miscarriages, all the pain those experiences had brought her, all the sleepless nights spent praying and sobbing for her losses, were released in those tears. Those tears that no longer tasted bitter and salty but were sweet as honey, precious as only a mother's happiness can be when holding her baby.

After that first word, there was no more stopping me. I turned out to be quite the Chatty Cathy, and probably as curious as Curious George. In fact, I would drive my parents crazy by asking them, "What's that?" over and over and over again. However, that incessant questioning on my part was a good distraction for both of them, as it allowed them to momentarily take their mind off a reality that could no longer be escaped: Their marriage was over. If they had to be honest with themselves, it had been over for quite some time; but they did not want to admit it to one another, as it was going to be too painful for both of them. They had known each other their whole lives. They played at the park together, pushing each other on the swings. They had bought ice cream together from Mr. Mangioni. They attended school together and acted in school plays together. They made such a great couple. The whole neighborhood had cheered them on when they got engaged. Their friends and family members grieved with them when they suffered those miscarriages, and they celebrated all together when I was born. But it was over now; it just had to be. Tom and Donna no longer made each other happy, and still in their early twenties, they had their whole lives ahead of them. It was only fair to move on.

One day, Donna decided to pack up her things and move out of the house she and Tom shared for a little while. Tom was devastated but agreed with Donna that this was indeed going to be for the best for the two of them, and especially for me. Besides, although they did not work as a married couple, they still remained very close friends and were actually great at co-parenting. When Mary and Leo heard the news, they insisted Donna, and I move in with them, but she was a very independent woman and wanted — or maybe needed — to be on her own for a while.

* * *

Donna was excited about the new apartment, although she was a bit scared, too. She was a proud woman, so she tried her hardest not to let it show that she was second-guessing her decision. But people close to her could feel her hesitance. After all, she had been living either with her parents or with Tom her whole life. They thought it was only normal she'd feel a bit perplexed, since this was the very first time she'd lived on her own, and to make things more complicated, she had an infant to worry about. A few weeks before moving, she had spent her time apartment-hunting, reading all the for-rent ads in the newspaper. After much looking and searching, she found one on Brighton Avenue, in Belleville, New Jersey. It was a basement apartment, and if you looked out the kitchen window, you could see the parking lot in the back, but the rent was reasonable. As soon as we moved in, she began cleaning and tidying it up so that it looked and felt like home to us. Outside the front door, there was a very big hall, which she thought would be the perfect place to put all my toys so that I'd have a big playroom.

The area wasn't bad either, as it was on a one-way street leading to Newark Avenue, with cars lined up along both sides of the road. The neighborhood was buzzing with young moms and children. As soon as you stepped outside, you would find older ladies sitting on their lawn chairs, gossiping and having tea and an overall enjoyable time. There was also a little grocery store at the end of the street, which turned out to be handy for quick small purchases like a bottle of milk or diapers.

Valerie used to come over often, and when the parking lot in the back was empty, she would park there so she could come straight in the house from the kitchen window. This was nothing to be surprised about since Valerie was known as being a bit out there, but you could always count on having a good time whenever she was around. Plus, she made the transition for Donna that much more bearable, as she would take her mind off the divorce and everything else related to that. It had become a tradition for the two best friends, every Wednesday at lunch, to bring the kids to Bloomfield Avenue, to JJ's Hot Dog Truck. Valerie would get her hot dog with onions, while Donna chose to put pickles on hers. Plain hot dogs with ketchup or mustard were for the kids, who actually got to spend a lot of time together. In fact, whenever Valerie was around, she'd bring her daughters, Marlana and Monique, and the two girls would have the best time taking care of me. Since I was still a baby, I guess I looked like a dolly to them, and they would take turns reading me stories and keeping me entertained.

On occasion, our moms would take us to the Friendly's on Broad Street in Bloomfield for ice cream, a very enjoyable treat that would usually be followed by a trip to Brookside Park, where we would have fun feeding the ducks. After tiring ourselves out, there was a quick stop at the store for some chips, and we would all head back home where Donna and Valerie relaxed in front of the TV watching *The Mary Tyler Moore Show*, while us kids would get some well-deserved rest.

Even though those were challenging times for Donna, it was also a period filled with laughter and giggles, which resulted from days spent hanging out with her best friend. After all, who better than Valerie, whose marriage had also ended around the same time as Donna's, could better understand where she was coming from? The two ladies were often joined by Diane, who used to stop by any chance she had to help Donna make pierogies and watch TV together, listen to music, or go out for a walk. Diane had recently become the mother of a bouncy baby boy named Ronnie. Since then, there was this new, more profound bond between the two sisters, who could now relate to each other in a deeper way than they could while growing up and being seven years apart. In fact, Diane would often help Donna feed me. I was told that while I loved eating grapes, I wasn't really a big fan of the skin, so my aunt, with endless patience, would actually peel them for me.

* * *

It was October 1975, and Valerie had been spending a lot of time over at her best friend's house. One night, after the kids had been put to bed and the two women were done watching *The Midnight Show*, Valerie said, "Hey, have I told you about this new guy I met?"

"What new guy?" Donna asked, curious.

"Steve," Valerie answered.

"Mm…no, I don't remember you mentioning a Steve." Donna added, "So, what about this guy? Is he cute?" She teased her friend.

"Oh, c'mon, get your mind out of the gutter," Valerie replied, "I met him a couple of months ago through J. He was her boyfriend."

"*Was*, huh?" Donna asked, winking at Valerie.

"Would you stop that?" She admonished Donna, slightly pushing her away by the elbow. "I'm not into him. But he is *such* a nice guy. Imagine that—when J moved to Allentown in Pennsylvania, he helped her even though they had already broken up."

"He sounds like a genuine guy," Donna noted.

"I really think he is," Valerie replied. "Plus, he comes from a good family. He's originally from Upper Montclair, New Jersey. His father is an orthodontist, and his mother is a housewife."

"Does he still live in Upper Montclair?" Donna had grown curious about this man.

"No, he has his own apartment on Grove Street, in Bloomfield," Valerie answered.

"Oh really? So, he lives close by," Donna pointed out.

"Yep," Valerie said. "Wanna know what he looks like?"

Valerie could tell by the look on her friend's face that she had become interested in this guy, so, she began teasing Donna, and the two exchanged quite a few subtle smiles and giggles.

"Sure, if you want to tell me." Donna was trying to play hard to get, but it wasn't working with Valerie. After all, they had known each other almost their whole lives, so they could read each other's expressions and always see what was hiding behind the façade.

"He's *taaall*…" Valerie prolonged the sound to highlight Steve's appealing physical quality. "And he's got dark hair, brown and gentle eyes, and a mustache."

"Oh, yeah?" Donna pretended not to be too much into the topic, looking down in the sink while she washed dishes that had been left there from dinner.

"Yes." Valerie knew Donna wanted to know more. "He is a very good-looking, nice man."

"I see," Donna replied, still with her hands in soap and water, but with a slight smile on her face, thus giving away the fact that for the first time after her divorce, she had finally reached a point in her life where imagining herself with another man wasn't such a foreign idea.

"Steve and I often talk on the phone, and I can tell he's feeling lonely since J left." Valerie tested the territory before adding "Maybe you two should meet."

"You think so?" Donna could no longer hide her excitement about the possibility of a happier future.

"Yes, I think you two could get along well."

"All right." Donna raised her gaze from the sink and looked at Valerie. "You should bring him over some time."

The two friends smiled.

A few days later, Valerie called Steve to let him know that Donna had agreed to meet him. Valerie had been telling him all about Donna, and Steve had grown interested in meeting her. She sounded lovely: beautiful, family-oriented, kind, and just an all-around fun person to be with. When Steve arrived at Valerie's house, he noticed that she had just changed her hair color. She now had dark hair, but he told her she should go back to her blonde hair. She looked prettier that way. As the two of them made their way to Donna's house, Valerie could tell Steve was a bit nervous. He couldn't seem to keep his fingers from trembling.

When they finally arrived at Donna's house, Steve walked a few steps behind Valerie. He was wearing a green T-shirt, jeans, and work boots. After Valerie introduced the two of them, Donna invited them all to sit at the kitchen table. She offered her guests some cookies and coffee, which they all enjoyed. The mood was very serene, and the conversation flowed naturally. It seemed as if they were all longtime friends, which was reassuring to all involved. They were having such a good time that nobody noticed over two hours had gone by. When Valerie glanced at the wall clock in Donna's kitchen, she suddenly said, "Oh, man, look at the time! I gotta go pick up the girls! They had a play date."

"Oops, sorry!" Donna said, "Call me later?"

"Yeah, no worries," Valerie replied.

"It was nice meeting you, Donna," Steve said as he got up to leave. "Would you like to meet up again sometime?"

Donna smiled. She felt a heat wave come up to her face, and she silently prayed that she wasn't blushing. That would have been embarrassing.

"Yes, that would be nice," Donna replied with a soft tone.

Once the three of them had waved goodbye at the front door, Donna went back in the kitchen, took a deep breath, and smiled. After all, this time being alone and spending restless nights over her failed marriage, it was nice to finally be with a potential companion to spend her days. As she cleaned the table of their mid-afternoon snack, she could not help but think that life was good and that hopefully, it would soon get even better.

As days went by, Donna and Steve spent more time together. Usually, Valerie was there as well since Donna was her best girlfriend and Steve her best boyfriend. She couldn't help but be proud of her match-making skills; after all, she had successfully brought two lonely souls together, and she was pleased to see that they had hit it off right away. The three of them had lots of fun together, dancing at clubs, sipping cocktails, and just having an overall carefree good time. Steve was such an interesting person to talk to. He was well-traveled, and he enjoyed telling Donna all about his fun trips, from skiing in Vermont to going down to California, where he had some friends.

Before they knew it, months went by, and Steve and Donna had moved on from spending lots of time with Valerie to just hanging out on their own. There was definitely something there; both of them could feel it, and Valerie certainly could see it, so she made sure to give them space to be alone and figure out if this relationship had the potential of becoming something more. They would often go to Dodd's in East Orange, where they enjoyed listening to cover bands playing rock music classics like Queen, Elton John, Pink Floyd, and Led Zeppelin. They used to spend so much time there that the bartenders had gotten to know their tastes in cocktails, and would go ahead and prepare what had become known as "the usual" — meaning Seven &7 for Donna and cold beer for Steve. Whenever my dad, with his new girlfriend Janice, babysat me, Donna and Steve would go out to catch a movie or go on a date at a nearby diner.

Steve was also very helpful with me. In fact, he would take my Mom and me to Brookside Park, which was close to where we lived. If I was sick, Steve would help Mom take me to the doctor, or keep me entertained when Donna had housework to take care of. He also took her down to Long Beach Island, where he had close friends who owned a service station. They had known Steve since he was a kid, and when they heard he had a new girlfriend, they immediately invited both of them down to LBI for a barbeque, which Donna appreciated and enjoyed very much. Steve had often mentioned to Donna how much he liked it there, and how he hoped someday soon to move there so he could spend more time with his childhood friends. He had even tested the territory one day with Donna, just to see where their relationship was at, and mentioned that possibly he'd like to move there with me and her—maybe in the near future—as a married couple. While Donna did not give a definite "Yes", she did not give a definite "No" either, so Steve remained hopeful.

With Christmas around the corner, Donna began feeling very optimistic and excited about the future. Christmas was definitely her favorite holiday, so she started decorating a couple of weeks in advance. This was the first Christmas my Mom, and I would spend together in the new apartment, so she went above and beyond to make it special for the two of us. Choosing the perfect Christmas tree was one of her favorite rituals. The pine tree had to always be the right height, with needles secured, and even the perfect coloration and freshness. This year, Steve joined her in the search, and once she was done choosing the perfect tree, he helped her bring it back to the house.

Things between them were going very well, and Donna thought he was truly one of the nicest guys she had ever met—not that she really had anybody besides Tom to compare him to. After all, Tom had been the first and only boyfriend she had ever had. But generally speaking, Steve seemed like a truly genuine person. In fact, she even invited him to spend Christmas Eve at her parents' house. She was actually quite nervous to ask him; they had only been going out for a few months, and she didn't know if Steve thought it was too soon to get so involved. She had been building up the courage to invite him for a few days before she actually asked him, and to her immense surprise, he accepted, adding that he thought it was a great idea. Donna was overjoyed.

On Christmas Eve, Steve, Mom, and I made our way to my grandparents' house, which was about ten minutes away. As on every Christmas, the house was filled with relatives who had brought a lot of food that now sat on the table. Everybody was having a good time, and the whole house was filled with laughter, joy, and giggles that echoed through Martin Street. Donna, who was sitting next to Steve at the dining table, glanced at him and saw tears in his eyes. Worried he was not feeling well, she placed her hand on his knee and asked, "Are you okay?"

Steve nodded.

"Something wrong?" Donna whispered.

"No," Steve replied in a soft tone while looking into her eyes. "I am happy to be here because I have never spent a holiday so filled with love and happiness. Thank you for inviting me."

Donna was incredibly touched by his words. She felt that everything in her life was falling into place, and she was looking forward to the future now more than ever. My grandparents appreciated meeting Steve, and they were ecstatic at the fact that this year they had two grandchildren to celebrate the holidays with. At the end of the very filling meal, Leo gathered everyone around and began telling them the Ukrainian spider web story, just like he had done every year since Donna was born. While Ronnie was just a baby and had no clue what was going on, I had become a bit of a handful compared to last year's Christmas, as I was attracted by those bright lights on the tree, the colorful wrapping paper of gifts, and that big tree in the living room. My grandmother spent a lot of her time and energy making sure I would not pull the tree down or destroy all the gifts. While she made it seem like it was a hard task to keep up with me, she wouldn't have asked for a better pastime than taking care of her little granddaughter.

After a long yet amazing night, it was time to go. Steve picked me up from the couch where I had fallen asleep, exhausted after keeping Grandma occupied for so many hours, and gently carried me to the car. Donna had her hands full of bags filled with delicious leftovers that were likely going to last us a few weeks. Before leaving, Steve made sure to go back inside and thank Mary and Leo yet again for having him over and for showing him such a good time. My grandparents were pleased to have met such a well-mannered, genuine man who seemed to be making their daughter happy. Although they were heartbroken by the fact that her marriage to my Dad did not work out, they remained hopeful that Donna would eventually find happiness with someone else. Could that be Steve? Only time would tell.

After arriving home, Mom changed me into the Christmas pajamas she had bought weeks in advance. She put me in bed, softly moving my hair to the side, and kissed my forehead before whispering goodnight. As she went back to the living room, she stopped to turn the radio on.

Elvis's song "Blue Christmas" was on. This was surely one of her all-time favorite songs. She just loved the Christmas spirit because it made her wish and hope that better times were on the horizon. She sat down on the couch and listened to Elvis's melodic voice,

I'll have a blue Christmas without you
I'll be so blue just thinking about you
Decorations of red on a green Christmas tree
Won't be the same, dear, if you're not here with me

Those words hit her hard in a very unexpected way. She couldn't help but think about Tom and their failed marriage. Tears began coming up in her eyes, and she allowed them to spill down her cheeks. She grew up in a tight family that was filled with love and everlasting respect. She knew that nothing was ever going to break her parents apart, and she was sad and disappointed in herself that she was not going to be able to provide that for me. She often wondered how having divorced parents would affect me later on in life, but she found solace in knowing that she and Tom had become great at co-parenting. Lost in her thoughts, she barely noticed Steve had joined her on the couch. He could see that something was bothering her, but instead of asking her if she wanted to talk about it, he held her hand. Donna quickly pulled herself together, and they spent the rest of the night listening to Christmas songs and admiring the decorated tree.

Christmas morning was finally here. Everybody, me included, woke up early to see if Santa had come and, to my enormous surprise, not only had he come, but he also must have thought I had been on my best behavior that year judging by all the gifts he brought over for me. However, he may as well only have brought wrapping paper, since that's what I seemed to be mostly excited about. There was a small gift underneath the Christmas tree. Steve picked it up and handed it to Donna, who was surprised to receive it. She quickly unwrapped it and let out a happy gasp when she saw a pair of gold earrings with a small diamond in the center, paired with a gold heart necklace. She had yet to regain her control after such a wonderful surprise when Steve handed her a few more gifts, including three tops he noticed Donna admiring when they went to the store and an off-white, faux-fur jacket. Donna was over the moon. She did not expect to receive so much from him, and she was simply blown away. She couldn't help but feel very optimistic about her future with Steve. She knew she was developing stronger feelings for him, and judging by how much time they spent together and how attentive he was towards her, Donna knew he was feeling the same way about her. The rest of the day was spent in a very joyful atmosphere. Steve left earlier to go to his parents' house for dinner, while Mom and I went back to my grandparents' house. That evening, Dad came over to bring gifts that Santa had left at his house for me, and the two of us got some quality daddy-daughter time. Watching the two of us play in harmony, Mom thought that life was good and even better times were surely ahead.

***

The relationship between Donna and Steve had progressed enough for Steve to move in with us. My mom was radiant, and people who knew her could tell from a mile away that it was all due to her newly-found happiness with her boyfriend. She had always been a very wifey kind of gal, one who loved the simple life and found joy in simple things, like the fact that now she had another person to cook for and that there was another toothbrush in the bathroom. She didn't know where this relationship was heading, or if there were wedding bells in the future for her and Steve, but she surely enjoyed watching it develop into something more serious.

However, soon after Steve moved in, his behavior began to change—nothing major at first, but he did seem to be a little off. Before giving up his apartment, he would find any excuse to come over to our house and spend time with us. Now that he lived there, he found every excuse to get out. He justified his absence to my Mom by reminding her he had three jobs since he had never relied on his parents financially. Apparently, he had moved out of his parents' house at a very young age and had learned how to make it on his own, picking up odd jobs here and there. He had also mentioned something about a trust fund from a great uncle who had passed away years ago, but Donna never questioned him to get more details. This odd behavior slowly progressed into him being absent from home for weeks at a time. However, he always seemed to make up for it whenever he came back, by becoming the male version of a Stepford wife. He would go grocery shopping, making sure I had enough diapers to last me a while; get the coffee machine ready in the evening so Donna would have a fresh cup of coffee in the morning; and so on. He really made a good family man. At the beginning, Donna, who had noticed Steve's odd behavior, would brush those wondering thoughts away by blaming herself for thinking ill of such a wonderful man. She would justify it as something to be expected, given that he had gotten into a rather heavy situation. After all, she was no longer just a girl who enjoyed carefree days. She came with baggage, which she was well aware of. She was a divorcée with a kid to raise, so taking on this package deal all at once would have proven to be a challenge even for the kindest, most committed man on Earth.

Yet his off behavior persisted. One night, Diane slept over. Steve was supposed to be out of town, so Diane shared the bed with Mom. While the two women slept peacefully, Steve came into the apartment and walked into the bedroom. He stayed there at the foot of the bed, staring at them for quite some time, before my mother slowly opened her eyes and jumped up in fear, letting out a suffocated gasp which woke up my aunt. After the initial shock, it took a while for the two women to fall back asleep. While tossing and turning, Donna kept thinking of how weird Steve was at times. Who *does* that? What kind of normal person just stays there, staring at people while they sleep? Something was surely off. Confused and startled, Donna made the decision to take a step back in her relationship with Steve and be a bit more watchful of this change in his personality. As much as she enjoyed his company and having his help, she had a baby to think about first and foremost, and she would have never allowed anything or anyone to put my safety at risk.

Months went by, and the nonsense did not stop. On the contrary, it was escalating to a point where things no longer just looked weird but were totally insane. Steve, who would often disappear for weeks upon end without even saying a word nor mentioning where he was heading, began telling my Mom that he was sure our phone line was being tapped by the FBI. Donna had no idea of where some of these allegations were coming from, but she had made up her mind that the relationship was closely reaching its expiration date. In May of 1976, Donna, who had had enough of Steve's nonsense, decided to face him after his umpteenth allegation that the whole apartment was being surveilled by the FBI.

"That's enough!" Donna began.

"What is enough?" Steve questioned.

"I can't put up with these absurd claims of yours!"

"You think these are absurd claims?" Steve raised his voice, "You have no idea what I'm going through here, trying to deter those agents from monitoring my life! The apartment is wired; this whole apartment is under scrutiny by the police, and the FBI agents, and God knows who else!"

Steve was becoming physically agitated. His palms were sweating, there was a tremor in his voice that suggested his nerves were up in flames, and he looked rather jittery.

"You are crazy!" Donna had had enough.

At the sound of those words, Steve stopped shaking. He took a step closer to Donna, who could now see the fury building up in his eyes. Her heart rate started going up, and her mouth had suddenly become paralyzingly dry. She swallowed fear, which made her lungs shut down in panic. She had never seen a more menacing look into anybody's eyes. Before she had a chance to react and step away, Steve spit in her face. His nasty, threatening saliva hit her right on her cheeks, the same ones that had tasted her tears many times before but that now burned with the pain of betrayal. Shock paralyzed her body, while anger started to poison her blood. Just as her mind began to formulate thoughts of revenge and self-defense, Steve punched her in her right eye, shocking these thoughts out of her mind all at once. The blow was so hard that she hit her back against the wall and fell down.

Pain. My eye...pain.
Panic.
"Tina...Don't cry, baby..."
Pain.
Gasping for air.
Help.
Help...

***

It was the second Sunday of May and, as usual, children all over the country were rushing to prepare the perfect gift to proudly give to the most important woman in their life: mother. Steve spent Mother's Day at his parents' house. He was outside the front porch, sitting down on the steps that led into the house. A neighbor, who had known Steve for a long time, waved to him, but Steve did not even attempt to greet him back. He was just there, staring into space. Wondering if the young man was okay, the neighbor walked closer to him. Nothing. Steve did not even glance at him to acknowledge his presence a few feet away. *That's weird*, thought his neighbor. He then asked Steve if he was okay, but his words went lost in the spring breeze.

Later that day, Steve stepped back inside the house, went to the kitchen where his mother was and, out of nowhere, said, "My girlfriend thinks I'm crazy." He sounded monotone.

"Girlfriend?" His mother was surprised. "I didn't know you had a girlfriend, Steve. Who is she?"

"I have the devil inside of me," Steve mumbled, completely ignoring his mother's question.

"What?" His mother was confused. "What are you talking about, Steve? Who's this girlfriend, and why does she think you're crazy?"

Silence.

"Steve?"

Silence.

"Are you okay?"

"I don't know why I say or do those things," Steve mumbled again. "Mom, should anything happen to me, make sure to tell my sister and my friends that…" he didn't finish.

He turned around quickly and left his parents' house. His mother tried following him to the front door, begging him to stop, yelling at him to go back inside and finish the conversation; but he had already left. For the next few weeks, Steve went up and down the West Coast, couch-surfing at his friends' houses and constantly on the move. His odd behavior only escalated from that point on.

***

Ring.

Ring.

"Hello?" Donna answered the phone.

Silence.

"Hello?" Donna repeated.

Silence.

"Anyone there?"

"It's me," Steve answered in a monotone voice.

"Steve?" Donna jumped up. "What do you want?"

"I wanna talk to you."

"Yea? Well, I don't wanna talk to you!" The tremble in her tone gave away the fear brought by their last encounter.

"I wanna come see you." He sounded rather dull.

"Don't. I don't wanna see you." Donna gained her composure and was now confident in her ways.

"I'm in San Diego. I wanna come see you."

"Stay away from me, you hear me?" Donna screamed at him. Then, she hung up.

A few days went by after the phone call, and life for Donna had started to regain its normalcy, which made her feel very positive. Her days were mostly spent with Valerie, who was now on the hunt for a new man in her life. She and Donna would spend their free time going on "spy rides" in Newark to look for a guy Valerie had developed a crush on. It was fun for them, because it took their minds off what had happened between Steve and Donna. Valerie couldn't help but feel responsible for how their relationship had ended. After all, she was the one who introduced her to him. In her defense, she had no clue how damaged he was, and how could she? He had never shown any signs of mental instability — or had he?

When June rolled around, Mom was very busy planning for my second birthday. Mary and Leo had offered their house as a possible party location, and Donna happily accepted. She wanted to get out of her apartment. Steve kept up with his random phone calls from many different states, and Donna had grown tired of him and his odd behavior. The party was held early in the afternoon, and the house was decorated with lots of birthday balloons, which I proceeded to grab and pop, scaring myself with the *bang* noise. Lots of people came by, including my dad, who brought me lots of gifts. Seven children had come to the party bearing gifts for me, and they all had a good time, especially when it was time to eat the cake. Mom surprised everybody in attendance when I began singing along with the birthday song. She hadn't told anyone that she had been practicing singing it with me for weeks in advance so I'd be ready for my party. My grandparents had teary eyes when they heard me singing along, and they all clapped when I somehow managed to actually blow out my two candles. It was a very joyous afternoon for everyone.

Once my birthday was over, it was time to get ready for my mom's, which was at the end of the same month. Although she did not have any big plans, her parents invited us over to their house for a good meal and fun times spent with family and friends. Later that evening, Valerie and her daughters came over to our apartment, and they surprised Donna with a birthday cake and an impromptu mini- birthday party. That day, my mom had two birthday parties and two birthday cakes. She was over the moon, and so touched by how everyone around always made her feel special. She was excited to enter her twenty-fourth year of life. When she went to bed that night, she crossed her arms behind her neck and, looking up at the ceiling, went through all the things she wanted to accomplish over the next year. Spending more quality time with me, and taking me to the zoo and out for ice cream, were high up on her list. Being a mother had always been her number one priority, and she took great pride in watching me grow up and achieving my little yet fundamental milestones.

Between my birthday and hers, Donna thought June flew by quickly. It was now July, and the summer heat of New Jersey was causing quite a few people to choose to stay inside rather than going out—but not Donna and Valerie, who were busy making plans for the Fourth of July. There was supposed to be a huge celebration, since these were the Bicentennial fireworks of 1976. The two ladies decided to spend the day on James Street, as the fireworks were going to be held at Foley Field. Everyone there was waiting with great anticipation, especially us kids who had never seen fireworks before. The countdown to the fireworks had begun, and my Mom picked me up in her arms.

"All right, baby," she said, "I need you to look up there in the sky for me, okay?" she told me, pointing up.

My gaze followed her index finger, and right when my eyes had settled on the dark patch of sky above us, the fireworks began—bright noisy and absolutely terrifying! I started screaming so hard that my mother had no idea how to calm me down. She was not expecting such a reaction from me; but in my defense, I was only two, and the fireworks were *loud*! Donna glanced at Valerie, who was now dealing with very upset daughters as well. In fact, both of them were yelling with fear, and Donna thanked the heavens she only had one screaming child to handle. The two friends exchanged a quick look, and they immediately knew what the other one had in mind: We all went back home right away, making that long-planned trip one of the shortest ones we had ever taken together.

August was shaping up to be a very fun month for both Donna and Valerie, who had been planning their one-week getaway to Wildwood. This was going to be the very first time the childhood friends took a trip together, even though they had talked about it for years. However, life happened, and one thing led to another, and the two never got around to actually taking the ladies-only trip—until this year. They had found a cute place to stay and even put down a deposit. It was right on the beach, which was ideal considering they planned on spending their days working on their tans and their evenings having fun and enjoying live music. They were both so excited about their vacation they could hardly wait for July to finally end.

On July 13, Donna received another phone call from Steve, who begged her to meet with him since he was now back in New Jersey and staying with his longtime friend in Long Beach Island. Donna, who wanted to put a definite period on her relationship with him, knew that he wouldn't let go of her until she told him face-to-face that it was over, so she agreed to meet with him at her parents' house that same evening, since her sister and brother-in-law were staying at her apartment. He accepted the invite and showed up at around seven in the evening. Donna had been building up the courage to tell Steve it was over between them, but this was no easy task for her. She had truly loved this man, to the point that she had even pictured a more serious future together, but he had betrayed her in the worst way. She had never witnessed domestic violence in her life, since both her parents and Tom had always treated her with nothing but white gloves even during the bad times. Being assaulted by him had turned her world upside down; her self-confidence had been shaken and her self-esteem shattered. She spent nights crying over him, wondering if she had done something to trigger his irrational behavior; but in her heart, she knew she had absolutely nothing to do with his mental instability. He was sick, and he needed help immediately. Should she tell him? No, that wasn't going to be part of her conversation with him. She wanted to cut him out of her life once and for all, and she wanted absolutely nothing else to do with him. He was no longer her concern. She had herself to think about, and a young daughter to take care of. She needed a stable, responsible man by her side, not one who could switch up his personality in less than a second. She did not want anything else to do with him, and she was determined to make that clear to him.

When Steve heard the news, his head fell into his open palms. He did not utter a single word after that. He just kept shaking his head in what looked like a rather mechanical move, almost as if his body was moving by default. Then, after Donna told him he had to stop by the apartment at some point to gather his belongings, Steve just got up and left the house. Donna was puzzled by his reaction—or, actually, lack thereof. He didn't even try to justify himself or apologize for his behavior. He just stood there as if present in body but not all there in mind and spirit. He seemed to be focusing on other things that were going on in his mind while Donna was explaining the reasoning behind her decision. *What a weird person*, she thought to herself after he left.

The night was peaceful, and Donna got some good rest even though she slept with both me and Ronnie. We all woke up early for breakfast, and Valerie joined us as well. Once Diane and her husband had made their way back to pick up their child, Donna and Valerie said goodbye to everyone and headed back to the apartment. Before going back home, however, they made sure to stop by the store to grab a few bags of chips and, since it was Wednesday, the ladies knew we were going to have JJ's hot dogs for lunch. They both loved that ritual, because at times it was one of the few good things going on in their life. After arriving at the apartment, Mom put me down for a nap, and she went to the bathroom. She noticed that a couple of tiles were down and that the room was messy. Irritated, she cleaned it up fast. She hated seeing her house untidy, because a clean house gave her peace of mind and made her feel serene. As she was getting her cleaning supplies ready, the phone rang.

"Hello?" Donna said.

"Hey, Donna, it's me." She recognized the voice. It was her brother-in-law. "Listen, I'm here with Diane at your parents' house, and I'm calling to let you know that Steve was just here."

"Steve?" She was perplexed. "What was he there for?"

"I'm not sure, but he was looking for you."

"Okay." Donna felt unease.

"I told him you were back at your apartment, so he might be showing up soon."

"Okay. Thanks for letting me know," Donna replied.

"Are you going to be okay?" he asked, worried by the unusual tone of her voice that gave away the fact she was rather uncomfortable about seeing him again.

"Yeah," she murmured. "Yes, sure. Thank you for calling."

"No worries. Bye now."

They hung up. Donna, who was standing by the phone looking anxious, turned towards Valerie, who, meanwhile, had gotten close to her friend. She was holding me in her arms, since the phone ringing had woken me up.

"What's wrong?" Valerie asked.

"Steve's coming here." She barely whispered.

She slowly walked to the couch, sat down, placed her hands between her knees, and bowed her head.

"Are you all right?" Valerie asked her friend, who was visibly agitated.

Before she had the chance to reply and tell Valerie what was going on in her mind, the doorbell rang. Steve had arrived.

Interlude

Dear Reader,

Before we move on with a story whose ending I cannot change, let me briefly press pause. Allow me to be two years old for a little while longer. Grant me permission to keep my mother with me just for another brief minute. I am not ready to let go of the leading lady in my life. Don't let the curtains close just yet. Don't turn the lights off on this amazing and promising stage that has been her life. I am not ready to stop looking at her beautiful face. I am not ready to be left without her comforting hugs, her gentle kisses, and her reassuring voice. Let me listen to one last lullaby before I drift away in my sleep. Let me be with my mother one more time. Just one more time.

Donna Lee Litchfield. June 30, 1952-July 14, 1976.

Chapter Four

911, What's your emergency?
[BREATHING HEAVILY] Yes…um…
Hello? What's the address?
19 Brighton Avenue…um…
Okay, ma'am, I need you to calm down. What's your name?
Sorry, I think I dialed the wrong number.

Suddenly, all went silent in the apartment. One moment Steve and Donna were screaming at each other, yelling and arguing, and the next moment all was quiet. Not a noise. Nothing. Had they made up? Valerie wasn't sure. She had seen Donna struggle in the bathtub, trying to defend herself against Steve, who was hitting her repeatedly. That was the scene that prompted her to call for help. Yet, as soon as she dialed the emergency number, the two of them had gone completely silent. Had something happened?

***

Ten minutes earlier:
"Marlana, since you are the oldest, I'll leave you in charge, okay?"
"Okay, mommy. Where are you going?"
"I'm going back to Auntie Donna to make sure she's safe, all right?"
"Okay."
"Now, listen to Mommy. Do not open the car door for anybody but me, got it?"
"Got it."
"Nobody! Not even Steve, all right?"
"Yes, mommy."
"Okay. I will be back soon. Take care of Monique and Tina in the meanwhile."
"Okay, mommy."

* * *

"Steve, open the door!" Valerie yelled while hitting the bathroom door with a thump.

Silence.

"Donna, are you okay?" Valerie screamed, catching her breath. "Donna!"

Silence.

"Steve!"

"Who is it?"

"Who do you think it is? Open the door!"

The bathroom door makes a squeaky sound as it opens, revealing Steve standing behind it, Donna's legs hanging outside of the bathtub.

"Donna's dead," he says.

* * *

"Good afternoon, ma'am. What can I do for you today? Oh, lovely girls you have there!" A man in his late fifties greeted Valerie at a nearby gas station.

"Call 911!" She yelled.

"I'm sorry?"

"Call 911! My girlfriend's been murdered!" She could barely breathe.

"Oh, my God!"

With shaky hands, the man grabbed the phone and dialed the emergency number. What followed is all a blur for Valerie.

* * *

The first people to arrive at the scene were the Emergency Medical Services and the firefighters, who were in the area. As they rushed in the apartment building, Steve was walking out. They asked if he needed any help, noticing he was soaking wet, which they found rather strange; yet he did not bother answering their question and just kept walking.

"Do me a favor, write down his license plate," one fireman told his colleague.

Steve's wet footprints led to Donna's basement apartment, so they followed them. They noticed my toys out in the hallway and proceeded to knock on the door that opened at the slightest touch. Inside, they could see the kitchen, whose floor was covered with bloody water. The whole apartment was later described as a bloodbath. They saw my playpen in the living room, but no signs of a child. They checked the bedroom; nobody in there. Then they entered the bathroom. The fully-clothed, lifeless body of my beloved mother was face up in a bathtub filled with water. There were no signs of the murder weapon.

When the police arrived, they informed the firefighters that I was with a family friend who had taken me away from the apartment before the murder happened. Since Valerie could testify that Stephen was the killer, there were no questions as to who murdered my mother. The real question, however, was: Where did he go? Quickly, the police put an APB out on his vehicle. The hunt for Stephen Moore had begun.

The police had the difficult task of calling my grandparents to tell them about their daughter. My father was also called, as well as my Aunt Diane, who told law enforcement that Steve spent a lot of time at his friends' in Long Beach Island. She remembered that one of his closest friends owned a service station there, and gave police his name. Not long after they had become aware of the service station, LBI police confirmed that the suspect's vehicle was spotted at that location. The officer who had found the car waited outside the service station until Belleville policemen arrived.

Once they made their way inside the location, they identified Stephen Moore. They asked him if he knew why they were there, and if he had been in North Jersey earlier that day. His answer was a simple "Yes." Meanwhile, they obtained permission to search him and his vehicle and found that neither contained blood, but they did find soaking wet clothes in the back of his car. Policemen took note that he was wearing a flannel shirt — a rather odd choice given that it was July.

"Mr. O'Dell, are you the owner of this service station?" The police questioned him.

"Yes," he replied, confused about what was happening.

"Do you know this man, by the name Stephen Moore?"

"Yes, he's been friends with my son for many years."

"Did you notice anything strange about Mr. Moore's behavior today?"

"Hmm...no. just that he was a bit quieter than normal, and he seemed to be smoking a bit more than usual. Why? Did something happen?"

"Mr. O'Dell, do you recognize the knife in this picture?" The policeman showed him a photo of the murder weapon.

"Yes, I do. It's a knife we keep here in the shop."

"Were you aware that the knife was missing?"

"No, not at all." The man took a deep breath and shook his head. "Stephen must have taken it this morning. It's really nothing you look for unless you need it."

After hearing Mr. O'Dell's words, the policemen placed Stephen Moore under arrest for the murder of Donna Litchfield. His car was taken for further investigation.

* * *

A-8 The Herald News, Thursday, July 15, 1976 • Serving North Jersey

'Boy friend' held in murder

By KENNETH MOORE
Herald-News Staff Writer

BELLEVILLE — The jilted boy friend of a young mother was seized Wednesday night in a South Jersey resort town, hours after her knifed body was found in the bathtub of her Brighton Avenue apartment, police said.

Steven C. Moore, 26, was arrested in Surf City after the slaying of Donna Litchfield, 24, during a "vicious fight" in the bathroom of her basement apartment at 19 Brighton Ave., according to police.

Reconstructing the incident, police said Mrs. Litchfield apparently was cleaning the bathroom when Moore arrived and the fight began.

A woman friend of the blonde-haired victim, who was divorced, hurried Mrs. Litchfield's two-year-old daughter, Tina, and another child out of the apartment and called Belleville police shortly after 2:30 p.m.

THE FRIEND, whose identity was withheld by police, returned to the apartment, where she witnessed the final moments, said Anthony Mautone, assistant Essex County prosecutor in charge of homicide.

When police arrived, they found the fully-clothed body lying face up and half-submerged in the full bathtub, Mautone said. A hunting knife with a six-inch blade lay beneath the body, he said.

"There was a rather large, gaping, cutting wound in her throat," Mautone said. "There were about 10 to 12 stab wounds, along with defensive wounds on her hands and arms."

The defensive wounds and "blood spattered on the far wall of the room indicated a pretty vicious fight," Mautone said.

FRIENDS of the victim told police Moore had acquaintances in Surf City, and local police notified authorities there, said Det. Thomas Glisenan of the prosecutor's office.

Almost immediately, Surf City police noticed Moore's car parked in front of a residence across the street from the police station, Glisenan said.

Moore, the son of a Montclair dentist, offered no resistance when arrested, Glisenan said. A search warrant will be obtained for the Surf City address, he said.

Moore was to be arraigned this morning in municipal court here on a murder charge, authorities said.

NEIGHBORS on Brighton Avenue, which is dominated by the large Brighton Estates garden apartments, knew little about Mrs. Litchfield. According to Belleville Det. Lt. Raymond Kimball, she moved into the complex about a year ago.

This was a murder that shook the entire community. News of what happened was spreading quickly. Many newspapers wrote about it; radio stations and TV channels covered it as well. People were left wondering: Who would commit such a brutal murder? What kind of person would take a mother away from her two-year-old daughter? Who would be capable of such violence towards a young woman with her whole life ahead of her? No matter how they formulated the question, the answer always had the same name and surname: Stephen Moore.

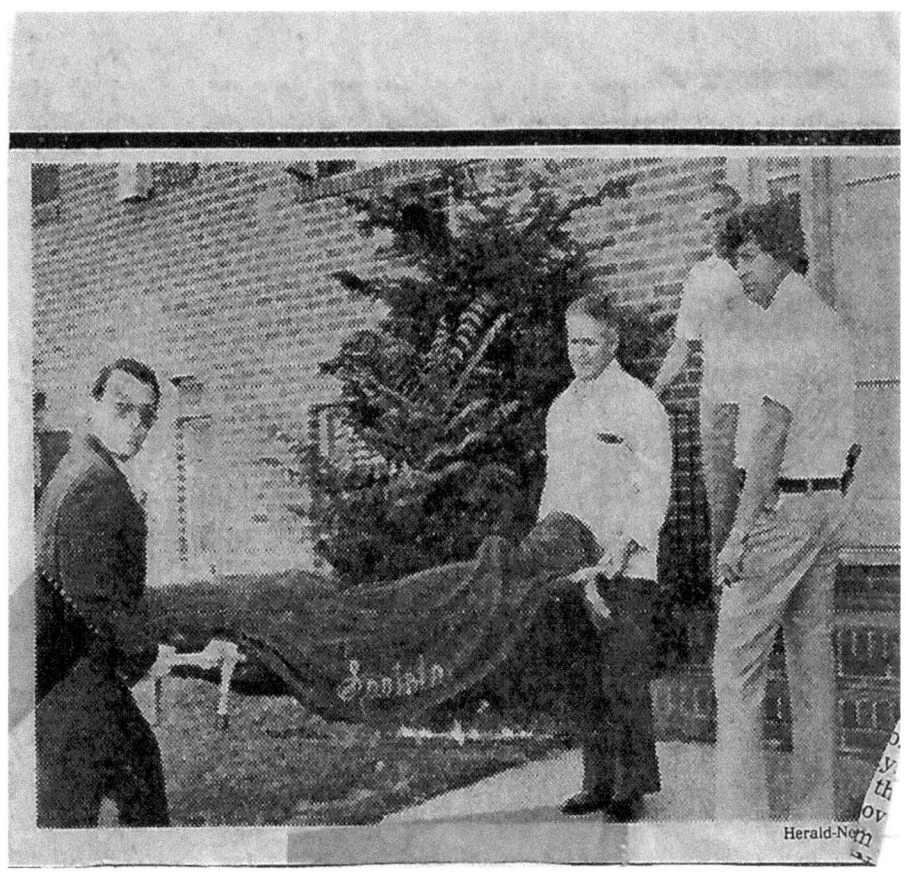

Authorities carrying the body of Donna Litchfield out of her home.

Chapter Five

Bail denied suspect in Belleville murder

By KENNETH MOORE
Herald-News Staff Writer

BELLEVILLE — Stephen Moore, 26, was ordered held without bail Thursday, charged with Wednesday's stabbing murder of his girlfriend, a young Belleville woman.

Moore was arraigned in connection with the murder of Donna Leitchfield, 24, during a brief session in Belleville Municipal Court before Judge Salvatore Intintola.

Five hours after Mrs. Leitchfield's body was found Wednesday afternoon in the full bathtub of her Brighton Avenue apartment, Moore was arrested in Surf City, near Atlantic City.

The mother of a two-year-old daughter, Mrs. Leitchfield was separated from her husband, said Anthony Mautone, assistant Essex County prosecutor in charge of homicide.

ALTHOUGH Mautone declined Thursday to discuss a motive for the murder, early police reports said the victim had tried to break off her relationship with Moore.

A friend of the victim was in the apartment when Moore arrived Wednesday afternoon and began arguing with Mrs. Leitchfield, Mautone said.

The friend, whose identity is being withheld by police, left the apartment to call police, returning at the closing moments of the fatal attack, Mautone said.

"She's just about an eyewitness," Mautone said. "Absent her having seen him inflict the stab wounds, there couldn't be a better witness."

MOORE, dressed in blue jeans and a plaid shirt, made no statement during his arraignment except to curtly acknowledge the charge.

The suspect's last known address was on Grove St., Bloomfield, police said, but "he had been all along the West Coast in the past seven weeks," according to Mautone.

"Indications are that he called Mrs. Leitchfield from San Diego and Oregon," Mautone added.

Police found Mrs. Leitchfield's fully-clothed body Wednesday bearing "at least a dozen stab wounds, including a gaping slash wound in the throat," Mautone said.

According to Belleville police, Mrs. Leitchfield had moved into the Brighton Avenue apartment about a year ago.

Steven Moore

The pre-trial hearing for Steve was set for late October. Given all the momentum that had been building up around this case, people were waiting for the pretrial outcome with anticipation. At the time, I was obviously too young to grasp the magnitude of what was going on in the months following my mother's murder. My father was actually doing an admirable job of keeping me sheltered from it all. For that, I will be forever thankful to him.

When pre-trial began, people tuned in on TV news channels and radio stations and bought newspapers to read all about the man who had so brutally killed a young woman, mother of a two-year-old baby girl. Although most people who heard the news had never even met or seen my mother, there was definitely something so emotionally shocking about this situation that it really grabbed the attention of many — and provoked emotions of sorrow and compassion in all.

The pretrial hearing began October 28, 1976 at the Essex County Courthouse. The case, State of New Jersey v. Stephen Moore, was set before the Honorable Ralph Fusco. That Thursday, the sun was shining, and the average temperature registered 53 degrees. Everyone who was present in court stood up when the judge entered the room.

"All right, Mr. Prosecutor, will you indicate the name of the matter we are considering, sir?" Judge Fusco began.

"Yes, your honor," Dennis Mautone, Assistant Prosecutor replied, sounding confident. "We are here for an indictment against one Stephen Moore, charging the crime of murder while armed. Indictment 4406 the '75 term and this is a pretrial for that case."

Judge Fusco looked around the courtroom, then down on the documents in front of him, and while scribbling something on a piece of paper, asked, "And for the defendant?"

"Your Honor," said a man dressed in what looked like a rather expensive suit. "Edward Schutzer, from the firm of Schwartz & Fielo, Belleville, appearing on behalf of the defendant."

"Now, you had an opportunity this morning to talk to your client. Is he cognizant of the proceedings you have taken, and those you are now indicating of the motion to have the court make a determination on whether Mr. Moore is competent to consult with counsel?" Judge Fusco inquired, looking at Steve, who was sitting next to his lawyer.

"I have conferred with my client. He is aware of the fact that I made the motion for a competency hearing, and he is apparently in accord with my judgment that he wishes to proceed to go to trial. He has indicated to me he *does* wish to go to trial; however, he is afraid anything he says will be held against him, although I have advised him that this will not be the case. He is ready and prepared to go to trial."

"It's not that I am afraid," Steve said, all of a sudden. "I just don't understand."

"I didn't hear you," Judge Fusco replied, sounding surprised by the abrupt interruption.

"It's not that I am afraid; it's just that I don't understand the proceedings of the court. I understand what I say counts against me; that's why I am having Mr. Schutzer speak for me."

"Go ahead, Mr. Schutzer," Judge Fusco said, releasing what sounded like a rather exasperated sigh.

"Your honor, although, as Mr. Moore indicates to the court, he doesn't understand because he is a layman, I think Mr. Moore is fully aware of the role of the lawyer as to judges and whatever. He indicated to me not only his willingness but his fervent desire, to consult with me and to have me direct the defense in this trial," Mr. Schutzer briefly glanced at Steve while talking in a failed attempt at making eye contact with this client. Then, after picking up a paper from his folder, he stood up and continued. "I refer the court to reports of both my doctors, Dr. Kern and Dr. Gelsinger, indicating the personality structure of the type whereby this defense can easily crumble and loosely reintegrate itself to the extent Mr. Moore can operate at a low level of functioning in a structured environment."

As he was done reading, Judge Fusco invited him with a hand gesture to continue speaking on the matter.

"I refer the courts as well to the last page of Dr. Latimer's report, where he says that from the formal standpoint, it is possible that the patient's condition does not match the requirements of competence to stand trial—inasmuch as he knows what the charges are and the dangers involved, as well the roles of the participants in the trial. Dr. Latimer indicates he discussed the matter greatly with Mr. Moore." Mr. Schutzer briefly paused as he took a sip of water from the glass sitting on his desk. "In addition, your honor, I refer the court to the final page of Dr. Kern's report, the state psychiatrist, wherein he said, 'Mr. Moore is oriented to time, place, and person.' These, your honor, appear to be the essential prerequisites for the defendant, who wishes to stand trial and to assist intelligently with his counsel in the preparation and execution of his defense."

"Now Mr. Moore," Judge Fusco said, "your lawyer made an application to me, reported by two reports by doctors, indicating that you may be too ill…"

"I saw three doctors," Steve interrupted.

"Pardon?" Judge Fusco questioned, surprised.

"I saw *three* doctors."

"You saw three doctors. I know that. That's all right. Your lawyer made an application to me reported by two doctors who tell me he thought that you didn't know enough about the case and what was going on so that you can confer with him, and help him with your defense."

"Your Honor," Steve continued. "I would like to work with the warden and change some of the rules in this institution, or jail."

"What you want to do with the warden?" Judge Fusco asked, blinking twice.

"Well," Steve said, very nonchalant, "I would like to talk with him; change some of the rules, some of the food conditions and living conditions."

"I have no control over the warden," Judge Fusco informed the defendant. "I'm sure that one of the guards can arrange for you to discuss with the warden or send him a note as to what your problem may be with the conditions, but the court has no control over that."

"I wrote letters to get an answer," Steve persisted. "No mail. I tried to talk to the officers; no response. That's why I'm mentioning it to you."

"I don't run the jail. That's the warden's responsibility," Judge Fusco reiterated in the hopes of quieting Steve's issues.

"Could you put a note in?" Steve had no intention of being quiet. "I'd like to see him."

"I can't make that request. That's between you and the warden. Your lawyer says to me he discussed it with you, that you know what you are being charged with—and by the way, what *are* you being charged with, do you know?"

"Supposedly alleged homicide."

"*Alleged* homicide?"

"Yes."

"What do you mean by alleged homicide?" Judge Fusco sounded curious.

"I don't understand the term, but supposedly to take a life."

"You know homicide means to take a life?"

"Right."

"Do you know when this alleged homicide is supposed to have taken place?"

"Supposed to have taken place July 13 or 14," Steve said, looking at the judge.

"1976?" Judge Fusco completed Steve's sentence.

"Yes, sir."

"Where is it supposed to have taken place?"

"In Belleville, sir. I don't know if this person is alive or dead."

"Pardon?" Judge Fusco was caught off guard by the defendant's admission.

"I don't know if the person is alive or dead," Steve repeated.

"I understand you don't, but I mean, you do know that you are being charged with committing a homicide, and it says here of one Donna Litchfield. I realize that if the State wants to establish your guilt, they have to prove not only that you did it, but they have to prove the person is dead." Judge Fusco glanced at Steve's lawyer and then asked, "How do they say you allegedly committed this homicide in the indictment?"

"It's on a paper I gave him," Steve replied.

"What does it say?"

"I don't have it. He has it." Steve said, nodding towards his lawyer.

"What does it say?" Judge Fusco inquired, "Do you remember?"

"Under the conditions I got arrested."

"In the paper, doesn't it say you did it with a knife?"

"Supposedly." Steve sounded bothered by the judge's question.

"That's what the paper says; I am not saying that you did," Judge Fusco reassured him. "So, you know what you are being charged with. Do you know who your attorney is?"

"Mr. Schutzer."

"Are you satisfied with the advice you are getting from him?"

"Well, he says my father appointed him." Steve still sounded bothered.

"Are you satisfied with his advice?"

"Well, I have a couple other lawyers I would like to work with him."

"Who are the other lawyers?"

"I don't have them. I haven't talked to them."

"When are you going to talk to them?" Judge Fusco asked, curious to know more.

"I want to contact Mrs. Kerry in New York, Meyer Lofsky in Paterson, and Bennett & Bennett in Newark," Steve affirmed.

"Have you talked to Mr. Schutzer about that?"

"Yes."

"Did you tell him?"

"Just before we came in here," Steve answered, briefly looking at his lawyer.

"You can wait until the night before the trial. When are you going to talk to the other lawyers?"

"I tried to make a phone call; I couldn't make any phone calls to get out of here. $300,000 bail." Steve mumbled.

"Has your father been in to see you?"

"I don't know if he is dead or alive."

"Pardon?" Judge Fusco was surprised to hear his statement.

"I don't know if he is dead or alive."

"Has he been in to see you?"

"He is in Montclair, hasn't come." Steve brushed it off.

"He hired Mr. Schutzer, though." Judge Fusco reminded Steve.

"I am paying for Mr. Schutzer." Steve sounded upset by the judge's statement, "I am over 21, but I mean, he says my father contacted him to represent me."

"You are saying you are paying for Mr. Schutzer?"

"Yes." Steve raised his voice a little bit, "Why should my father pay for him?"

"I am asking. I don't know." Judge Fusco cleared his throat and then proceeded to pick up the conversation where he had left off. "I indicated to you, Mr. Schutzer now says that from his conversations with you and everything he knows about this case…"

"I don't know what his fee is," Steve interrupted him again, "What is your fee?"

"That's between you and him." Judge Fusco dismissed him. "I don't get involved in that."

"I don't understand the different charges and fees. I'm not trying to be wise. I don't understand the law procedures."

"Mr. Schutzer tells me after reading the doctors' reports and talking to you, he feels you know enough about what is going on so that you can go to trial on this case. Do you understand that?"

"Yes. I want to go to trial, and you know…"

"You *want* to go to trial?" This time, Judge Fusco interrupted Steve.

"Yes. I want to get jail," Steve affirmed.

"What is the trial date?"

"November 7th?" Steve asked his lawyer.

"The 8th," Judge Fusco corrected him.

"This man told me November 7th," Steve said, pointing at the lawyer standing next to him. "He wrote it on a piece of paper: pretrial the 7th."

"I will correct it," Judge Fusco reassured him. "By the way, this girl was supposed to have been your girlfriend?"

"Yes."

"What is her name?"

"Donna Litchfield," he said. "If she is alive, I want to see her, you know—but on the other hand, if she is dead, you can't see her. Can't you bring her back to life if she is dead?"

"You tell me," Judge Fusco said, looking at Steve.

"I don't know."

"Well, as I said, the State is going to prove it."

"I mean, is it possible I could be framed, that this person is dead?" Steve asked.

"Certainly, you could be framed. That's what your lawyer is here to protect you from, being framed." Judge Fusco humored him.

"She could be hiding someplace. Somebody could be paying her to put me in jail or something."

"Mr. Moore, I have already indicated Mr. Shutzer thinks that you are aware enough of what is going on to stand trial. Do you have any objection, and are you willing to try case beginning November 8th?" Judge Fusco asked in a firm tone.

"I want to go to trial, get it over with so that I can get jail." Steve dismissed him.

Judge Fusco looked down on his papers. He took a deep breath and took his glasses off. After rubbing his temples, he cleared his throat and said, "Gentlemen, in view of the action by defense counsel and my opportunity to converse with Mr. Moore, I can say he is cognizant of the charge that the alleged homicide played on or about the 13th or 14th of July 1976, that the alleged victim was one Donna Litchfield, and the alleged charge of homicide arose by reason of use of a knife; and the defendant's further observation that he has retained counsel, is satisfied with counsel of his choice, and is desirous of going to trial. I am going to dismiss the motion heretofore filed returnable October 21, 1976, requesting that a hearing be held to determine competency of the defendant to stand trial."

"Your Honor…" Steve interrupted, once again.

"Yes, Mr. Moore?" Judge Fusco sounded irritated.

"I would like to go book President Ford."

"I beg your pardon?"

"I would like to press charges against President Ford. I want to broadcast I didn't find any paper to be broadcasting ABC. My lawyer told me my conscience is being read aloud over television and CBS radio. I want it to stop," Steve rambled on.

"All right." Judge Fusco dismissed him. "Is there an alibi defense?"

"No, your honor, there isn't."

"You have already indicated you are going to interpose an insanity defense?" Judge Fusco asked the defense attorney.

"Yes, your honor."

"How many witnesses do you contemplate calling prosecutor?"

"Twelve to fourteen, sir."

"Mr. Schutzer?"

"Your Honor, at this time, six or seven."

"All right. How long do you think it will take prosecutor?"

"Eight days, sir."

"Mr. Schutzer?"

"Your Honor, I think about seven or eight days."

"All right," Judge Fusco said in a closing statement, "Thank you, gentlemen."

***

The trial date was fast approaching. Many people were interested to learn of the killer's fate. Amid speculations, fake news, allegations, and gossip, one thing played as the common denominator among all those who knew about the trial: for justice to be served! The entire courtroom was packed with people and security guards. Among all of the witnesses that would be called to testify, including firemen who first responded to the 911 call and Mr. O'Dell, who had unknowingly provided Steve with the murder weapon, nobody was more anxious than Valerie. She was the key witness, and she was aware that her deposition was the one everybody was waiting to hear.

The trial finally began November 15, 1976. Dennis Mautone was Assistant Prosecutor for the state of New Jersey, and Edward Schutzer was still appointed attorney for the defendant. In the courtroom, tension was definitely high. Mautone, dressed in a very elegant suit, stood up and walked in front of the jury. He quickly adjusted his tie, cleared his throat and began his opening statement,

"Judge Fusco; Mr. Schutzer; ladies and gentlemen of the jury; my name is Dennis Mautone. As you know, I am the Assistant Prosecutor in Essex County. I am charged with the responsibility of presenting a case to you — a case that is brought before you by indictment 4406 of the '75 term. This indictment is the spark, the catalyst, to bring us all here to decide the issues based on the testimony we will hear come from the witness stand and from whatever evidence will be introduced in this case. By this indictment, Stephen C. Moore is charged by the grand jury of the state of New Jersey 1976 in the town of Belleville that he did willfully, feloniously, and with malice aforethought kill and murder Donna Litchfield; and in count two of the indictment, the grand jurors charge that Stephen did have and place and in the jurisdiction set forth in the first date in his possession a dangerous knife during the commission of that unlawful killing in New Jersey.

"Ladies and gentlemen, all unlawful killings are considered to be murder in the second degree. There are certain proofs that will be used from the witness stand which may either elevate the crime to murder in the first degree, and those proofs will be necessary in order to find a case of murder in the first degree. We all have a very important function in the determination of this case. Mr. Shutzer is here to ensure the defendant has proper legal representation. Your Honor Judge Fusco is charged with the responsibility of making certain legal judgments and rulings during the pendency of these proceedings, and with charging you as to the law that you are to apply to the case or to the facts of the case that you here testify to. My responsibility as the assistant prosecutor in charge of this case is to present it to you as clearly and consistently as I can. I will do everything in my power to do so. Responsibility, ladies and gentlemen, if that responsibility of that fact. You will be asked to listen to the testimony that comes from the stands; you will be asked to sift through the evidence that is produced in this case; and you will be asked to come to a fair and just conclusion based on the law as the judge tells you, and as applied to the facts that you hear. Now, when making these determinations, you will be asked to go into the jury room. Do not, I implore you, do *not* leave your common sense, your reasonableness, your everyday experiences, without bringing them in there with you. They will be very important and very useful in determining the true issues in this case.

"I want to outline for you very briefly what the state intends to prove in this case, so that you will have more to assist you in following the testimony as it comes forth. The State's case essentially will revolve around July 13th and July 14th, 1976. On July 13th, 1976, we will show you, Stephen Moore, the defendant, in this case, united with the victim, Donna Litchfield, at the home of her sister in Bloomfield, and that during the visit Donna told Stephen she did not want to see him anymore. You will hear how Stephen reacted to that rejection, and what that defendant did, and how he left that house, and how he proceeded to Surf City, New Jersey. He went to the house of his friends, the O'Dells, and he spent the evening with them; and the next morning, with his plan developing and knowing what he intended to do, Mr. Moore took a knife from the service station of his friend Mr. O'Dell. And with that knife in his possession, he proceeded to North Jersey; and, aware of his intention to take the life of Donna Litchfield, he went to the bank in Montclair, New Jersey, and withdrew the sum of $1,000.00.

"He then proceeded to the last place he'd seen the victim, but she was not there. He was informed that she had gone to her own apartment in Belleville, and then he proceeded to that apartment; and, knowing his intention, he entered the apartment and he was met by the victim. A friend of hers, Valerie Iacobucci, will testify, and you will hear how there were three children in the apartment, and that Mr. Moore was engaged in a conversation with the victim, and the victim was cleaning the apartment, and he went into the bathroom; and you will hear how the victim went into the bathroom and continued cleaning, when Mr. Moore then affected the purpose he had in going to Belleville. He killed

Donna Litchfield. Donna Litchfield fought for her life, ladies and gentlemen, but to no avail. Mr. Moore then left the bathroom and went into the kitchen, washed the blood from his person, and left the apartment with his getaway money in his hands. He proceeded to Surf City, New Jersey. The police officers arrived, gathered as much information as they could, and were able to contact the Surf City police in New Jersey.

"Testimony that you will hear and evidence you will see produced, will lead you to a conclusion, ladies and gentlemen, that Mr. Moore, on July 14, 1976, intended and planned the murder of Donna Litchfield, and he did, in fact, murder her. When the testimony comes in, I will ask you to evaluate a when you go into the jury room. Usually common sense is your reasonableness, your everyday experiences, which will give you no trouble rendering a fair and just verdict. This allying was very brief. You will hear the testimony, and you will be asked to evaluate. I will speak to you again at the conclusion of the case. Keep an open mind and listen to all the testimony. That's all the State asks. Evaluate here, and evaluate fairly based on the law. Thank you very much, ladies and gentlemen.

The jury, which had been listening intently during the prosecutor's opening statement, now turned their attention to Judge Fusco who, inventing the prosecutor to go back to his seat, said, "Thank you prosecutor. Mr. Schutzer, whenever you're ready."

Mr. Schutzer stood up when called, walked towards the jury, and began his speech.

"Thank you, sir. Ladies and gentlemen of the jury, it's been said that the trial by jury is a tool which we use in our society to extract the maximum amount of truth from conflicting sources of the story. Now, you have just heard a story from the prosecutor, who asked what the State intends to prove to you people. The problem is that there is more here than meets the eye. The problem is that there is a whole iceberg. There is ninth of an iceberg beneath the tip, which the prosecutor has just indicated to you. He has just indicated a very credible story about a seemingly normal—if there is such a thing—crime. My point is this, ladies and gentlemen: What the prosecutors told you, what I am telling you now, is what we intend to prove, but we don't know. We weren't there.

"With due respect to Mr. Mautone, he wasn't there; I wasn't there; you people weren't there. We are going to have to describe this case, or *you* are going to have to decide this case, based upon what you hear from the witness stand, based upon the evidence which is presented. You are going to have to decide this case on what we call credible, believable testimony and credible, believable evidence, ladies and gentlemen. The fact that Mr. Moore sits there accused of this crime doesn't indicate that he is guilty in the matter that the prosecutor says; doesn't indicate anything more than he is being charged with this crime. It doesn't indicate he planned to murder or that he killed Donna Litchfield. It doesn't indicate anything at all, and I ask you ladies and gentlemen to consider that. There also must be a degree of mental in other words, as it's been put in the past, and must not only be an evil doing parent, that evil meaning mind. Ladies and gentlemen, Mr. Mautone is going to indicate to you that because Mr. Moore, my client, was there at the scene of the crime; that because certain acts he may have committed were in fact committed by hand—that this indicates Mr. Moore knew what he was doing, and that this indicates that Mr. Moore knew what he was doing was wrong. Well, I'm going to submit to you people frankly that is not the case. Appearances deceive. Every single day, we hear that people really don't know what they are doing. This is not just a defense which sprung up in order to give you an excuse to acquit a man.

"This is very serious business, because I am indicating to you that Mr. Moore may not have known what he was doing on July 13th and 14th—and even before that. The prosecutor's case centers on July 13th and 14th. Ladies and gentlemen, I'm going to ask you to consider long before that. Because Mr. Moore appears to have done certain things on the 13th and 14th, I'm going to ask you not to consider that so much as to consider the whole picture.

"Ladies and gentlemen, when we talk about insanity, and that's what we are talking about, there are all kinds of insanity, all kinds of mental illness, emotional disturbance; doctors can hardly define them, but what we are talking about in this particular case is the fact that whatever Stephen Moore may have done on July 13th and 14th, he really didn't know. And why is that? Because he was acting under what the doctors call, for lack of better word—and it's a technical term—he was acting under delusions, hallucinations.

"This is not a joke. It is a very serious crime, and I'm not attempting to lessen what happened to poor Donna Litchfield by saying to you, well, he didn't know what was happening. The point is that Stephen Moore didn't know what he was doing. The point is that he didn't know what he was doing was wrong, as the law defines it. He acted under certain premises, which you people—and I and the judge—which we normally don't act under. He acted under a whole different set of rules. What were the delusions of Stephen Moore? Suppose I were to give you a compass, any one of you, and I were to say, you are a great navigator, you know your way around, here is a compass. I want you to go do northeast—but what you don't know is that the compass is off by 10 to 15 degrees. And so you take the compass, being a perfectly good navigator, knowing full well what you have to do, and you take it, and you proceed along a course thinking that where you are going is due northeast, but you are not going due northeast; you are really going east, and you may find that you are off by about 30 miles. Ladies and gentlemen, this is what happened to Stephen Moore. He started off from a false compass reading. He got information that you and I don't have access to. He started out from what we call false premise.

"Everything he did after that may have looked normal, may have appeared like he was sane, but he wasn't. He was traveling in a completely different direction. It's the same thing as if we were going to play a game of solitaire, only the deck is smudged so that the suit and the denominations are mixed up. And we sit there, and Mr. Moore is going to play a game of solitaire, and he knows the rules and he knows the sanctions, and he proceeds to play it in a rational manner, but what he doesn't realize is that he is making mistakes. This is the only way I can describe it to you, ladies and gentlemen; this is what happened to Mr. Moore, and this is not a joke. Mr. Moore was playing with a partially smudged deck. He was making mistakes. He was proceeding from false premises.

"Now, I indicated to you earlier that whatever evidence in this case is going to come from the witness stand, I am going to allow you people to see the evidence there is to present in this case. I am not going to go into it, because I think you are going to see for yourselves how sick Mr. Moore was on July 14th, and I think you are going to see for yourselves how sick he still is. We are not talking about sick like being somebody who has a hoarse throat or a cough or a rash. This is a disease of the mind Mr. Moore suffers from. It can happen to any one of us. You will find that it happened to Mr. Moore, how it developed, what it is, and how it manifests itself; but we don't have any observable physical criteria to observe the disease—we don't have the coughing, the hoarseness, or the rash.

"We have what you are going to see when the defense presents its case: the testimony of his friends and relatives as to behavior which he has had in the past. You are going to see how bizarre some of the behavior was, and you are going to hear from doctors, ladies and gentlemen, doctors who are used to observing certain criteria just like x-rays or blood tests who are used to observing a particular person in a particular manner in order to detect mental illness.

"You're going to hear from those doctors how sick Mr. Moore was on July 14th, and how sick he is today, and you're going to hear why Mr. Moore cannot possibly have been responsible as to the law for conviction of a crime for the commission of the act which the State charges. But because the tests employed are not objective, and because they are not like X-rays and blood tests and the like, I am going to ask you people not to disregard that though the defendant may still be sick, he is in fact sick mentally.

"I am going to ask you people to consider throughout this trial the reason I demonstrated for you, with the examples I did. I'm going to ask you people to consider at every stage of the trial the delusions, the false premises Mr. Moore may have labored under, that we are going to prove to your satisfaction he did labor under on July 14th. We are going to ask you to consider whether under our laws, as the judge will charge you, ladies and gentlemen, Mr. Moore can be considered legally responsible for having committed this crime. Now, we are not going to deny his presence at the scene; we are not going to deny that he removed money; we are not going to deny he did any of the things that Mr. Mautone says he did. The point is this: Because a person is insane—and you will see that from the testimony of the doctors—because a person is insane doesn't mean he is not intelligent, he can't act rationally; it doesn't mean he can't function in a normal way, apparently, physically, observably.

"The point is that he is not normal; he is not really functioning in a normal way. The point is this, ladies and gentlemen: Mr. Moore's delusions, his false premises, his hallucinations, made him the way he did. Intelligence can be put to the service of our delusions, and you will see that. You will see that insanity does not preclude intelligence. You will see that insanity does not mean a person is incapable of planning something. I can plan to walk from here to there, and that's a plan, and it's a premeditated plan; but by walking from here to there based upon a delusion, based upon a false premise, the result is going to be I am doing something that I really have no control over. I am doing something that I totally don't have a cognitive understanding of. I'm doing something I don't really know the consequences of.

"Now, you are going to see a lot of evidence in this particular case, and some of it is going to be extremely unpleasant for most of us. Many of them are going to be photographs, I imagine. This particular crime is an ugly crime. The defendant is not denying that. I'm here to say to you, well, it doesn't mean a thing! Life is important. It is very important, ladies and gentlemen. But I'm going to ask you in fairness not to allow your sympathies for the victim—and we will have sympathy; I have sympathy—I'm going to ask you not to allow your sympathy for the victim, not to allow your stomach when you look at pictures or when you hear the testimony about this case to override your eyes and your ears, your intelligence, your common sense; not override the function which you people have, to decide fairly, to get at what I originally spoke to you about, to get at the truth.

"We are here to get at the truth, not to convict a man, not to get a man off. We are here to find out what happened, and to deal with it in the most appropriate manner. I'm asking you, ladies and gentlemen, again, in fairness to the State, not for sympathy for Stephen Moore because he is sick. No, I'm asking you to consider this in a rational light. Consider the proofs that the state presents, and that the defendant will present, as you must, without any passion, without any prejudice, without any sympathy or emotion; and it's going to be a very, very difficult job—perhaps even more difficult than Mr. Mautone's job and my job. It's going to be very difficult to sit there and say, well, I know this was a brutal crime. I know that it was gory, and I know I wouldn't want it to happen to me or somebody in my family. But still, sit there, and say that I have a duty. The law imposes upon me a duty when I was sworn in the jury box to decide fairly; to decide upon the facts, the evidence—the credible evidence—presented from the jury box.

"It's going to be very difficult. It's going to be particularly difficult in view of the fact, as I indicated to you before, that none of us really know what went on that day. None of us will ever know for sure what went on in Stephen Moore's mind. We can only estimate to some degree of reasonable certainty—reasonable medical certainty—that Stephen Moore was not playing with a full deck in his mind; and I think that when all of the evidence is in, including the case, I think when you hear the testimony of his friends, and his relatives, and the doctors, you are going to find that there is a preponderance of evidence, a greater amount of evidence, that shows that although Mr. Moore looked sane and acted sane, that he was not sane.

So, ladies and gentlemen, I'm going to ask you to consider all of these things as you listen to the testimony in this case. I'm going to ask you not to listen to your stomach or with your heart, but with your eyes and your ears and your minds; and I'm going to ask you to try to be fair. I realize that this case, as in every case, is extremely important, because we are not just dealing with Donna Litchfield's life."

* * *

The next day, everybody was back in the courtroom. Today was the day that Valerie was going to testify. She knew she was about to be asked very uncomfortable questions, and she knew she had to remain calm and collected so as to make sure that justice was indeed going to be served. That morning, Valerie could feel her heart beat in her throat. Her whole body was shivering and she was having a hard time keeping her hands still. She did not want to show she was nervous, but the harder she tried to keep calm, the more aggravated she became.

Before long, time to think was over for Valerie. The jury had just entered the courtroom when she heard her name being called to the stand to testify.

"Call your witness, prosecutor." Judge Fusco said.

"Thank you. Good morning, sir." Mr. Mautone then added, "I call Valerie Iacobacci."

The walk down the aisle to the stand felt like the longest walk she had ever taken. But she had to pull it together. She had to remain strong for Donna, and especially for me. Donna deserved justice. I deserved justice. Once she sat down, she was sworn in. Then she took a deep breath, rubbed her hands dry of nervous sweat on her pants, and looked up at the prosecutor.

"Ms. Iacobacci, where do you live?" He began with the questions.

"East Passaic Avenue, Bloomfield."

"Do you know a man named Stephen Moore?"

"Yes," she replied with confidence.

The prosecutor kept asking questions back to back, and Valerie answered all of them the best she could and as calmly as she was able to manage. Valerie told the jury of how she had introduced Donna to Steve, and how their relationship had evolved into something more serious, to the point that a probable marriage was not something to completely exclude from their future together. She also told them of how Steve had become physically abusive towards Donna, and how he had been slowly checking out of the relationship, disappearing for long periods of time without even mentioning where he was going or with whom.

Then the hard part came, when Valerie was slowly brought to the day of the murder. This was the part she had been dreading all along, but she had to do it. She had to make sure she reported the facts clearly, so there would not be any doubt whatsoever that Steve had premeditated the murder and killed her best friend. She took a deep breath, closed her eyes for a moment to gather her composure, and then went ahead with confidence answering questions.

"Now, when Donna initially went to the bathroom, did Mr. Moore go in with her?" Mr. Mautone inquired.

"Yes."

"And did Donna or Mr. Moore ever come out of the bathroom?"

"Donna came back out and she got paper towels."

"How long after they first went into the bathroom did Donna come out?"

"About a few minutes; maybe five minutes at the most."

"What did she do after she got paper towels?"

"She went back into the bathroom." Valerie felt her legs going numb from the stress. To her, this seemed almost like an out-of-body experience. This couldn't be happening to her. This couldn't have really happened to her best friend.

"Now, when Donna went back into the bathroom the second time, was there anything that drew your attention to the bathroom?" Mr. Mautone asked her.

"She started screaming." Valerie swallowed air, which felt quite painful in her throat.

"Did you hear her scream?"

"Oh, yes." Her mouth was now completely dry.

"Did you go to the bathroom?"

"No, I didn't go into the bathroom."

"Did you look into the bathroom?"

"I saw in the bathroom." Valerie had a flashback of what she saw in the bathroom that day. She had been having nightmares almost every night after witnessing such a horrible and brutal murder. She closed her eyes briefly to regain her focus.

"When you looked into the bathroom, what, if anything, did you see?"

"I saw Donna in the bathtub, and Stephen hitting her."

"What was she doing?"

"Fighting with him."

"And what was Stephen doing?"

"He was hitting her."

"And you saw this. What did you do?"

"I took the kids and took them out of the apartment."

"What did you do with your children when you took them?" The prosecutor asked, pacing around.

"I locked them in my car," Valerie replied, following the prosecutor with her eyes.

"After locking the children in the car, did you do anything else?"

"I went back into the apartment."

"What did you do when you returned to the apartment?"

"I picked up the phone and I called the police."

"What did you tell the police?" Mr. Mautone inquired.

"I told him I thought I had the wrong number, or something like that." Valerie began to feel dizzy and her heart rate was going up.

"Why did you say that?"

"I didn't hear anything else, all I heard was water, the water running, and I didn't know if they made up or what they did."

"What did you do after you told the police you had the wrong number?"

"I hung up the phone, and went to the bathroom door."

"Was the bathroom door open or closed?"

"It was closed," Valerie said, then took a deep breath to keep calm.

"What did you do when you approached the closed bathroom door?"

"I knocked on the door."

"Did anything happen?"

"Nobody answered at first."

"Then what did you do?" The prosecutor looked straight in her eyes when he asked her this question.

"I knocked again. Stephen asked, 'Who is it?' And I said, who do you think it is? And he opened the door, and he said 'Donna is dead'." Valerie delivered this sentence in one breath.

"What did he say?"

"'Donna is dead.'" Valerie whispered as if, had she spoken those words using a louder tone, then they would have made the entire situation turn into a reality. Pronouncing those words out loud would have actually confirmed that Donna had been killed. She had been killed. Everybody in the courtroom heard her words. Now they all knew. It was true. It was actually true now. No turning back.

She felt tears filling her eyes. She closed them to prevent them from coming out and rolling down her cheeks. Although she knew she was in a courtroom, she felt as if she was at Donna's apartment, standing in a state of shock by the bathroom door, hearing Steve pronounce those horrible words that forever changed the course of not only her life but of everyone involved from family members to friends and acquaintances. Anybody who had ever been in contact with Donna, or had ever even had just one conversation with her, had been truly shocked by what happened to her and the tragic end her promising life encountered.

* * *

After many long and tiring court days; after all the witnesses had been called to the stand; after all the evidence had been shown, some of which included raw and terrifying scenes from the day of the murder; it was time for the jury to deliberate on the verdict. It was 3:30 p.m. when the Jury retired. After only half an hour, the jury entered the courtroom again. They had a verdict. At that moment, it felt as though everyone was holding their breath.

"Mr. McTernan, would you please receive the verdict?" Judge Fusco asked. "Members of the jury, have you agreed upon your verdict?"

"Yes, we have, sir."

"Mr. Foreman, is your verdict unanimous?"

"Yes, it is."

"Mr. Foreman, what is your verdict with regard to Count One, the willful, deliberate, and premeditated murder of Donna Litchfield?"

"Guilty."

"Which degree of murder?"

"First degree."

A sigh of relief could be heard throughout the courtroom.

"With regard to Count Two, possession of a dangerous weapon, what is your verdict?"

"Guilty."

"All right. Do you desire the jury to be polled?"

"Yes, your honor. I do."

"On both counts, Mr. Schutzer, or on each one separately?"

"On each separately, please."

"Will you please poll the jury on the verdict of guilty of first-degree murder?"

"Members of the jury, the court has ordered the jury to be polled. As your name is called, each answer yes if this is your verdict, or not, if it is not your verdict."

With regard to Count One, the jury was polled; each juror answered "Yes."

"Members of the jury, in the same manner, you will be polled with regard to count two. If this is your verdict say yes; if no, say no."

The jury was polled once again, and each juror answered "Yes."

"Ladies and gentlemen of the jury," Judge Fusco said, "I want to express my appreciation and thanks to you for your having sat beyond your usual tour of duty. I hope you have had an interesting and worthwhile experience. I am going to excuse you now, wish you a happy Thanksgiving, and happy holidays for the end of the season. Thank you and good night."

The judge then waited for the jurors to leave the room and, once they were all gone, he turned his attention to the defendant.

"Mr. Moore," he called him, "Do you want to say anything to me before I impose sentence?"

"Sentence me," Steve told Judge Fusco. "Get it over with, judge. I tried everything I could; this is my lawyer, he did nothing for me, went through the whole proceedings."

"Is there anything else you want to say, Mr. Moore?"

"Nothing to say. I am asking with my two ears what did I do? I have no choice, I am innocent and you didn't bring in the body, I wanted the body in to see how it was killed and see what you are all talking about. Frankly, I don't know."

"Your Honor," the defense attorney interrupted Steve's rambling.

"Yes, Mr. Schutzer?"

"I am requesting something in line with what Dr. Latta here has indicated to the court. I really would like to see, for the time being, Mr. Moore placed in Martland Medical Center, and extensive neurological tests."

"Oh, no!" Judge Fusco said in a firm tone, "The jury found him sane, Mr. Schutzer. This court isn't going to take action over the jury's verdict." Judge Fusco looked at each lawyer and then concluded, "Thank you, gentlemen. A very well-tried case."

Stephen Moore was sentenced to life in prison without the possibility of parole. Justice had been done.

Slayer found sane and guilty

Nov 24 1976

By DONALD WARSHAW

Rejecting a defense of insanity, a Superior Court jury yesterday convicted Stephen Moore of Belleville of the stabbing murder of his 24-year-old girlfriend. The judge immediately imposed a life sentence.

The jury deliberated nearly six hours at Essex County Courthouse before convicting Moore, 26, of the murder of Mrs. Donna Lee Litchfield of 19 Brighton Ave., Belleville. Mrs. Litchfield, mother of a young daughter, was separated and awaiting a final divorce decree.

The victim died July 14 of loss of blood in her bathtub after receiving 69 cuts and stab wounds, most of them superficial, Assistant Essex County Medical Examiner testified.

Moore never took the stand, and the defense was based solely on the claim of insanity.

Judge Ralph L. Fusco immediately imposed a sentence of life in prison, and Moore, who mumbled and ranted throughout the trial, was led quietly from the courtroom.

Psychiatrists for both the state and defense testified Moore was a "paranoid-schizophrenic."

Assistant Essex County Prosecutor Dennis Mautone, however, in summation emphasized the facts in the case proved Moore was sane under the legal test in New Jersey — that he knew "the nature and quality of his acts."

Mautone argued Moore planned the crime by taking the murder weapon from a gas station owned by friends and taking $1,300 from his Montclair bank account to finance a getaway.

Moore was about to head west when arrested in the Surf City gas station owned by Mr. Rodney C. Odell, Mautone said. Odell and his wife, Jean, appeared as defense witnesses and testified about Moore's mental deterioration over a seven-month period prior to the murder.

On the day before the killing, Mrs. Litchfield told Moore she did not wish to continue their relationship, another witness testified.

Chapter Six

At the age of two, I found myself having to live the rest of my life without my mother. Tell me, does that sound fair to you? My father's life changed dramatically as well. He now had to be both mom and dad to me, but he was up for it. He has always been the best father a daughter could ever ask for. When I went to live with him, my grandparents Audrey and Pete, lived downstairs. I must say that as unlucky as I was to have lost my mom at such a young age, I was lucky enough to be surrounded by family members who loved me and who took great care of me.

My childhood was filled with everyday activities that made time go by quickly. I helped my grandparents in their garden, where I was in charge of picking tomatoes right off the vine and bringing them back inside for my grandma to wash and use in a salad. I was also tasked with picking blueberries and raspberries, but they soon discovered why not many of them made it to the kitchen. It's because I would eat them all before they had a chance to be shared with other family members. My grandmother was such a great cook! Her apple cake was something else. I watched her make it so many times that I eventually picked up the recipe, which I still hold close to my heart today. One day, I'll share it with my children, so they too can keep making the most delicious apple cake and carry on this family tradition.

Martin Street was the setting of my childhood days, just like it had been for both my parents. Mornings were spent playing at Pulaski Park on the swing set and making mud pies. Afternoons were usually busy with chasing down the ice cream man, who, however, was no longer Mr. Mangioni, as he had gleefully retired. Summer evenings were filled with lightning bugs, which my father and I would catch in a glass jar. And my nights? Well, those were spent crying. I missed my Mom. Falling asleep was always hard. I would sob for hours before I would finally close my eyes and drift away. It was heartbreaking for my father to watch me being in so much pain. Are you a parent? If you are, take a moment to think about it. Pause reading this book and look at your child. Can you imagine witnessing your most precious gift going through so much emotional distress and knowing there is absolutely nothing you can do to help?

Losing my mother so suddenly affected me on a much deeper level than anybody thought at the time. I suffered from separation anxiety as a toddler, to the point that my father had to take me out of preschool because I would spend the entire day crying my heart out while at the facility. My grandmother quit her job to stay with me at home until it was time for me to go to kindergarten. I attended Franklin School, but my childhood had been marked by significant trauma, and as much as my grandparents and father tried to shield me from pain and hurt by having me live as normal a childhood as possible, the shock would manifest itself in other ways. For example, I became an incredibly shy and introverted young girl. I didn't trust anybody, and making new friends seemed almost like an impossible task for me. Being the "kid with no mama" didn't help either.

One day, my father and Janice decided it was time to approach the topic in an attempt to alleviate my pain, so they sat me down on the couch. They looked very serious, and I wasn't sure what was going on. Then my father held my hand and said, "I want to talk to you about your mom."

His tone was very sweet, but I wasn't ready. As soon as I heard the word "Mom", I immediately put my hands on my ears. I did not want to hear it. I did not want to know about her. My father stared at Janice with his big eyes wide open, as if unsure of what to do. How was he supposed to know I was going to react like that? He was completely caught off guard. He didn't want to add to my pain, so Janice nodded that she agreed to simply let the topic go—at least until I was ready to learn more and face the truth. I did not know this at the time, but it would be many years before I would ever have a conversation about my mom with my dad.

Eventually, one day led to another and then another one, and in the end, I was able to slowly come out of my shell and begin to make new friends. As years went by, I started seeing more of Valerie and her two daughters as well, especially at birthday parties. Valerie had dissociated herself from the family for a few years in a reasonable attempt to heal and overcome the trauma that she too had to endure. The holidays eventually began to go back to what they used to be before my Mom's passing. To the eyes of a child, Thanksgiving seemed the closest thing to magic. How could so much food be prepared all at once? I thought it was some kind of spell that made it all appear on the dining table. I had no idea how much work my grandmother and her sisters put into cooking for days upon days just so we could all sit together and enjoy so many delicious dishes on that one specific occasion.

Christmas was just as exciting. Santa always seemed to think I was the best girl around. Not that I complained about it! He would leave presents upstairs and downstairs for me. One year, I got a new bike; and boy, did I love it! Winter weather could not stop me from getting bundled up and going outside for a ride. It was the cutest bike ever, with its little basket on the front and its bell. Another year I got a skateboard, and, given that our house was on top of the hill, you can imagine the fun I had riding on the skateboard all the way down Martin Street. Let's just say that I spent many hours in the emergency room, and I have plenty of scars to proudly show from my daredevil days as a child. I also had more toys than an actual toy store. I had tons of toys upstairs already, and the sun porch downstairs at my grandparents', which is where I spent most of my days, was filled with even more toys. I'm not sure if my father and grandparents were trying to overcompensate for my mother being gone. They probably were, but all these toys always came with lots of quality time spent with all three of them, as they would take time to play with me to make sure I was growing up in an emotionally stable environment.

One day, as I was spending the afternoon at my grandmother's house, the phone rang. I rushed to answer it, because in the mind of little old me, answering the phone was about the coolest thing a kid could possibly do. At the time, I was probably five or six years old.

"Hello?" I cheerfully said, feeling like a big kid because I had properly answered the phone just like I had seen grown-ups do so many times before.

Silence. There surely was somebody on the other end, because I could hear what sounded like either a light breeze or someone breathing in the speaker.

"Hello?" I repeated, this time a bit more determined to get an answer.

"Hi, Tina," an unfamiliar voice said.

"Hi," I replied, not sure who was speaking to me. "Who is this?"

"I'm…" the mysterious man cleared his throat before adding, "it's Daddy."

"Daddy?" I was young, but I knew that man wasn't my father.

"Yes," he asserted.

"You don't sound like Daddy," I admonished him.

Meanwhile, my grandmother had grown curious about this strange exchange, and she had come into the living room where I was.

"Who is it, Tina?" she asked me.

I looked back at her and shook my head. He says he is Daddy, but it is not. Then I shrugged, gave her the phone, and five minutes later, forgot all about that awkward call. It wasn't until many years later that I found out who the man on the other side was: Stephen Moore. He had escaped from the maximum security prison, Trenton State, where he had been sentenced to spend the rest of his life — or so we thought.

* * *

When I was seven years old, my Dad got remarried to a woman named Janice. I had known her all my life, pretty much, because she and my Dad began dating not too long after my parents separated. I always liked her, and she took her responsibility of step-mother very seriously and to heart. They both worked at All-State Can in Clifton when they met. After they were married, we moved down the shore to Lanoka Harbor, New Jersey. We lived in a big old white Victorian house, which was absolutely gorgeous. It had a huge wrap-around porch, and the bathroom was big enough for me to do cartwheels in — not sure why I did them, but I did! I used to love going up to the third-floor rooms, which were filled with lots of cool psychedelic posters made of neon, left behind by people who lived in the house before us. During those years, I began cheer-leading, playing softball, and taking horseback-riding lessons. It was all so much fun! Janice coached the softball team; she was a very hands-on stepmom. I liked playing softball, especially because my Dad had played for years and I used to watch him play as often as possible. He was always a champion in my eyes because he was able to pitch very fast.

During the lazy days of summer, we spent time at Cedar Creek, on the beach, where Janice worked on her tan, and I made sandcastles. Janice's niece and nephew would come down and visit us during the season so we would get passes to Great Adventure, where Janice's cousin and her husband worked as vets for the safari. It wouldn't be an exaggeration to say we pretty much spent the whole summer there. It was just so much fun being there, especially because they had concerts in the evening.

Even though my father, stepmom, and grandparents never left me wanting for anything as I was constantly showered with love and affection, I always felt a painful void inside of me. The more I grew, the more aware I became that the void had been left by my mother's passing. The older I got, the more conscious I was of the fact that, no matter how long I waited, no matter how hard I prayed, she was not coming back to me. At times, the thought of not going through life with her was too much for me to bear. You might think that not having her there to witness my most important milestones—such as scoring my first run in softball, or my first game cheerleading, or dealing with my first crush—was the hardest part. But oddly enough, those major milestones were not the moments when I missed her the most. On the contrary, I missed her the most during my daily routine. I missed her reminding me to brush my teeth before bed. I missed her asking me if I wanted a special breakfast on Sunday mornings. I missed her taking me to school and walking me to my classroom holding my hand. You see, this kind of pain never goes away; you just learn to live with it.

* * *

Mom, were you there when I had my first communion? Remember, I was at the church, and I kept glancing up at the ceiling; I'm not sure why. Maybe I was hoping I'd see you. Did you like my dress? Dad said I looked like a beautiful princess dressed in my white dress and veil.

Mom, do you like tulips? They are my favorite flower. What's yours? Would you just take a moment to come with me in the yard and admire how gorgeous these tulips are? Just a moment, Mom, please.

* * *

Even though I was not happy to be so far away from my grandparents, I began to like Cedar Creek. In spite of being very shy and not willing to trust new people, I was able to make friends who lived nearby. We spent lots of time at Seaside and Point Pleasant, both on the beach and the Boardwalk. Although I wasn't a big fan of rides, I still enjoyed playing games at the arcade. After a day of fun, my friends and I would go get pizza at one place that had the best pizza ever and the biggest slices! But you cannot call a day fun unless your dinner is followed by ice cream. Wouldn't you agree? We made sure to always get our scoops in.

For my eleventh birthday, I invited all my friends over for a party. After spending some time outside playing in the back yard, we went in to enjoy some delicious cupcakes; then it was time to open the presents. There was one boy, Kenny, who was rumored to have a crush on me, and I was totally into him. I mean, I was so much into him that my whole notebook was pretty much filled with lots of teeny tiny hearts that framed his name! Yep, I was one of *those* girls. What are you gonna do? It's like a rite of passage. Anyway, he gifted me this amazing bracelet whose design was rather popular at the time. I was absolutely smitten with this present. I mean, you'd think the boy had given me an engagement ring for how big my smile was the rest of the day! When it was time to say goodbye to all my friends, Kenny waited in a corner until all the others had already left. Then, as I approached him to thank him for coming, he gave me a quick kiss. I was in shock! I turned six shades of red, and I couldn't understand how one person could feel like falling down in an endless well and flying high in the sky at the same time. It's safe to say I didn't get much rest that night, I was so happy!

My father spent the next few years working up in Bloomfield and Montclair, where he would deal antiques and buy out the contents of houses. Given the distance between his workplace and home, he would commute back and forth, although he would often stay over at my grandparents' house and just come home on weekends. If I have to be honest, I wasn't a big fan of this whole routine. I missed my dad, and I wanted him to be close by. Janice also was becoming impatient with this back and forth and began pushing to move back where we used to live before. At least that way, we would be together all the time. I was definitely cheering for moving back, but I had made a few good friends over the years, and I wasn't looking forward to leaving them. I was still very shy and making new friends for me at times seemed like an impossible task to accomplish; but, at the same time, I had family members back on Martin Street, as well as Valerie and her daughters, who still lived nearby.

I don't know if it was the move back to Bloomfield, or the fact that I was growing up and become more aware of who I was as a person, but after we moved, I began to daily experience sadness. I missed my mother so incredibly much that at times it became physically painful. I also started asking lots of questions that went unanswered, no matter how many times I tried with both my grandparents and my father. Talking about my mother seemed to be something nobody ever wanted to do. Was it because of the reaction I had years before when my dad tried to approach the topic? I wasn't sure, but I needed to know. I felt ready now. I wanted to get to know her so I could understand myself. I felt the need to find out even the smallest details. What was her favorite color? What did her laughter sound like? But these questions bothered many people. As a result, "Mother" became synonymous with "taboo," and I soon found myself being caught in a make-believe world that functioned on the notion that if we didn't talk about the issue, it was as if it never happened.

Meanwhile, my social skills were not getting any better. Not only did I still suffer from separation anxiety and having a hard time making friends, but I also noticed that I had deep trust issues. Why should I trust strangers? After all, wasn't it a stranger who took my mother away from me? As a result, I only had very few people around me, and that was okay with me. Few, but good, you know? When I started going to middle school, I found out that my guidance counselor had actually known my mother. That was an incredible surprise to me because up until that moment, I had never met someone who had known my mom. I wanted to ask her all sorts of questions; I wanted to know everything she knew about my mom. But something kept me from doing so. Was I too scared to break the unofficial pact I had going on with all my family members that "We never speak about your mom"? Was I afraid to find out something about her that would upset me? After all, I wasn't even a teenager yet. Was I ready to receive this information? I didn't know, so I waited.

***

It was May of 1988 when I experienced another terrible loss. My beloved grandmother Audrey passed away. To say I was heartbroken wouldn't even begin to describe how lost I felt without her. Part of me felt like I had just lost my mother all over again, but what made this worse was the fact that I would always remember losing my grandma. She was so much more than just a grandmother to me. She was my best friend. To take care of me and make sure I'd grow up to be a strong woman, she quit her job. We spent years together, and she taught me all about being a girly-girl. She loved Avon, and she would have weekly get-togethers with her girlfriends, who would come over to her house and try new Avon products, play games, and prepare delicious food for everybody. She taught me how to cross-stitch, and to always go after what I wanted. I remember one time when I had told Janice that I really wanted this pair of stretch pants, but she wouldn't buy them for me because, according to her, they didn't look good on me. When my Grandma heard about that, she called a cab—because she didn't drive—went all the way to the store where I had seen them, and bought me a pair. Can you imagine the joy that I felt as a pre-teen when she showed up at the house with this gorgeous pair of stretch pants? She was simply unbelievable, the best grandmother a young lady could have ever asked for.

After losing my grandma, my Grandpa Pete suffered multiple strokes. Since he needed constant care, he moved in with my uncle and ended up selling his house. Had I been a few years older, I would have surely bought that house. I had so many memories there; it was painful to see it up for sale and have another family move in. As years went by, I began to not enjoy school at all. All I wanted to do was getting out of there and travel the world. I had been so fascinated by those incredible places photographed in *National Geographic* magazines that all I could think of was getting out of Jersey and exploring the world through a camera lens, taking gorgeous photos of remote locations that would then be published in those glossy pages and make children all over the country dream of being there.

But my reality was pretty different from my daydream. I did not spend time discovering unknown worlds. My afternoons were mostly made of walks to the local McDonald's, and my nights were filled with sleepover dates at my friends' houses. Following in my mother's footsteps, I was very much into changing my hair color and trying out new styles. It was actually pretty fun, as it gave me a chance to explore who I was and what my personality was like. The holidays were usually spent at my friend's house, watching *Mary Poppins*. I feel safe in saying I knew that movie by heart. After all, it was on every single year around that time; but no matter how many times I watched it, it was always so much fun!

For my seventeenth birthday, my father surprised me with a white Cavalier convertible. It was my very first car, and I absolutely loved it! Driving gave me much more confidence and the freedom to go wherever I wanted, which at the time was pretty much the 7-Eleven down the street and Brookdale Park; but hey, my friends and I looked pretty cool cruising up and down Broad Street all day long. Time was definitely flying by, and before I knew it, it was time to start my senior year in high school.

* * *

All my life, I have always felt like I have missed out on not one of, but *the* most important experience any human being is entitled to have: growing up with my mother by my side. Although over the years she had always been a constant thought in the back of my head, she became my only focus when I started my senior year. I am not sure why, but something in me switched. I wanted to know more. I *needed* to know more. Looking back now, I realize that it was my subconscious way of letting myself know I was ready to understand what had happened to her, and why she was no longer with me.

That year I began what would eventually turn out to be this book: a desperate search for truth and justice. One day I went to the Belleville public library to see if I could find anything there. I was not counting on it, honestly, because my previous attempts at requesting information from my most direct sources—my family—had gone nowhere; but I had to try. And to my great surprise, my determination paid off. It took time, and lots and lots of reading, but eventually I found what I had gone there for: newspaper articles covering the crime. As I read word by word slowly, the black ink would jump up from the old page that had turned yellow. A knot suddenly formed in my throat, and I felt like I was choking. I kept swallowing to get rid of the knot but to no avail. Words that used to make sense no longer did, and I was forced to close my eyes for a second, open them again, take a deep breath, and read the same sentences over and over again just so my brain could process them properly. I had to sit down because the room started spinning when I saw those gruesome pictures from the scene of the crime. My stomach was cramped and my whole body shook. My mind was so foggy I couldn't even remember my own name. Have you ever been in a situation so shocking that your body shuts down and gives out on you? That's how I felt. I had finally found information on my mother, and what I found was something that could never be unseen.

Once I regained enough control of my emotions and my body, I grabbed the articles and headed straight for the copy machine, which turned out to be out of order. Not knowing what to do, I sat back down so I could think properly and make a logical plan. Yes, I had it! I would call up the newspaper and ask them to send me copies of the articles I needed. Days went by, and I finally got hold of the newspaper staff. The person I spoke to sounded rather cooperative, and I was assured those copies would eventually come my way, but they never did. Instead, the newspaper chose to do a reprint of the original story.

Soon after, Janice, who worked at the Clara Maass Hospital in Belleville, right down the street from where the crime happened, was approached by a coworker who blatantly asked her, "You are not Tina's real mother, are you?" Janice was shocked. You see, we had never told anybody that Janice was my stepmom. She was caught off guard and had no idea where this information was coming from. Then her colleague proceeded to wave a copy of the article in front of her eyes. At that point, she knew I had something to do with it. When she came back home that evening, she came to my room and asked me to join her and my father in the living room. She had a copy of the article in her hand. When I saw it, I understood what was happening; I looked at both of them, took a deep breath, and confessed I had been secretly looking for information on my mother. I think what shocked them the most was learning just how much I already knew.

"Tina," my father began, not really knowing how to approach the topic, "Would you like to know where your mother is buried? Maybe you could visit her."

"Dad, I *know* where she's buried," I interrupted. "I have already been there to visit her."

Silence.

"Would you like us to reach out to your other grandparents?" Janice asked. I had not been in touch with them since after my mother's murder. At the time, I wasn't sure why.

"Yes, please."

"You know, they live over…" Janice offered the information, but I stopped her.

"I know where they live," I told them.

Janice volunteered to put me in contact with my grandmother Mary. I appreciated his gesture because I know how hard it must have been for them to face such a topic. I am pretty sure this was the conversation they had been dreading since I was two years old. After all, this was no easy conversation under any circumstances. But the moment had finally arrived. I was no longer a girl who was too afraid to learn the truth. I was a young woman who needed to know what happened. I wanted to learn why she was with him in the first place; I wanted to know his name; I wanted to put a name and face to the person who singlehandedly robbed me of my mother. I wanted to know that he was paying for what he did to her—and to me. I wanted to know he was spending each waking second thinking about what he had done. I wanted to know that justice had been served. Yes, this was the moment that I made up my mind I was going to learn all there was to know about my mother and her involvement with this man. This was the moment where my search for truth and justice began. This was the moment the soul of this book was born. But this was only the beginning of what turned out to be a very long road, one I have yet to finish walking.

Chapter Seven

There are certain moments in life when you witness an event so catastrophically traumatic that your brain somehow takes a photo of that very specific moment, and will replay it for the rest of your life when you least expect it. Some call it post-traumatic stress disorder. I am not sure what name to give these flashbacks; all I know is that, after reading those articles, I keep seeing them fresh in my memory and in my nightmares, where they come back to haunt me.

After reading the words that so vividly described my mother's efforts to defend herself and the 69 wounds he inflicted upon her that eventually took her life away, I felt sick to my stomach. I was constantly dizzy, and I experienced shortness of breath, as if the more I tried to take deep breaths, the less oxygen got into my body. Yet I was not going to stop; I needed to know more. But where could I start?

After giving it some thought, I decided to call the New Jersey Prosecutor's Office. That day, I was home alone. I sat down on the couch in my living room and dialed the number. A woman, who introduced herself as the secretary, told me in a somewhat impatient way to wait on the line while she inquired about the case. As I patiently listened to the hold music, I could honestly feel my heart beating in my neck. I closed my eyes for a moment, secretly hoping the irritating tune would soon end. No such luck; it seemed to be going on forever. How hard was it for this woman to inquire about my mother's case? Where did she go that it was taking her so long? Was I supposed to be taking her prolonged absence as a positive or as a negative sign? She could have been busy collecting all the paperwork she was going to give me after cordially inviting me to the office to pick up the documents that would let me finally understand what actually happened; or maybe she just took her time and made herself some coffee before coming back on the line to tell me there was nothing there. The wait was becoming rather aggravating to me. I caught myself tapping my fingers on the end table, making an irritating noise as my nails touched the glass top.

"Ma'am, you still there?"

I jumped up. Finally, she was back!

"Yes, I'm here," I said, making a conscious effort not to sound too frustrated that she made me wait for what felt like hours.

"I'm sorry to tell you I didn't find anything about the case in question." She sounded so nonchalant. She had just given me terrible news that did not even make much sense to me, and she had the nerve to sound so mellow about it. Didn't she know what this meant to me? Easy for her to be so careless and tone-deaf. It wasn't *her* mother who had been brutally murdered.

"How is that possible?" I asked, surprised at my own tone of voice, so broken from holding back tears I didn't even notice had started running down my cheeks.

"I don't know what to tell you, ma'am." She concluded, "Have a nice day."

Have a nice day? *Have a nice day*? How can you tell me to have a nice day when you just slammed a massive door in my face?

"Yes. Bye." I didn't have the strength to reply, so I just hung up as fast as I could.

I couldn't tell you exactly for how long I remained there, sitting on my couch, staring at the phone. I guess I expected this search to be easier and smoother. I assumed all I had to do was to look for answers that were going to be readily available to me. I just didn't realize how hard I actually was going to have to work to get those answers and clues. First, the articles were not sent to me as I had specifically asked the newspaper. Then, the prosecutor had no files on my mother's murder. It felt like the universe was plotting against me. I mean, this case obviously happened. I was not crazy. I was not making this up. I knew this happened. So why was it so hard to get answer? Was it because it made people feel uncomfortable? Well, tough luck! I wanted to know the truth, and I was going to get it, no matter how uneasy people felt about it. Do you think it made me feel happy and satisfied having to dig up so many horrible things about my past? Not at all, but I had to. I had to do it for my mother because she deserved justice. I had to do it for me, for my own sanity and my own family. I was on a mission, and nothing and nobody was going to stop me from finding out what I had set my mind to.

* * *

Determined. Stubborn. Over the years, people have used both adjectives to describe my never-ending quest for knowledge and justice. Some of them have praised me for being on this mission, telling me how much they admire my strength. Others have cursed me, yelling at my face for opening up this Pandora's box that has inevitably spilled over the life of many family members and acquaintances who would much rather no longer relive this tragedy. I understand both sides. Having to continuously think about my mother and what happened to her is no easy task for me, but I have no choice. I have to have justice. I deserve it. My mother deserves it.

Without a doubt, my biggest support system through this whole ordeal has been my own family. When I felt like quitting and giving up, they stood by me, reassuring me that eventually justice will be served. My husband Kevin has been supportive. We have known each other for such a long time, I can honestly say he witnessed my mission for justice since day one. We met when we were both working at Dale's in Bloomfield. We were friends for many years before we went out on a date. Our wedding was incredibly special; we had it in Ireland, where I have lots of family members. I love Ireland. Have you ever been there? Just now, as I sit at my desk typing these words, I can see those breathtaking landscapes right in front of me. The rolling green hills, the salty breeze coming from the sea, the craggy cliffs; the people are unbelievably friendly, too, and I don't say this just because my family members will be reading a copy of this book. They are all so genuinely kind and welcoming that it becomes painful to leave them. It's also probably due to the Irish accent, which has a melody that is hard to find anywhere else, so even if they said something mean to you, the musicality of their accent would make it all sound so pleasant!

It may sound odd to you but, I had very little to do with my wedding day. I was told by my Irish family that all I had to do was show up with my groom. They took care of everything and surprised us with an outdoor wedding in this gorgeous open garden that went on and on until infinity. There was a marquee set up in a very elegant way, delicious food catered for all of us, plenty of flowers that set the ambiance, and great music we all had fun dancing to. Then, we took photos at what is possibly my favorite spot in the whole world: Castle Roche. While admiring the ruins of such an important historical landmark and smiling for the camera, I remember wishing my mother had been there to witness it all. Although I really did not have a chance to get to know her, I am sure she would have loved being there. Would she have cried tears of joy watching me walk down the aisle? I like to think she would have. It was my big day, and I know she would have done her best to make it extra-special. After all, it was truly a magical day, one of the top three most important days in my entire life. What? Oh, which ones are my other two, you ask? Well, the birth of my two children, of course! I have a daughter and a son.

While having children was always something I had desperately wanted since I was a little girl, I did not expect it to be so hard on me. You see, when you grow up without a mother, there are certain things you just don't know how to do, because nobody ever taught you. I had no idea how to bathe my little girl when I brought her home from the hospital, and I had nobody there to show me. When my son had a high fever as a baby, my mother was not there to let me know everything was going to be okay. When I felt overwhelmed with two small children in the house because all I really wanted to do was take a shower, my mother was not there to watch them for me. There were definitely moments when I felt out of place and had no clue what to do.

But my biggest fear was not being there to watch them grow up. I still remember the moment the doctor gently placed my daughter in my arms, and I hugged her for the first time. I closed my eyes; tears of joy were falling down my cheeks, and my lips were trembling as I kissed her tiny forehead. In that moment, I prayed to God to let me live long enough that she would remember me. I begged Him not to take me away so soon because I didn't want my daughter to grow up without a mother like I did. Experiencing my childhood without my Mom was an incredibly traumatic event that I don't think anyone could possibly fully overcome and move on from. Even though I have been fortunate that my Dad did all he could and more to give me the best upbringing—something I will forever be thankful for—there is nobody in this world that could ever replace Mother. When my son was born, I remember thanking God for giving me another precious gift, but I made sure to have the same conversation with Him. My mother left only me behind, but I was now mother to two children, and I was twice as scared of something happening to me that would force me to leave both my babies.

You see, over the years, I realized just how deeply and irreversibly I had been affected by the tragedy of losing my mom. I grew up with trust issues, fears of abandonment, and feeling inadequate in some of the most natural roles that women are blessed with — especially motherhood. Nightmares have been a constant staple in my life, as well as sudden flashbacks and the behaviors of a socially awkward child who had a hard time making new friends. This is what I wish I could tell Steve.

In fact, Steve, if you are reading this — as I hope you will one day — hear me out: you have taken away, in the most brutal way, the most important person in my entire life. In doing so, you have ruined me. I have had to deal with so much trauma, so much pain, and so much distress because of you. That day, you decided to take my mom away, a tragedy that unfortunately did not end there. A young life — my life — was affected as well; so deeply, in fact, that to this day I deal with the consequences of what you chose to do to my mom. But this is where it ends, Steve. This is it. I have the most wonderful children, and I am determined to break the cycle. This is why I am writing this book: because I want justice. I want to show my children that while I was severely punished for your decision to take my mother away, *they* will not have to suffer. I will not allow you to make them victims as well because you have also taken their grandmother away. By translating my feelings into written words, I hope to turn those same words into a powerful weapon for change, so that other families out there who have suffered through similar pain, and have been victimized further by a broken justice system, will be able to hold on to this book and to these words and fight for what we all know to be true: We deserve justice. I deserve justice. My mother deserves justice.

Interlude...

"There is but one and only one,
Whose love will fail you never.
One who lives from sun to sun,
With constant fond endeavor.
There is but one and only one.
On Earth there is no other.
In Heaven a noble work was done,
When God gave us a Mother."

Old Irish verse

Chapter Eight

I spent many years searching for answers. I was determined to uncover everything there was to know about my mother's case, but I had no idea how hard it was going to be for me to find answers to my many questions. I kept calling the prosecutor's office, year after year after year, but the tune was always the same: they had nothing on file. The more people shut the door in my face, the more resolute I became. I was not going to give up.

In 2011, after recovering from my many failed attempts to find information, it became obvious to me I had to take a different approach. One day, while I was over at my grandmother Mary's house, she told me that she heard Steve had actually been transferred to the Marlboro mental hospital. This was shocking news to me. Wasn't he supposed to spend the rest of his life in a maximum-security prison? That's what I had read in those newspaper articles. That's what my family members knew. I mean, you, reader, just read the same articles; wasn't it clear to you as well that Steve had been found sane and guilty? How could it even be possible that a murderer, who had been found completely sane and had had the mental clarity to premeditate the murder, was no longer in prison, but had been moved to a mental institution? Something was wrong. Really wrong. So I started digging.

I began doing research on the Marlboro mental hospital. What I found was troubling, to say the least.

From the *Matawan-Aberdeen Patch*, 2011:

Today, the Marlboro State Psychiatric Hospital is a contaminated site. But for about 67 years, it was a state-run institution for the mentally disabled. After more than six decades of the hospital running under state funding, it was shut down after a state investigation, prompted by an undercover operation. On July 1, 1998, the state hospital closed its doors for good.

Closing the state hospital came 11 years after State Senator Richard Codey went undercover in the hospital, hired as an orderly. Codey chronicled his experience saying he witnessed "inhumane care and treatment of mental patients," as well as poor living and working conditions.

Codey's undercover work sparked a Senate Task Force in 1994, which investigated the inner-workings of the hospital, from environmental practices to the use of funds designated for patients.

The hospital, built in the 1930s, came under scrutiny as the Senate team found evidence of illegal environmental practices, bribery and a "range of irregularities," that the task force reported had been going on since the late 1980s.

The task force's 1994 executive summary said, "The results of the investigation reveal a tableau of waste, fraud, thievery, and corruption in which the squandering of taxpayer dollars virtually has become business as usual at this institution." According to the Senate's executive summary, the Marlboro State Psychiatric Hospital was one of seven state-run psychiatric institutions in New Jersey. In its final years, it served 780 patients per day and employed 1,157. The report cites the hospital's 1995 state budget, which was $55.5 million.

The closing of the hospital was the first in a series of changes, as the state re-evaluated its state-run institutions and investigated de-institutionalizing the mentally ill. According to Codey in New Jersey Monthly, many of the task force's suggestions became state law.

But the closing of the hospital did not come without opposition. A July 1998 New York Times article said unionized workers at the hospital, as well as families of patients, opposed the closing of the doors. Neighborhood groups also worried that patients that were not transferred to another hospital and instead determined they could live alone would be a danger to communities.

The Marlboro Township history book, published in 1999 by Arcadia Publishing, said, "Security issues for the facility were long a local concern. State mental health practice in the 1990s focused on getting patients into 'community' settings,' with a reluctance to maintain costly in-patient hospitals, regardless of the ongoing need."

Marlboro Township documents cite more than 780 calls for police between 1988 and the closing of the hospital in 1998, many of which were reports of patients leaving the grounds without authorization. Patients were transferred to non-permanent treatment, state-funded independent living, and other psychiatric hospitals. Currently, the Trenton Psychiatric Hospital holds the medical records of former patients, and accounts records are held at the New Jersey Division of Mental Health Services.

Can you imagine how many questions I had after reading this news about the Marlboro mental institution? First of all, why was Steve there? Wasn't he supposed to be serving a life sentence in prison—and where was Steve now, since the institution closed? The article said that patients were transferred, but where to? I just couldn't believe it. I had to find out why Steve was no longer in prison. He had been found sane during the trial; that much I knew. I had read it. You've read it, too.

After many sleepless nights spent doing research, I finally found a department named Victim-Witness within the prosecutor's office, so I decided to call them.

"Hello, Victim-Witness Office. This is Lisa; how may I help you?"

"Yes, good morning, Lisa," I began. "This is Tina Ann Healey. I need help finding information regarding my mother's case."

"Sure; what is your mother's name?" she asked, sounding kind.

"My mother was Donna Litchfield," I replied. "She was a victim of murder at the hands of Stephen Moore."

Saying that sentence out loud hit me like a ton of bricks. There was a brief pause from Lisa, and then she invited me to tell her all the information I already had regarding the case. It felt really good to find someone who was at least interested in listening to me, without hanging up as soon as I mentioned my mother's case. She sounded genuine and willing to help and vowed to call me back once she had answers.

Time went by and, truth be told, I never expected to hear back from her. So many people before her had told me they would eventually call me once they had more information to give me, but my phone never rang. As I type this, I can see myself sitting on the couch by the end table, just staring at the phone, silently praying for it to ring. I spent many years trapped inside a whirlwind of emotions and was angry at those who could not or had no interest in helping me. I feel guilty for spending so much time consumed by this desperate search for answers that took too much time away from my family, and completely drained me because of the incessant struggle to find people willing to lend a hand.

One day, while I was busy washing dishes, my phone rang. Without even checking to see who the caller was, I just answered.

"Hello?"

"Hello, is this Tina?" The voice sounded familiar.

"Yes, this is she." I turned off the water so I could hear better.

"Hi, Tina. This is Lisa from the Victim-Witness Office."

The sponge I was holding in my right hand dropped in the kitchen sink and I quickly dried my hands.

"Hello, Lisa." I felt like I had to hold my breath and brace myself for more bad news to come any second now. My silence must have made Lisa understand I was very tense, so she took charge of the conversation—something I was hoping she'd do.

"Tina, I am calling to inform you we have found an entire box full of records, court transcripts, and more on your mother's case."

Finally!

"You have? Oh, my! Thank you!" I could barely hold it together.

"Yes. So, would you like to come here?" she asked politely. "We can go over them together."

"Yes, absolutely!"

"All right. You will have to come when the Prosecutor is here as well, for legal reasons. Are you available this Thursday?" she offered.

"Um..." it took me a moment to remember what day of the week it was, what my work schedule was like, and what sports practice my children had on Thursdays before I could confirm. "Thursday sounds good. At what time?"

"I have an 11:30 open."

"Oh, um...11:30 is fine by me."

"All right, we'll see you on Thursday at 11:30."

"Yes, thank you!"

After we wished each other a good day, I sat down at the dining table. I felt so much lighter. My neck and shoulders suddenly felt so relaxed, I almost had no control over them. My whole body felt as though somebody had just lifted a truck off of it, and it was now free from so much pain, struggle, and tension. That night, for the first time in many years, I slept well.

* * *

At 6:00 a.m., my alarm went off. It was Thursday. Let me tell you, I couldn't get to the prosecutor's office fast enough! The whole drive there, my heart was pounding out of my chest, my mouth was severely dried out, and my temples kept pulsing, giving me a horrible headache. After parking, I took a deep breath and walked my way inside the building. I was welcomed by Lisa, who looked as kind and sympathetic as she sounded. Then, she introduced me to the prosecutor, who explained to me that he ran a check on Steve but could not find out his whereabouts.

"It looks like he never even applied for a driver's license," he explained.

I simply nodded, as I was at a loss for words.

"Mrs. Healey," he continued as he ushered me into his office, pulling up a chair to invite me to sit down, "From our search, it looks like Mr. Moore escaped from Trenton State Prison."

"He escaped?" I exclaimed in disbelief. My hands had suddenly become soft like butter, and they let go of my purse, which accidentally fell on the floor. I picked it up slowly because I felt rather dizzy. "May I please have a glass of water?"

"Of course," Lisa replied. "Here you go." She handed me a glass of water, which I sipped as I tried to get my breathing to slow down.

"Mr. Moore was on the run for five years," the prosecutor continued. "He eventually turned himself in while in California."

This made no sense to me. He was in a maximum-security prison. How could he escape? As the prosecutor kept telling me details of what his search had produced, I struggled to keep my focus. He mentioned precise dates of when Steve escaped and when he then turned himself in. Suddenly, it hit me: when I was a child, one day I answered a phone call while at my grandmother's house. The man on the other line told me he was my dad, but I instinctively knew he was not my father; then my grandmother took the phone away from me. It was Steve! Steve had called my grandmother's house! As I realized this, cold chills ran up and down my spine.

The prosecutor had been talking to me all along, but his voice had basically become a distant noise in the background. Nervous he might be upset with me for not paying attention to what he was saying, I forced myself to focus on his words, staring at his lips moving so to understand better what he was talking about.

"And apparently," he said as I began following him, "his life sentence was overturned on what seems to be the technicality that an insanity test had not been administrated."

When I heard him pronounce these sentences, I was in disbelief. How could his sentence have been overturned? He was found sane. Had tests been done after the court hearing? This was unbelievable.

"According to the files in this box," the prosecutor said, indicating the large box sitting on his desk, "the technicality was actually brought up by Mr. Moore's lawyer."

"But..." I mumbled, having a hard time putting into words the chaos going on in my mind.

"Mrs. Healey, under New Jersey law, if you are aware of the nature and quality of your actions, you are not considered insane. Obviously, there were no doubts that Mr. Moore had mental issues; but his lawyer and the two psychiatrists who were asked to testify all assured the court that the defendant was able to stand trial. I mean, even Mr. Moore himself told the judge he was able to stand trial."

Lisa, who was sitting next to me, offered me another glass of water.

"Mrs. Healey, are you sure that neither you nor other family members were made aware that Mr. Moore had escaped?"

I just shook my head no. "Um..." I said, trying to regain my composure, "So, what happened after he turned himself in?"

"Well, he turned himself into a minimum-security prison. Then he was shipped off to the Marlboro institution, and then...we don't know where he is right now."

Tears were quickly flooding my eyes. I tried to hold them back as much as possible. My whole body felt so heavy I had a hard time getting up after Lisa invited me to follow her to a room where I was finally offered the chance to view the files in that box. I spent three hours in that room. I was not even able to get through one-quarter of the box. Nothing in my life could have ever prepared me to face such a harsh reality. I wept as I read through newspaper articles. I felt nauseous as I skimmed through court transcripts describing Steve's outbursts and incoherent statements. I sobbed as I came across his mother's testimony that proved everyone in his family was well aware of his mental issues.

Then I read reports stating that while he was in Trenton State Prison, he tried to commit suicide. I am glad he did not succeed, because suicide, in my opinion, is the coward's way out. He has to pay for what he did to my mother, and to so many other people who have gone through life suffering for their loss. He does not deserve to get a free pass and check out. According to those same reports, Steve manifested very weird behavior while in prison, like drinking his own urine and more disgusting things. I guess these details served him well when his lawyer appealed the sentence and was successful in overturning it due to insanity.

"Tina," Lisa called me, shaking me out of my focus. "I am afraid it is almost time for us to close."

"Oh, yes, of course," I mumbled. "Can I bring these files home with me?"

"I don't think it's possible. I'm sorry," she informed me. "But you can fill out this form and fax it to our office to release the records to you."

"Thank you." I felt relieved.

*　*　*

On my drive home, my head was foggy. I tried hard to let my photographic memory work with me in keeping as many details about those files as possible stored in my mind. I wanted to write down all the newly-learned information as soon as I got home, so as to have records of my own.

Once at home, I filled out the form I had been given and faxed it over to the prosecutor's office. Expecting to hear back from them in a very short amount of time, I became increasingly impatient when days turned into weeks without an answer. Then I received a letter in the mail to inform me that there were no records on file for this particular case. No records? But I saw them! I touched them! I went through them! Irritated to the point of no return, I phoned Lisa who, kind as ever, told me I had faxed it to the wrong address, and I had to send the request to the Criminal Records Department.

"Tina, let me know once you have faxed the request," she told me, "I will keep the box right here on my desk so that nobody will misplace it."

Hopeful that I was finally on the right track to have these documents released to me, I waited patiently to hear back from the Criminal Records Department. Finally, after a few days, I received the call I had been waiting for.

"Mrs. Healey, I regret to inform you that this is listed as a missing case in our system." The female voice that so nonchalantly delivered the bad news was very irritating to me. It had the tone of voice people have when forced to do something they really don't want to do.

"Well, this isn't right," I insisted. "This cannot be a missing case. I spoke with Lisa from the prosecutor's office, and she told me that the box is sitting on her desk. Can you please get in touch with her? I'm sure she can help."

"Uh, ah…" she said, sounding like she was chewing gum with her mouth open. How rude!

A few weeks went by before I heard from Ms. Polite-Manners again. I remember dreading to talk to her, just because her tone made me shiver like when somebody scrapes their nails on a chalkboard.

"Ma'am," she said, loud chewing going on still. "I should have never gotten involved with this case. Sorry, but there is nothing I can do to help you." She sounded very nasal.

"What…what do you mean?" I was confused. "Did you talk to Lisa?"

"Ma'am, I'm not at liberty to give you any details, but you'll get a call sometime from my colleague, who's the Victim-Witness manager, all right?"

"Okay." I was at a loss for words. How could this be? The box was sitting on Lisa's desk, and I had touched those files. I read through some of them. Why was it so difficult for them to release these documents to me? I seriously just felt like screaming. It felt as though everything and everyone was plotting against me, and I had no idea why.

Once again, days turned into weeks. Then, while my family and I were vacationing in Florida, I received the call.

"Ma'am, I am sorry, but I have some bad news." The lady on the other side of the line thought this was going to be the best way to break the ice between us. I have no clue why these people don't get to take a lesson on tact when they are hired. "There was a mistake. You should have never been allowed to view these documents. You will have to hire a lawyer if you wish to view them again."

"But why? I don't understand," I knew I was raising my voice, but between you and me, I really couldn't have cared less about being tactful at this point.

"It's because of HIPAA."

"The what?" I asked confused.

"The Health Insurance Portability and Accountability Act. We are not at liberty to release those documents because of medical records that are protected by U.S. law for privacy matters."

"But I don't want his medical records; I don't care about those. I just want the court transcripts, and…"

"Sorry, ma'am," she interrupted. "Have a nice day."

Yes, sure…have a nice day. Like that's even possible after everything I had been going through! Easy for her to say; she was getting paid to give me that call full of bad news. She didn't care about my case. She didn't care about the reasoning behind my frustration. Angry at the world for conspiring against me and my fight for justice, I searched online for what this HIPAA was all about. I found out that the privacy act was not in place in 1976, the year of the murder; so, the court records should not have been under the HIPAA seal. More determined than ever, I proceeded with my search.

* * *

After getting in touch with the New Jersey parole board, I found out that in the state of New Jersey, if you are found guilty and sane, then you get paroled. However, if you are found guilty but insane, you are *not* given parole. Confused? Yes, so was I. You see, one would think that if you find a person guilty of a crime, whether they are sane or not, you'd want to keep an eye on them when they are released from prison—wouldn't you agree? I guess not, according to the parole board in New Jersey.

During my chat with the parole board, I also discovered that the New Jersey prison's interest in Steve ended on September 10, 1980. According to the lady I spoke to, this might be the date he was transferred to the mental institution, or maybe when he escaped from prison. Either way, those dates did not add up. As time went by, the situation became even more complicated and confusing instead of becoming clearer. I found myself having more questions than answers.

Steve never made it on the Department of Corrections' website, either. I know the crime was committed in the middle of 1976, and there was no internet, but there are people on there who committed crimes way before my mother was killed. So why wasn't he on it? I mean, if he escaped and then turned himself in after five years of being on the run, that would bring him well into the 1980s, meaning he should have been added to the website. I know this was a long time ago, but we are not talking about the Ice Age here. This case was not handled correctly. I was not sure by whom, but I had to figure it out.

I felt like I was just going in circles, never really ending up anywhere. I took a couple of Post-It notes and wrote down the following,

Prosecutor's Office = no records.
Parole Board = little to no info.

So, what now? I tapped the pen on the table while trying to figure out what my next move was going to be. Should I try to contact the medical examiner's office to see if I could get a copy of the autopsy result? More than likely it was going to be another flop, but I had to give it a try. I sent my request to the medical examiner's office, and not too long afterward, I received the following letter back:

Sept.13, 2012
Re: Deceased – Donna Litchfield
Date of Death - July 14, 1976
Dear Ms. Litchfield:
At the present time, there are no medical examiner records available prior to 1982, the year this office took over the duties of the Essex County Medical Examiner. Prior to that time, the Essex County office was located elsewhere in Essex County. Our office had tried, unsuccessfully, to locate any Essex County medical examiner records. However, we will keep your file request should old records become available.

I am not even sure why I was so surprised to get more bad news; but if they didn't have the autopsy report, then who did? Could it be that the report was in that famous box probably still sitting on Lisa's desk at the prosecutor's office? I had to figure something out. Back to the drawing board:

Prosecutor's Office = no records.
Parole Board = little to no info.
Medical Examiner = no autopsy report.

Suddenly I remembered reading in a newspaper article that the case had been later referred to the Attorney General's office, so that was my next step. After getting in touch with them, I found out that the lawyer who represented Steve had gone to work for the New Jersey prosecutor's office, meaning they were banned from handling the case. The detective I spoke to then said, "Mrs. Healey, I do have a folder on Mr. Moore here, but…" He paused briefly as if trying to figure something out. Being on the other side of the line, obviously, I had no clue what it was, so, I waited patiently for him to continue. "This is so bizarre. There is only one piece of paper in this folder."

"Only one? How's that possible?" I was puzzled. "What is the paper for?"

"It's a transfer form," he said.

"Transfer form?" I was so confused. "Transfer to where?"

"Um…" The detective no longer sounded comfortable answering my questions. "Mrs. Healey, can I get your phone number, please? I'll call you as soon as I find more information regarding this form and the case."

I told him my full name and phone number, which he assured me he wrote down.

Five years later, I am still waiting for him to call me back.

Chapter Nine

My children were growing up quickly, and I was having a hard time keeping up with them. I kept repeating to them to slow down, but they did not listen! While carpooling them to school, taking them to sports practice, and buying them a new pair of shoes (next size up, please!) pretty much every other day, time was going by fast. Yet when it came to me finding out new information regarding my mother's case, it felt like I had been stuck in the same spot for years.

The thing is, I *had* been, and I was becoming increasingly impatient and aggravated about that. How was it possible that as soon as I found one person willing to help me, he or she felt like they had gotten into a situation way bigger than them, and gave me the boot? How was it possible that Steve had somehow gotten away with everything, and I had no luck in even figuring out where the heck he was?

Not knowing his whereabouts made me always fear for my safety, as well as for my family's. I remember one day when I had to go get groceries: I was at the checkout counter and this man who stood in line behind me, kept staring at me. My heart began to beat so fast I thought the vein in my neck was going to explode. He had a mustache that resembled the one Steve had in that photo from the newspaper article. Remember? I mean, he was even wearing a plaid shirt. His hair was more of the salt-and-pepper shade, which made sense since that photo — where he had dark hair — had been taken many years ago.

"Ma'am!"

A squeaky voice made me jump out my skin. The cashier, a young woman in her early twenties with an unnatural blue hair color I had only seen on a fairy godmother in cartoons, was staring at me. Her left eyebrow was raised, and her right eye was almost completely shut. Her lips were also curled up in an awkward way — definitely not a smile. She did not look happy nor fulfilled. I could tell she would have much rather been anywhere else but there, stuck behind the counter, waiting for me to come back to reality and hand her my debit card.

"Sorry," I said in a low tone, trying not to let the Steve lookalike hear me.

"It's $30.55," she said, pronouncing it *thaa-dy fiddy-fah*.

While waiting for her to give me the receipt, I saw that he only had one item to pay for. Shaving cream. Hmm…was he going to shave his horrible mustache off so to disguise himself better? Was this all a ploy to be able to follow me around without being noticed? What if this was really him? Was my life in danger? Did he have a knife hidden somewhere behind his back?

I couldn't walk out of there fast enough. While heading towards my car, I looked back, and I saw him walk just as fast. He was following me! All of a sudden, my nose felt all stuffed up, and no air was getting through it into my lungs. Unconsciously, I opened my mouth and began taking short, quick breaths—still no air in my lungs! I turned back again: he was getting closer! I now held onto my purse, whose strap was sliding off my right shoulder. I squeezed the two plastic bags full of groceries, and I ran towards my car. How did he even remember that Donna had a daughter? He was mumbling and rambling about all sorts of nonsense during the trial, but he remembered I existed? This made no sense. Yet, he was here…he was *right* here—wasn't he?

I turned around again. He was gone. Where did he go?

My attention was caught by the sound of a truck door slamming shut. I looked up and saw him through the car window. Where was he going? Why was he leaving? Why was he driving in the direction away from my home?

* * *

I wish I could tell you that was the first and only time I ever freaked out in public—or in private, for that matter—about the chance of seeing Steve. I felt ashamed for reacting like that towards a complete stranger who, for all I knew, could have been the most genuine person in the whole world. However, for years, I have been looking behind my back, scared of finding Steve just standing there. I always felt like he was somehow keeping track of me, where I lived, where my family and I spent our vacations, which school my children attended.

I guess it was mostly because I had no idea of where he was. The more I tried to figure it out, the more complicated it seemed to become. It was as if people were scared of helping me out—as if having to deal with a case like my mother's was going to somehow rub off on them like an infectious disease. At first, everyone seemed so willing and open to lending a hand and do their best to cheer me up. Then, once certain— read *gruesome*—details about that horrible day would come up, those same people couldn't hang up the phone fast enough, or pretend like they dropped off the face of the Earth along with all the documents I had been looking for.

It was truly a bizarre situation, one that really didn't help me with my sleeping problems. I had been wasting my time making phone calls and filling out requests to have official documents and transcripts released to me, and guess what? It had gotten me nowhere. I decided I no longer needed to look for another office to call or another approach to take; I needed to get help. I was in desperate need of a lawyer who would ask for these documents on my behalf and who would make these phone calls for me.

It was going to be expensive, sure; but I had to do this. As far as I can remember, I have always known I was never going to allow anything nor anybody to stop me from finding out what actually happened to my mother and seeking justice on her behalf.

As I sat down at my desk, I began to think back on which person, if any, had seemed a bit more willing to help me. Who seemed a bit more human? Well, the only person who I felt I had developed a genuine interest, in this case, was Lisa, but she also sort of disappeared once things turned official, didn't she? Oh, well; I had to give it another try. The last shot, I told myself. I opened the left drawer and began sorting through little notes I had been collecting through my years of investigating the case. Gosh, not only was I not the best investigator, I was terrible at keeping track of who I spoke with!

After my momentary self-scolding and silent New Year's resolution of improving my organizational skills, I found it: Lisa's phone number. Excited and nervous at the same time, I went back to the living room, sat on the couch, and dialed.

It was ringing.

No one was picking up.

What time was it? Could she already be out of the office?

Oh, wait…someone picked up!

"Hello, you've reached the Victim-Witness Office…"

"Hello, Lisa—"

"We are now closed. Our hours of operation are from…" Answering machine.

I hung up.

I lay back on the couch, rested my head against the wall, and took a deep breath.

Would I ever be able to find answers?

I was honestly starting to doubt it.

* * *

A new day brings new opportunities. I always believed that. So the first thing I did when I got up was look for a lawyer. I didn't need the first kid out of law school who barely passed the bar; I needed somebody with a track record of smashing hits, somebody who wasn't afraid of stepping up for clients. You know, I've heard that you only get what you pay for; so I paid. I paid a *lot*. But I knew I was getting the biggest big shot in the world of law and order. I had heard about her. Apparently, she was quite the shark! Ms. Krasby looked to be over six feet tall, with shoulders as broad as a football player, thick blonde hair, and exotic facial traits—an absolutely stunning woman. Rather intimidating, though.

I was happy to have found a woman to represent me. I was sure she was going to be the only one capable of truly understanding my struggle and where I was coming from. During our first meeting, she sounded very confident. Her brain seemed to function in bullet-point lists. She was able to turn every part of the conversation into a "Point A to Point B" sort of deal. She told me in a categorical manner exactly what I had to do. She reminded me of a living instruction manual. If you do Point A, you will then move on to Point B, which will lead you to Point C.

All right. If Ms. Krasby, who did not like to be called Mrs. because, as she specified in a rather harsh tone, you'd have to be a married woman to be a Mrs. which was something she was very proud *not* to be, as if she had somehow managed to avoid getting this terrible disease that afflicted humanity. She was confident her plan was going to work, then who was I to judge her ways? When I went back home, I wrote down the following:

Point A: Call Lisa and tell her I've lawyered up.

I went to the living room, sat down on the couch, and dialed the number.

"Hello, Victim-Witness Office. This is Lisa, how may I help you?"

"Lisa! This is Tina Ann Healey; we spoke a while ago."

"Oh, hi, Tina!" She sounded genuinely surprised. "I have been waiting to hear from you! How've you been?"

"I'm okay, thank you," I am not the type of person to make small talk. As a matter of fact, small talk makes me uncomfortable. I never know what to talk about. Every small-talk topic seems so empty and, well, *small*.

"I'm calling because my lawyer told me to let you know she will be contacting you shortly to have those files released to us." I did my best to highlight the word "lawyer"; I'm not sure if it worked.

"Okay, wonderful," she replied. "Just let her know to fax a document proving she is representing you."

"I sure will, thank you."

"My pleasure, Tina." She then took a pause and added, "I still have that box sitting on my desk."

She sounded kind when saying these words, which made me feel hopeful and warm inside. Could this finally be a change of wind in my favor?

* * *

A few weeks later, I called the New Jersey Parole Board on my lawyer's recommendation to see they had any updates. What I found was rather disturbing. Apparently, Steve had only spent four years at Trenton State Prison. Four years! Can you believe it? That's not all: He was not charged with murder, either, and I have no clue what he *was* charged with. I was truly speechless. I mean, this felt like my mother had been killed all over again.

How could this be happening? He was sentenced to life in prison for the murder. And now, over thirty years later, I found out that he was only at the maximum-security prison for four years. People who shoplift serve almost as much as he did. This man killed a woman! And not by accident—he stabbed her to death. They found 69 wounds on her body, and many of them could be categorized as self-defense wounds. My mother tried to fight him to stay alive so she could come back to me—so that she could still be my Mom.

But he took her away, and justice had been served when he was sentenced to life in prison. He was also found mentally sane—at least, sane enough to stand trial and be prosecuted. When I heard the man on the phone tell me that Steve had spent only four years at the prison, I felt like the ground had been pulled away from under my feet. I was then recommended to call the New Jersey District Attorney to see if they knew more.

More determined than ever to finally get some answers to oh, so many questions, I just went to the District Attorney's office and basically demanded to be seen. A woman dressed in a very elegant pencil skirt suit took me to a small room filled with furniture and lots of paperwork piled up on the desk. She asked me to wait there and offered me a cup of coffee. I declined. I was nervous already. I sure didn't need any caffeine in me.

"Mrs. Healey?" asked a man in his forties when he walked into the office.

"Yes," I said, standing up to shake his hand.

"Hello. Hope you didn't wait too long." He sounded nice.

"No, thank you."

After telling him everything I knew about my mother's case, he opened a folder and began reading bits and pieces of information from a whole bunch of paperwork. It appears that the case went to them for a second trial after Steve's lawyer claimed that his client's rights had been violated. I still can't believe he had the audacity to claim his rights had been violated; what about my mother's? What about mine?

"Here, this is the transcript of his second trial," he said, placing a document in front of me.

July 9, 1980. Closed hearing.

State of New Jersey vs. Stephen C. Moore, defendant

I have asked you to come up, gentlemen, because the court wants to resolve the application, the post-conviction relief petition for post-conviction relief, that has been pending here for some time. I think it is appropriate to cover first just a very short procedural history.

Stephen Moore, the petitioner, was convicted of murder of a former girlfriend, and the jury rejected an insanity defense that was made at that time. At a pretrial proceeding shortly before the trial that was conducted by the trial judge, Judge Fusco, the defense counsel, who had made a request for a competency hearing by motion supported by affidavits of his own doubts as to the defendant's competency and also by psychiatric reports of doctors who had examined him, brought to the court's attention that it was his desire to withdraw the request for a competency hearing largely based upon the desires of his client, Mr. Moore, to get on with the trial, essentially. And at the time, in a rather general way, the trial counsel indicated that he felt that Mr. Moore might qualify as being competent.

The trial judge refused leave to withdraw the request for a competency hearing, but after a brief interrogation of Mr. Moore along the lines which suggest that he was addressing himself to the subject of competency, he dismissed the motion, indicating he was not going to permit the withdrawal at that time. The prosecutor, while not objecting to that procedure, did suggest that under applicable cases, it might have been useful to conduct a normal full-blown competency hearing, but was not pressed by the State.

In any event, there was no special hearing with testimony by psychiatrists out, although the court did have the benefit of certain psychiatric reports and certain psychological reports of the conviction, and appeal was taken to the Appellate Division, which affirmed the conviction. Then there was a change of defense counsel, I believe, along about that time. New counsel sought on its efforts to secure certification by the New Jersey Supreme Court to raise a competency issue, but it does not appear that the Supreme Court considered it. They simply denied certification, and we don't know to what extent, if any, there was any consideration of this issue.

Thereafter, an application for habeas corpus writ was made in the United States Supreme Court, and thereafter, Judge Lacey wrote an extensive opinion which ultimately concluded that it was appropriate to defer to the post-trial conviction relief procedures that are available under New Jersey court rules. So, that has brought us here.

Now, I don't think there is any question that during the pretrial before Judge Fusco at the time that he dismissed the competency motion, the request for a competency hearing at the time that the motion was dismissed, and also during the course of the trial, there were a number of blatantly inappropriate outbursts and comments and physical actions clearly occurring. I will have some more particular reference to some of those incidents, but that does not appear to be in dispute here. To psychiatrists — Dr. Kern, who testified for the State at the trial on the insanity issue, and Dr. Latimer, who testified for the defendant — were present for significant portions of the trial and observed the defendant at a hearing that I held here on one of the return dates of the petition. These two psychiatrists were permitted by me to make a record, both as to their present views respecting the then-competency of the defendant, but also as to their pretrial opinions, as expressed in reports respecting the competency and other aspects of the mental condition of the defendant. And those reports are in evidence in this case. The principal thrust of the petition, I think, is narrow but pretty clear.

It is that Judge Fusco should have conducted a full-scale competency hearing, notwithstanding the attempted withdrawal of the motion by the defense counsel at the time, and notwithstanding the court's dismissal of the motion respecting competency. It is addressed in two stages. First, whether there was enough at the time of the pretrial for Judge Fusco to have taken this upon himself; and next, whether or not the events during the course of the trial, as they disclosed someone making both physical and verbal outbursts, gestures, and inappropriate outbursts — whether they disclosed a condition, taking into account the previous reports that were available to the court; a situation where such an action **sua sponte** *was required.*

I think what we should do first is take a look at the legal context in which an application for post-conviction relief arises, and some of the cases that have been decided in this area. This is brought under Rule 3:22, and it is clear that this is not a substitute for appeal. There has, of course, been an appeal previously taken, and Rule 3:22-4. It is clear that grounds of relief not previously raised in the proceeding cannot be raised on this type of application, but there are two exceptions that I think we have to direct ourselves to, whether enforcement of the bar that I have just discussed — whether hat would result in a fundamental injustice — and, of course, whether a denial of the relief would be contrary to the United States and New Jersey's constitutions.

The issue respecting the defendant's competency was raised below, and could reasonably have been raised in an appeal. It wasn't raised at the appellate division level, but efforts were made at the Supreme Court; but we can't tell whether that was considered. But one thing is pretty clear under the law: that a conviction of someone who's incompetent at the time would be a violation of the defendant's rights due to process. This is clear under 420 United States, Drope v. Missouri, 1975 decision, United States Supreme Court.

I should also address, in addition to the Rule 3:22 context, what the standards are for review of a trial court's failure to hold a competency hearing. Of course, while those are normally standards of a review on appeal, it seems to me that these same standards are appropriate in this case. In the New Jersey Supreme Court, they set up at the time a standard that the trial court's failure to inquire into a defendant's fitness to stand trial would not be reviewed on appeal unless it clearly appeared that the defendant was incapable of standing trial. The court noted at that time that the defense counsel would be in a far better position than the trial judge to know the defendant's mental state, and to the initiate a defense of such an inquiry. I have reviewed an Illinois statute, and held that where the evidence raises a **bona fide** *doubt as to the defendant's competency to stand trial, the judge, on his own motion, must — I underlined the word* **must** *— conduct a competency hearing.*

No words could describe how I felt at that moment. My head suddenly became very foggy, and I felt as if I was on a ship which was being harshly rocked side to side by giant waves.

"Were you or your family made aware of this closed hearing?" he asked me, shaking me out of my dizziness.

Without lifting my eyes from the document, I shook my head no.

"I also read here," he said, placing another document in front of me, "that Mr. Moore escaped from the mental institution he was sent to. However, he was later returned, and was unable to walk the grounds after that."

I glanced at him.

"Apparently, in 1984, a lawyer put in a request for a Krol commitment."

"A Krol commitment?" I asked, confused.

"Yes," he replied. "A Krol commitment is basically parole for the mentally ill. However, he was denied the commitment given that he was considered to be a substantial threat to himself and others. I'm afraid that's all I can tell you about him."

My eyes were watering up. I wanted to keep my composure, but my emotions were about to get the best of me. I felt so overwhelmed. I kept swallowing what felt like a bitter gulp of air that burned my esophagus as it went down. I tried taking a deep breath to let my tears go back where they came from. It didn't work. Before I knew it, my cheeks were wet with disappointment and heartbreak.

* * *

Eight months had passed since my visit at the D.A.'s office. I was still waiting on Ms. Krasby to get me those files from Lisa's desk. It was nervewracking waiting for that call to come. It seemed like every time my phone rang, my heart would skip a beat, hoping it was her, but no such luck.

Growing tired of waiting on her, I decided to keep investigating on my own; so I called the Department of Human Services to find out where Steve was.

"Sorry, ma'am," the lady told me, "there is a new law that prevents me from disclosing this information."

Frustrating. to say the least.

"But I'm not asking for his medical records," I pleaded. "I just want to know where he is now."

"As I told you, ma'am," she insisted, "I cannot tell you where he is. This is private information."

"Please, you don't understand." I was so upset. "I have got to find him, please!"

My begging took me nowhere. She basically hung up on me after barely wishing me a nice day. And yet, I did not give up. I called the Health Commissioner's office, but it didn't go any better there. I was shut down rather quickly after being told she was going to pass my name and number along and I would be receiving a callback. I highly doubted it.

As you can imagine, during this investigative journey of mine, I have spoken with hundreds of people regarding my mother's case, and I have heard plenty of suggestions from the majority of them. Some of them encouraged me to keep going and to not stop until I reached my final goal. Others seemed like they couldn't have cared less; a few apologized and felt genuinely sorry for not being able to help me as much as they had hoped to; and I won't deny that I have heard a couple of "Lady, you are crazy!" comments. One of the suggestions that kept coming up from quite a few people was that I should file a civil suit.

However, when I inquired about it to the prosecutor's office, as well as other lawyers I have contacted through the years, they all told me that there is a two-year statute of limitations.

"I know that," I replied the last time I heard this clause. "And I also know that, when it comes to murder, there is no such thing as a time limit."

At that point, I truly felt like I knew more about the world of law than these attorneys I spoke with.

"See," I said, pointing out to a document I took out of my own folder—yes, I eventually made my own folder filled with documents, which were sort of a chronological map to my investigative journey—"It is a new law, actually, that amends the 'Survivor's Act', and it reads: N.J.S.A.2A:15-3: To make the statute of limitations for lawsuits brought under that law consistent with the statute of limitations for actions brought under the Wrongful Death Act, N.J.S.A.2A:31-1 *et seq*. Specifically, the new law amends the Survivor's Act to provide that any action brought under N.J.S.A.2A:15-3 must be commenced within two years after the death of the decedent, and not thereafter, *except* that the action may be brought at any time if the death resulted from murder, aggravated manslaughter, or manslaughter for which the defendant has been convicted, found not guilty by reason of insanity, or adjudicated delinquent."

At the sight of his face totally baffled, I wished him a good day and walked right out.

There I was, day "I-lost-count" of this over-thirty-year journey, and I felt like I had more information when I first asked my father about my mom than I did now. Over the next few months, I called the New Jersey Bar Association, who referred me to a lawyer in Montclair who was apparently a specialist in family issues. Big fail. So I called different departments in Trenton, Camden, and Essex Counties. Another big fail.

Friends and some family members have tried to dissuade me over the years from moving forward, mostly because they care about me and they saw me in pain every time I felt helpless and hopeless when met with yet another door slammed shut right in my face. They kept begging me to just forget about what happened and focus on the future. As much as I have always appreciated them, I simply cannot stop looking for answers. I will seek justice for my mother for the rest of my life. If that's how long it's going to take me, then so be it! But please don't ask me to just forget about it. This is my beloved mother we are talking about, not my childhood pet who somehow went to a farm far away and never came back.

My mom was 24 years old when she was brutally killed. She left a 2-year-old orphan without a mother for the rest of her life. My children will never get to meet their grandmother. Someone has got to own up and admit mistakes were made in handling this case. I want people to step forward, place a hand on their heart, and confess that they overlooked a few crucial details, which then turned the whole case upside down.

* * *

It was a busy Tuesday when that phone call came. I had been waiting for it for so many months, I had basically lost all hope it would ever come. The phone rang, but I was busy with running errands, so I answered it without even checking who was calling me.

"Hello?"

"Yes, hello, Mrs. Healey." The female voice sounded full of herself and straightforward. "This is Ms. Krasby."

As soon as I heard the name, I stopped stone cold in the middle of the sidewalk. A young man who had been walking behind me holding a cup of coffee barely managed to stop as well, saving my brand-new coat and his breakfast in one quick move.

"Yes, hello." I was all shaken up. Was it going to be good or bad news? I felt like at that point I was more prepared to receive bad news than good ones. I had no idea how I was going to react to hearing good news. I hadn't heard any as of yet!

"Listen, I want to talk to you about those documents you want to have."

The beginning did not sound promising. However, nothing could have prepared me for what she was about to say.

"I really think that you were way too young when all this happened to your mother and, for that reason, you have sort of become fixated on this case."

Um, what? How dare she!

"So my recommendation to you is to go see a psychiatrist," she asserted in a cold-blooded way. "You need to get some help, but not in the form a lawyer. You need to get your mental health under control before you move on with this case, as I think you are really not thinking this thing through."

I will spare you the choice words I yelled at her over the phone. I will just skip to the part where I hung up the phone on her. All I needed her to do was to fax a letter to Lisa's office stating she was my lawyer. I guess it was way too much work for her. I had to wait over eight months for her to call me and suggest I go seek psychiatric help.

I was entitled to receive those court transcripts. I knew that; she knew that; heck, *Lisa* knew that! Lisa…wait, I should call Lisa and let her know that this letter is no longer coming? I dialed her number as fast as I could—I knew it by heart at that point—and she answered almost immediately. In one short and quick breath, I proceeded to tell her everything that happened with that Ms. Krasby, lawyer from Hell, and she sounded as confused and heartbroken as I was.

"Tina," she told me in a sweet tone, "what I'm about to tell you might cost me my job; but, I do believe Mr. Moore slipped through the cracks. I'm afraid this case was not handled correctly."

Those simple words made me feel validated. Finally, I felt like someone out there actually cared about my feelings. She did not think I was overreacting, or that I should just let go of this whole thing and move on with my life. It felt so good hearing those words from her that I looked up, closed my eyes, and took a deep breath. It had started drizzling by then, and my face was getting wet from the raindrops.

Lisa, if you are reading this book, just know that those words meant everything to me at that moment. You gave me hope when I felt like there was no more hope left. I guess what I am trying to say is: thank you.

Chapter Ten

I'm not going to lie to you. As you have witnessed so far, this journey of mine to seek justice for my mother has had its many ups and downs, and it has not come cheap, either. In fact, over the many years, it has taken me to get to the point where I am able to write a book about my story, I have spent more money than I can count. From attorneys' fees to just gas to go back and forth from their offices only to hear them tell me they couldn't help me, you can imagine I have actually invested a good fortune.

As I've already told you, I have a family of my own to consider. Time and time again, I have looked at my children, wondering how this restless search of mine has affected them. What if I never come to a conclusion? Will they resent me for taking so much time away from them, or will they be proud of me for not giving up? These are questions that, I must admit, I am a little afraid to answer. I don't want to look back on my life only to find out that the people I love the most somehow resent me for becoming so invested in this journey of mine that they think I forgot about them.

You see, the truth is, the reason why I have been so desperately seeking justice is not only for my mother but for my children as well. They deserve to believe in the law. They deserve to believe in the justice system, in the armed forces, in people who have the title "attorney at law" after their last name. I brought them into this world, and I need them to be able to count on the simple truth that bad people get punished and the punishment fits the crime. And given this story of mine I have been telling you about for some time now, can you blame me for fearing they will grow up not knowing what it means to live in a society that takes care of their own people?

I knew you'd understand.

***

Countless phone calls, paired with lots of waiting around, eventually led me to be able to file the Open Public Records Act (OPRA). I paid $800 in fees and faxed a request as soon as I was done. This request was supposed to help me get my hands on those court files once again—but this time, they would hopefully be coming home with me.

It was just one of those days, you know, when everything goes wrong. The Universe seemed to be at odds with me since the very minute I opened my eyes. I wanted the alarm to just shut up, so I slammed my hand a bit too hard on the nightstand, and instead of quieting the obnoxious sound, I threw my lamp on the floor. As luck would have it, it broke; and it doesn't end here.

I got up, frustrated as I could be, and guess what happened? Yep, I stepped on a piece of glass. I should thank my lucky stars that I did not get a piece of glass stuck under my foot. After looking at it carefully, I realized it was just a scratch; but not like a deep cut, just a small, horribly hurtful one, worse than a paper cut. I hate those.

My husband, who had been sleeping soundly, groaned while turning the other way and somehow falling back asleep, which made me feel even more frustrated because I mean, hello? I am here with a scratched foot, glass shattered everywhere, and you keep sleeping?

After taking a deep breath—through my nose, as I was told to never take a deep breath from my mouth or the air actually fills the stomach more than the lungs, go figure—I decided to power through and go shower. And what do you know: no hot water. The universe was winning three-nil.

To cut a long story short, my morning proceeded more or less like this: I spilled hot coffee on my brand new white blouse and got a flat tire on my way to work, where I arrived late. It just kept getting better. So when the phone rang, you can assume I was way past my metaphorical last nerve.

"What?" I shouted as I picked it up.

"Oh...um...is this Mrs. Healey?" a male voice, which sounded almost boyish, asked me.

"Yeah." I couldn't have cared less where I had left my manners.

"Hello, Mrs. Healey. I am calling in regards to the OPRA you recently filed."

I jumped up in my seat.

"OPRA?" I asked, just to double-check I heard right.

"Yes," he said, sounding more like a man in his 40s now that I started to calm down. "We have reviewed your request and are happy to tell you we have approved it."

I was speechless. All I can tell you is that, in that very instant, I forgave the universe.

"We apologize it took us so long to do so, but apparently, the papers you requested were so old we had to actually copy them one by one as they could not be scanned."

I didn't even care about the wait anymore. I was finally going to have those papers that had been sitting on Lisa's desk for pretty much years now! There was a light at the end of the tunnel. I just hoped it wasn't an oncoming train.

* * *

Finally, the papers arrived. Looking through them, I quickly noticed I did not receive all the documents I remember being in the box from when I visited with Lisa. Oh, well; I was just so happy to finally have *something*, I didn't really care if I had them all or was missing a few. I was still very curious to find out what Steve had been up to since he left jail, as well as when he escaped from Trenton State Prison. Nobody seemed to know what he did or where he stayed, but I knew that in due time, I would eventually find out. I just needed help. I had gotten as far as I could without a lawyer. I didn't think I could get any further, to be honest.

I started reaching out to potential lawyers whose description seemed to fit what I was looking for. Since all I had received in the past oh-so-many years were rejection letters and replies I was not a suitable candidate or that I did not have a solid case, I was truly surprised—dare I say shocked—when I received an e-mail back from Joe Bell, a lawyer in Dover, New Jersey. Apparently, my plea for help and description of my mother's case intrigued him, and he wanted to meet me right away. Oh—he also asked me to bring with me all the documents I had! He gave an appointment for Saturday!

That Saturday morning, you better believe I was more than ready to meet with the lawyer. I grabbed the box that contained all my hard work, all my non-returned calls, doors slammed in my face, so many "We can't you help", and walked out of my house feeling as hopeful as I had ever felt before.

When I entered his office, I found a man dressed to the nines, looking very professional.

"Good morning," I said in a soft-spoken tone.

"Good morning, Mrs. Healey." He welcomed me, inviting me to shake his hand by stretching out his right arm. "Please take a seat."

"Thank you."

"All right," he began, getting comfortable in his leather chair. "So, I am very interested in your case, and if you don't mind, I'd like you to tell me about it."

Music to my ears. I couldn't believe he had actually just asked me to tell him my story. Every time I attempted to even begin to tell my journey, I was shut down with a simple, "Okay, let's get to the point here." Whenever I heard this sentence, I just wanted to scream: "This *is* the point, you fool!" But my dad raised me right.

I leaned back a little to get more at ease, and I just poured my heart out. I told him everything: the ups and downs, the few victories and the many defeats, my purpose, my ultimate goal — my journey. Never once did he interrupt me. He listened intently, nodding from time to time while taking notes.

"Well," he said once I was done with my story, "I actually know quite a few people in Essex County, and I'm positive they will be able to help us locate Mr. Moore."

I couldn't believe my ears. I felt as if the weight of the world had suddenly been lifted off my shoulders, and for some weird reason, I felt tired. No, delete that — I felt *exhausted*. I needed to go to sleep right away.

"I'm going to need you to leave me this box, though, if it's okay with you."

"Um…" I was reluctant and not afraid to show him. "Mr. Bell, you see, it took me so long to finally get these documents, and…"

"You don't want to give them up." He finished my sentence for me.

I just nodded.

"Mrs. Healey," he began to say, but I interrupted him.

"Mr. Bell, I don't mean to be rude, but if it weren't for this box and everything in it, it'd be as if my mother's case never even existed. This is something that drives me mad, because, I mean, a person has been brutally murdered, the killer walked away scot-free, and my family was forever broken; so I care deeply about this box because it is my only lifeline to seeking justice for my mother." Only when I finished my sentence did I notice that I had pretty much yelled at him. I had gotten so worked up I could feel my neck pulsating from my raised heartbeat.

"You have nothing to fear. I will be giving you the box with all its content as soon as I am done going over all the documents."

His confident smile made be hopeful, so, I trusted him.

"I also recommend filing a civil lawsuit, by the way."

"Yes, many people advised me to go down that path, but I have no idea where to begin."

"Well, I would be happy to help," he said with genuine candor. "Mrs. Healey, I need to make something clear, though. While I promise you I will do my best to be successful and achieve the goals you have been aiming for the past twenty-plus years, you understand I cannot guarantee any positive outcome whatsoever. I just want to point that out, because, well, I don't want you to feel like you've just wasted your time, money, and effort in hiring me."

That surprised me, in a good way.

"Mr. Bell, to my eyes and heart as Donna's daughter, this journey has never been about money. I just want my mother to have justice for what Mr. Moore did to her."

He smiled.

"What about you?" I asked, "would you feel like you've wasted your time and effort if we don't succeed?"

My question caught him off guard, but he answered right away.

"Not at all. I am somehow intrigued by this case, and when I feel pulled towards a cause, I have to do something about it. Mrs. Healey, you can rest assured that I care about your case and your goal of making people pay for what they did so as to restore justice."

And just like that, I was happy. We shook hands, wished each other a pleasant day, and vowed to speak soon. The stars were finally aligning, and they were smiling at me. I'm sure mom had something to do with it.

* * *

Tuesday morning. Nine a.m. sharp. My phone rang.

"Hello?"

"Mrs. Healey, it's me, Joe Bell." I could hear street traffic in the background as he was walking down the street.

"Yes, good morning!"

"Mrs. Healey," he said, "I have great news."

My heart skipped a bit.

"The private investigator we hired," he paused briefly, "found Mr. Moore."

Oh. My. Lord.

"I'm sorry; can you repeat that, please?" I asked. I knew I had heard every word he said, and I was sure my brain had processed the information correctly. I just needed to hear it again.

"We have been able to locate Mr. Moore!" He sounded accomplished and proud.

"Where is he?" I felt short of breath.

"He's *not* in New Jersey." What a relief! He was not in my home state. I can't tell you how many times I walked into a bakery or a flower shop and thought he was following me. I truly believe I was close to crossing the line into becoming paranoid about being stalked by him. "He is in a private mental facility. Apparently, his mother had to sell their family home in upper Montclair years ago to afford this place. Oh, and get this: He is not in the mental institution for what he did to your mother."

What?

"Well, what's he there for, then?" I was puzzled and rather confused.

"We are not sure yet, but we plan to find that out," he assured me.

I couldn't believe he was in a mental institution; but most of all, I was shocked to learn he hadn't even been committed there for my mother's murder. What was he there for? A vacation? A way out of prison? I had to find out.

Once I got back home, I tracked down the old files I had from the Marlboro psychiatric hospital and called them. A lovely lady with a musical Spanish accent answered. I could tell she was a genuine person, and kind-hearted as well because she actually took the time to listen to me and my story. She felt for me. As soon as we were done exchanging information, she told me she'd see what she could do and that she'd call me back. I wasn't counting on it, given how many times someone had actually followed through after giving me that classic line. To my surprise, though, she did call back after only a few days, inquiring about more information she needed. I was relieved and happy to hear back from her. I was faithful she'd help me out.

However, after a few weeks went by without hearing from her, I decided to take matters into my own hands once again, and I gave her a call. No answer. I called her regularly for many, many months; no answer. So I decided to leave her a voice message, explaining to her I understood if she could no longer help me. I politely requested she'd give my information to her boss, or the legal department because maybe they could help. I highlighted that hearing back from her or anybody else from her department would have meant a lot to me. I almost begged her.

Several months went by, and I finally heard back from her.

"Ms. Tina," she stated, "you have to file a lawsuit to have these records subpoenaed."

"What?" I was surprised. Why would I have to file a lawsuit if these records should be available to me by law? "I don't see why I have to do that. I am not asking for his medical records. I just want to know how and why he was released. This has nothing to do with HIPPA, do you know what I mean?"

"I do," she said kindly. "I wish there was more I could tell you, but this is all I was able to come up with."

"I understand," I lied.

"I'm sorry."

"No worries; thank you for your time."

And just like that, I had hit yet another wall. You see, I think this is what it all comes down to: words. The confusion lies in the fact that I have never asked for his medical records. I just want to know the reason why he was allowed to leave prison and be shipped off to a private mental institution.

We are not talking about a man who was mentally insane. We are talking about a man who was *criminally* insane. There is a huge difference, and once you cross over to being a criminally insane person, you lose all rights that a mentally insane person would have. This is part of my fight for justice: I want authorities and governments to recognize the difference between mentally insane and criminally insane.

Stephen Moore was and is criminally insane. He should still be rotting in jail so he can pay the price for brutally killing my beloved mother. Instead, he has been treated with white gloves the whole time. *This. Is. Not. Justice*!

Conclusion

October 2017
New Jersey
   Dear Reader,
   First of all, let me thank you for allowing me to tell you my story. As you can see from this book, throughout the years it has been hard for me to find people willing to listen; so your time and patience do not go unappreciated.
   Let me tell you briefly what I have been up to lately: I have filed and won a wrongful death lawsuit against Stephen Moore, who now owes me one million dollars. My lawyers told me I will never see a single dime from him, though, because apparently, the killer has no money. This sounds fishy to me, because I am aware of his trust fund, set up by his uncle, and I know he had access to the money when he turned 35 years old. I still have lots of unanswered questions, including why and how he ended up in that private mental institution; but oh, well. What matters to me is that my cause has been recognized by the law in that courtroom.
   My children are growing up beautifully, and I am proud and honored to have the privilege of seeing them grow up. This is something my mother never had the chance to experience, so in a way, I am doing it for both of us. My husband is as supportive as ever, and I am one lucky woman. As for me, years ago I started volunteering at Domestic Abuse and Sexual Assault Intervention Services, a private nonprofit organization established in 1984 providing comprehensive services to survivors of domestic and sexual violence and their families in Sussex County, New Jersey.
   I have also contacted a few Senators and Congressmen in New Jersey to let them know about my story and my fight for justice. I have recently received the following reply:

Thank you for writing to Senator * and Assemblyman * regarding this horrible tragedy. I wanted to touch base to let you know that we are looking into your idea for legislation. I will keep you informed on how it progresses.

Thank you again,

It has been 2 years and I have not heard back from them.

* * *

And so, this is where my story momentarily concludes. I say "momentarily", because I want this book to simply be the beginning of another journey, one that will see me reach my ultimate goal: to get Donna's Law passed, first in the State of New Jersey and then in the rest of the country and bring back the Death penalty in NJ when it comes to murder. Donna's Law would do away with the verdict of "not guilty by reason of insanity" and make it "guilty by reason of insanity" in cases of murder. Changing this law and applying the guilt to the person, even if they are insane, will give the victim's family rights to information that they otherwise would not be privileged to. It is also a way for murderers to be held accountable for the atrocious crime that is committed. I wish people to remember that there is no statute of limitation when it comes to murder, no matter what anyone tells you.

I hope people can see the difference between the mentally insane and the criminally insane. The words "mentally insane" assume that the person is affected by a mental instability or disorder that he or she has absolutely no control over. Hence, they cannot be held accountable for whatever crime they might commit. However, the *criminally* insane are in control of their mental and physical abilities. They are psychopaths who are fully aware of what the consequences to their actions will be and still choose to go ahead and commit the crime. Stephen Moore is *criminally* insane, a deliberate and cunning human being who committed a premeditated murder. See the difference?

I remember when, years ago, a police officer told me "Don't expect to change the world." He was mocking me for my determination to see Steve pay for what he did to my mom. Well, I took his suggestion, thanked him, and kept going down my own path. I don't aim to change the world for the entire human race; I am not naïve. But if this book of mine helps even one person, then I will have reached my goal. I want to make a difference for people who, like me, are family members of a loved one who was a victim of a heinous crime and have yet to see justice. I want you — yes, you, reading this book — to know that I will do my best to make sure Donna's Law passes so that nobody else will have to go through what I have been going through since I was two years old.

You can rest assured that I will not stop until I can go to bed at night knowing that I have accomplished what I set out to do for my mom and for other victims' families. My journey doesn't end here; neither should yours. Given the nature of my book, in the upcoming pages, you can find contact information for domestic violence and sexual assault helplines.

With strength, determination and a bit of stubbornness, we can make a change.

Yours truly,
Tina Ann Healey

The Star Thrower

A man was walking on the beach one day and noticed a boy who was reaching down, picking up starfish, and throwing them in the ocean. As he approached, he called out, "Hello! What are you doing?"

The boy looked up and said, "I'm throwing starfish into the ocean."

"Why are you throwing starfish into the ocean?" asked the man.

"The tide stranded them. If I don't throw them in the water before the sun comes up, they'll die," came the answer.

"Surely you realize that there are miles of beach and thousands of starfish. You'll never throw them all back; there are too many. You can't possibly make a difference."

The boy listened politely, then picked up another starfish. As he threw it back into the sea, he said, "It made a difference for that one."[1]

---

[1] Eiseley, L. (1979). *The Star Thrower*. Mariner Books, 1st Edition. Retrieved from: https://starthrowerfoundation.org/about-starthrower-foundation/the-star-thrower-story/

Contact Information for Victims and Survivors of Domestic Violence and Sexual Assault

DOMESTIC VIOLENCE

Domestic Abuse and Sexual Assault Intervention Services.
Services are free and confidential.
24 Hour Helpline: 973-875-1211
TTY: 973-875-6369.

The National Domestic Violence Hotline
1-800-799-7233 (SAFE)
www.ndvh.org

National Dating Abuse Helpline
1-866-331-9474
www.loveisrespect.org

Americans Overseas Domestic Violence Crisis Center
International Toll-Free (24/7)
1-866-USWOMEN (879-6636)
www.866uswomen.org

National Child Abuse Hotline/Child Help
1-800-4-A-CHILD (1-800-422-4453)
www.childhelp.org

National Sexual Assault Hotline
1-800-656-4673 (HOPE)
www.rainn.org

National Suicide Prevention Lifeline
1-800-273-8255 (TALK)
www.suicidepreventionlifeline.org

National Center for Victims of Crime
1-202-467-8700
www.victimsofcrime.org

National Human Trafficking Resource Center/Polaris Project
Call: 1-888-373-7888 | Text: HELP to BeFree (233733)
www.polarisproject.org

National Network for Immigrant and Refugee Rights
1-510-465-1984
www.nnirr.org

National Coalition for the Homeless
1-202-737-6444
www.nationalhomeless.org

National Resource Center on Domestic Violence
1-800-537-2238
www.nrcdv.org and www.vawnet.org

Futures Without Violence: The National Health Resource Center on Domestic Violence
1-888-792-2873
www.futureswithoutviolence.org

National Center on Domestic Violence, Trauma & Mental Health
1-312-726-7020 ext. 2011
www.nationalcenterdvtraumamh.org

CHILDREN

Childhelp USA/National Child Abuse Hotline
1-800-422-4453
www.childhelpusa.org

Children's Defense Fund
202-628-8787
www.childrensdefense.org

Child Welfare League of America
202-638-2952
www.cwla.org

National Council on Juvenile and Family Court Judges
Child Protection and Custody/Resource Center on Domestic Violence
1-800-527-3233
www.ncjfcj.org

Center for Judicial Excellence
  info@centerforjudicialexcellence.org
  www.centerforjudicialexcellence.org

TEENS

Love is Respect
  Hotline: 1-866-331-9474
  www.loveisrespect.org

Break the Cycle
  202-824-0707
  www.breakthecycle.org

College Campus Safety Guide

DIFFERENTLY ABLED

Domestic Violence Initiative
  (303) 839-5510/ (877) 839-5510
  www.dviforwomen.org

Deaf Abused Women's Network (DAWN)
  Email: Hotline@deafdawn.org
  VP: 202-559-5366
  www.deafdawn.org

WOMEN OF COLOR

Women of Color Network
  1-800-537-2238
  www.wocninc.org

INCITE! Women of Color Against Violence
  incite.natl@gmail.com
  www.incite-national.org

LATINA/LATINO

Alianza
  1-505-753-3334
  www.dvalianza.org

Casa de Esperanza
  Linea de crisis 24-horas/24-hour crisis line

1-651-772-1611
www.casadeesperanza.org

National Latin@ Network for Healthy Families and Communities
1-651-646-5553
www.nationallatinonetwork.org

IMMIGRANT

The National Immigrant Women's Advocacy Project
(202) 274-4457
http://www.niwap.org/

INDIGENOUS WOMEN

National Indigenous Women's Resource Center
855-649-7299
www.niwrc.org

Indigenous Women's Network
1-512-258-3880
www.indigenouswomen.org

ASIAN/PACIFIC ISLANDER

Asian and Pacific Islander Institute on Domestic Violence
1-415-954-9988
www.apiidv.org

Committee Against Anti-Asian Violence (CAAAV)
1-212- 473-6485
www.caaav.org

Manavi
1-732-435-1414
www.manavi.org

AFRICAN-AMERICAN

Institute on Domestic Violence in the African-American Community
1-877-643-8222
www.dvinstitute.org

The Black Church and Domestic Violence Institute
1-770-909-0715
www.bcdvi.org

LESBIAN, BISEXUAL, GAY, TRANSGENDER, GENDER NON-CONFORMING

The Audre Lorde Project
1-178-596-0342
www.alp.org

LAMBDA GLBT Community Services
1-206-350-4283
http://www.qrd.org/qrd/www/orgs/avproject/main.htm

National Coalition of Anti-Violence Programs
1-212-714-1184
www.ncavp.org

National Gay and Lesbian Task Force
1-202-393-5177
www.ngltf.org

Northwest Network of Bisexual, Trans, Lesbian & Gay Survivors of Abuse
1-206-568-7777
www.nwnetwork.org

ABUSE IN LATER LIFE

National Clearinghouse on Abuse in Later Life
1-608-255-0539
www.ncall.us

National Center for Elder Abuse
1-855-500-3537
www.aginginplace.org

MEN

National Organization for Men Against Sexism (NOMAS)
1-720-466-3882
www.nomas.org

A Call to Men
1-917-922-6738
www.acalltomen.org

Men Can Stop Rape
1-202-265-6530
www.mencanstoprape.org

Men Stopping Violence
1-866-717-9317
www.menstoppingviolence.org

LEGAL

American Bar Association Commission on Domestic Violence
1-202-662-1000
www.abanet.org/domviol

Battered Women's Justice Project
1-800-903-0111
www.bwjp.org

Legal Momentum
1-212-925-6635
www.legalmomentum.org

Womenslaw.org
www.womenslaw.org

National Clearinghouse for the Defense of Battered Women
1-800-903-0111 x 3
www.ncdbw.org

Bonus Material Part I

Essex County Courthouse
Newark, NJ

October 28, 1976

The State of New Jersey v. Stephen Moore

Before: Hon. Ralph Fusco

Disclaimer: The following transcripts are official documents of which I, the author, am in rightful possession. The format of these transcripts has been modified to provide the audience with a clearer format than the original one; however, the actual content, including typos, spelling, punctuation, and more, has not been edited and will not be edited.

All right, Mr. Prosecutor, will you indicate the name of the matter we are considering, sir?

Yes, your honor. We are here for the record, assistant prosecutor Dennis Mautone, for the State – we are here an indictment against one Stephen MOORE, charging the crime of murder while armed. Indictment 4406 the '75 term, and this is a pretrial for that case.

All right. For the defendant?

Your Honor, Edward Schutzer, from the firm of Schwartz and Fielo, Belleville, appearing on behalf of the defendant.

All right, gentlemen. I have before me, one returnable October 22nd and the other is a notice of insanity defense served on the prosecutor dated October 11th, and I can't help but say that I received a telephonic communication from counsel for the defendant, indicating that it was the intention of the defendant through his counsel to with draw the motion.

Now tell me where we stand this morning on the motions.

Your Honor, with respect to the motion for the competency hearing, that motion was made by me at a time when I actually believed there would be the defense.

I am requesting that motion be withdrawn in as such as my doctors indicate Mr. Moore is, or likely to be competent to stand trial.

At the present time I understand Mr. Mautone may have an objection to my withdrawal of the motion but as it stands that is my position.

Well, you say withdrawn. I don't with draw anything. I either act on them or dismiss them. It becomes ridiculous to let you with draw and then five hours later you say you want to file it again. This matter has a trial date, doesn't it?

Yes, Your Honor.

What is the trial date?

November 8.

Now you had an opportunity this morning will talk to your client. He cognizant of the proceedings you have taken, and those you are now indicating of the motion to have the court make a determination on whether Mr. Moore is competent to consult with counsel? How about it?

Your honor, may I have a moment? I had discussed it with him. May I have a moment now to discuss it?

Let me know when you have it discussed.

(iterim)

All right, Mr. Schutzer.

My apologies to the court. I have conferred with my client. He is aware of the fact that I made the motion for a competency hearing, and he is apparently in accord with my judgment that he wishes to proceed to go to trial, he has indicated to me he does wish to go to trial, however, he is afraid anything he says will be held against him, although I have advised him that that will not be case. He is ready and prepared to go to trial.

It is not that I am afraid, that I don't understand.

I didn't hear you.

It is not that I am afraid, it just that I don't understand the proceedings of the court. I understand what I say count against me, that's why I am having Mr. Schutzer speak for me.

Go ahead, Mr. Schutzer.

Your Honor, although, as Mr. Moore indicates to the court, he doesn't understand, only because he is a layman, I think Mr. Moore having consulted with him and he with me is fully aware of the role of the lawyer as to judges and whatever. He indicated to me not only his willingness but his fervent desire to consult with me and to direct the defense in this trial, and I refer the court well to reports of both my doctors, Dr.Kern, the state's Dr., Wherein, for instance, in Dr. Gelsinger's report he indicates the personality structure of the type whereby this defense can easily crumble and loosely reintegrate itself to the extent Mr.

Moore can operate at a low-level of functioning in a structured environment.

Are you reading to us?

Yes, Your Honor.

Pick up the paper and stand.

This young lady– you gentlemen turned down and re-into your file and my reporter absolutely gets nothing from it. I am sorry, but they don't make any difference if I get it, but this lady right here needs to get it.

Yes. And I refer the courts as well to the last page of Dr. Latimers report, where he says from the formal standpoint it is possible patient's condition made me the requirements of competence to stand trial, as much as he knows what the charges are, the dangers involved, as well the roles of the participants in the trial.

Dr. Latimer indicates he discussed the matter greatly with Mr. Moore. In addition, Your Honor, I refer the court to the final page of Dr. Kern's report, the state psychiatrist, wherein he said, "Mr. Moore is oriented to time, place, and person." These, Your Honor, appeared to be the essential prerequisites for the defendant who wishes to stand trial, and to assist intelligently with his counsel in the preparation and execution of his defense. Under those circumstances, Your Honor, I was respectfully request that the court dismiss my motion with prejudice and that this matter proceed to trial.

All right. Prosecutor?

Your Honor, it was mentioned by Mr. Schutzer that I oppose the withdrawal of this competency hearing. I didn't oppose the filing of the motion. I don't oppose that withdrawal of the motion, I merely wish to point out that once the matters of this nature are brought to the attention of the court, that there may be imposed on the court a duty to make the determination as to competency, and I think that the court should consider the possibility that requirements in the law are for hearing to be held, and that's my only position.

Mr. Schuzter, when your motion was made and unfortunately it is not dated, so I don't know when it was made, but it was filed on October 12, returnable October 20, I have your own certification, and I have reference to Dr. Latimer and after Dr. Shellsinger, who examined your client.

I have your memoranda of law on the issue, and then you have Dr. Shellsinger's psychological report, and course Dr. Latimer's report.

Now as a result of these two reports, you file your notice of motion indicating that your client may not be competent to assist at the trial, and you desire that the court hold a hearing on the motion so that the court may make a determination whether the defendant was competent to stand trial.

Following October 19 you requested an adjournment, since you desire to have your doctors available to testify.

Following that, and unfortunately I don't have a reported record of the next action, but a day or two ago this office was in receipt of a call you desire to withdraw your motion. Now that is history of these proceedings down to this moment before you or the prosecutor have spoken.

Now I have, and I don't know a of the receipt, I have report of Dr. Kern directed to the prosecutor, dated October 20. Unfortunately, I don't know when the office received it. I don't know how it got to the file, because there is nothing to indicate it was mailed to me by anyone.

Your Honor, I delivered that to the court yesterday.

Okay, prosecutor. Send me a letter next time, so I know where it comes from. All I know is somebody slips at the paper file. The clerk had no record of it, and I don't know how it got to the file.

I shall.

Papers sent to me should have a letter saying," I am enclosing a copy," and did you send a copy to your colleague?

Being provided as part of discovery.

You don't send anything to the courts that don't send to your adversary.

Now Mr. Moore, your lawyer made an application to me, reported by two reports by doctors indicating that you may be to ill--

I saw three doctors.

Pardon?

I saw three doctors.

You saw three doctors. I know that. That's all right. Your lawyer made an application to me reported by two doctors tell me he thought that you didn't know enough about the case and what was going on so that you can confer with him, and help him with your defense.

Your Honor, I would like to work with the warden and change some of the rules in this institution, or jail.

What you want to do with the warden?

Well I would like to talk with him, change some of the rules, some of the food conditions, living conditions.

I have no control of the warden. I'm sure that one of the guards can arrange you to discuss with the warden or send him a note to what your problem may be as to the conditions, but the court has no control over that.

I wrote letters and get an answer. No mail. I tried to talk to the officers, no response. That's why I'm mentioning it to you.

I don't run the jail. That's the warden's responsibility.

Could you put a note in? I like to see him?

I can't make that request. That's between you and the warden.

Your lawyer says to me and he says he discussed it with you, that you know what you are being charged with, and by the way, what are you being charged, do you know?

Supposedly alleged homicide.

Alleged homicide?
Yes.

What do you mean by, alleged homicide?

I don't understand the term, but supposedly take a life.

You know homicide needs take a life?

Right.

Do you know when this alleged homicide is supposed to have taken place?

Supposed to Have Taken Place., July 13 or 14

1976?

Yes, sir.

Where supposed to have taken place?

In Belleville, sir. I don't know if this person is alive or dead.

Pardon?

I don't know if person is alive or dead.

I understand you don't, but I mean, you do know that you are being charged with on the 13th or 14th of July 19 allegedly committing a homicide, and it says here of one Donna Litchfield. Are you telling me you don't know if that person is alive or dead. I realize that if the state wants to establish your guilt they have to prove not only that you did it, but they have to prove the person is dead, and how do they say you allegedly committed this homicide in the indictment?

It's on a paper I gave him.

What does it say?

I don't have it. He has it.

What does it say? Do you remember?

Under the conditions I got arrested.

In the paper doesn't it say you did it with a knife?

Supposedly.

That's what he says, I am not saying that you get did, that's what the paper says. So you know what you are being charged with. Do you know who your attorney is?

Mr. Schutzer.

Are you satisfied with the advice you are getting from him?

Well he says my father appointed him.

Are you satisfied with his advice?

Well I have a couple other lawyers I would like to work with him.

Is the other lawyer?

I don't have them. I haven't talked to them.

When are you going to talk to them?

I want to contact Mrs. Kerry in New York, Meyer Lofsky in Paterson, and Bennett & Bennett in Newark.

Have you talked to Mr. Schutzer about that?
Yes.

Did you tell him?

Just before we came in here.

You can wait until the night before the trial. When you talk to the other lawyers?

I tried to make a phone call, I couldn't make any phone calls to get out of here, $300,000 bail.

Has your father been in to see you?

I don't know if he is dead or alive.

Pardon?

I don't know if he is dead or alive.

Has he been in to see you?

He is in Montclair, hasn't come.

Had he come down?

No, sir.

He hired Mr. Schutzer.

I am paying for Mr. Schutzer. I am over 21, but I mean, he says my father contacted him to represent me.

You are saying you are paying for Mr. Schutzer?

Yes. Why should my father pay for him?

I am asking. I don't know.

Yeah.

I indicated to you, Mr. Schutzer now says that from his conversations with you and everything he knows about this case—

I don't know what his fee is. What is your fee?

That's between you and him. I don't get involved in that.

I don't understand the different charges and fees. I'm not trying to be wise. I don't understand the law procedures.

Mr. Schutzer tells me after reading the doctors reports and talking to you he feels you know enough about what is going on so that you can go to trial on this case. Do you understand that?

Yes. I want to go to trial and you know--

You want to go to trial?

Yes. I want to get jail.

What is the trial date?

November 7?

The 8th.

Mr. Moore, what you say?

This man told me November 7, wrote it on a piece of paper, preliminary trial, November 1, and the other trial November 7, and the pretrial for this one, pretrial, and pretrial the 7th.

I will correct it. The original pretrial was scheduled November 1, but the trial date is on November 8, because we won't on a Sunday.

Now we are going to hold pretrial today.

By the way, this girl was supposed to have been your girlfriend?

Yes.

What is her name?

Donna Litchfield. If she is alive, I want to see her, you know.

But on the other hand, if she is dead you can't see her.

Can't you bring her back to life if she is dead?

You tell me.

I don't know, you know, it this person that are not.

Well, as I said, the State is going to prove it.

I mean, is it possible I could be framed, that this person is dead?

Certainly you could be framed. That's what your lawyer is here to protect you from. Being framed. She is not, the state is—

She could be hiding someplace. Somebody could be paying her to put me in jail or something.

That's right. Mr. Moore, I have already indicated Mr. Schutzer thinks that you are aware enough of what is going on stand trial. Do you have any objection to what the town may and are you willing we undertake to try case beginning November 8th?

I want to go to trial, get it over with, so that I can get jail.

Anything else you want to say, Mr. Schutzer, in this regard?

No, Your Honor.

My apologies to the court for having made my motion to withdraw this motion on such a short notice, but, I had a with Mr. Moore, and discussed great lengths with doctors in preparation for the compentcey hearing, and at the time he indicated they felt he probably would be capable of standing trial. I indicated to the court in my original certification with the moving papers only that I had a doubt, I was plagued by doubts as to the mental capacity, no I didn't stay on the second page that I will be my client could possibly stand trial, and at that point I was of that opinion; and I and stronger that opinion today.

I believe the court can cognizance Mr. Moore's ability to comprehend basic things concerning the trial of the case, even though as a layman he can't understand the legal technicalities.

I as a judge don't know what they are all about.

Now, prosecutor, do you have anything to say on this issue?

No, I have stated my position.

Gentlemen, in view of the action by defense counsel and my opportunity to serve Mr. Moore, and you have several colloquies with can in which he indicates he is cognizant of the nature of the which he being charged, to wit, he called it and alleged homicide, he indicates his cognizance of charge that the alleged homicide plays on or about the

13th or 14th of July 1976, and alleged victim was one Donna Litchfield, and the alleged charge that homicide arose by reason they use of a knife and the defendant's further observation that he had retained counsel, satisfied with counsel of his choice, and that he is desirous of going to trial.

I am going to dismiss the motion heretofore filed returnable October 21, 1976, requesting that a hearing be to determine competency of the defendant to stand trial. Such order will be entered.

Now ask to have any matters that we may dispose of now, if all possible and as a result of this conference, I would appreciate an order to evolve prepared by the prosecutor, following which it will be consented to as to for by counsel for the defendant, and can be agreed to the four I will settle this on Monday, November 1, without notice to any of the parties.

All right. At the outset let me ask whether there are any matters that you, Mr. Schutzer, feel that must be attended to in advance of the trial, that had not been attended to.

Your honor, the only one I do have this point, is the fact that I would like the opportunity to have the report of Dr. Kern, a psychiatrist.

I thought he said he gave it to you.

He did this morning, as I say this morning I haven't got it yet, but I have read it.

It's right there. It's his.

Wait a minute. Did you have him sign and a knowledge receipt of it? Have him do it now. You may never see again. Don't you have the original?
Yes.

Have him sign, "I hereby knowledge receipt of a true copy of this report," and for the rest of your life you will know he has it.

As of now, Mr. Schutzer doesn't know if he got it yet.

Your Honor—

Yes, Mr. Moore

I would like to go book Pres. Ford.

I beg your pardon?

I would like to press charges against Pres. Ford.
I want to broadcast I didn't find any paper- to be on broadcasting, A.B.C. my lawyer told me-my conscience being read aloud over television, and C.B.S radio.
I want it to stop.

Anything else, Mr. Schutzer, besides the doctor's report?

No. For the record, Your Honor, I will be I just acknowledged receipt of Dr. Kern's report.

I don't do anything about discovery. That's between you and the prosecutor. If you never got it I don't care. If you got it, I care less. Why are the record with something that is not part of the court's responsibility? Give the receipt to the prosecutor, let him file it. Tell me what else you feel you need that you may not have had.

At this point, Your Honor I don't need any more.

Prosecutor?

There were two conclusory reports in the Belleville Police Department, and an administrative report from the prosecutor's office detectives. Bowel reports we have and I had them Xeroxed, so I could provide to Mr. Schutzer this morning, and the only problem is that the entire middle of the report came out blank.

Why not give it to one of the detectives to type up and serve it to him today?
I don't want to do anything tomorrow we can do today. The Detectives have done nothing for six weeks except hide in my library. Fair enough?
Are there any emotions that are contemplated, Mr. Schutzer?

At this point, Your Honor, none.

All right.

Is there an alibi defense?

No, Your Honor, there isn't.

You have already indicated you are going to interpose an insanity defense?

Yes, Your Honor.

Now, prosecutor, are there any preliminary matters you feel must be to now that we have contemplated?

Your Honor, there were certain oral statements made by the defendant in the presence of at least detective Gilsensen from my office; I would contemplate introducing.

You are suggesting to me, we will have a Miranda problem.

Possibly, sir.

Involuntariness.
Yes.

And, Your Honor, that is introduced I will make lotion at the appropriate time.

All right, now you may have a alleged oral statements to your colleague?

Yes, sir.

Some of them are part of a report, into a knife and reduced to writing and, Your Honor. I discussed it with Mr. Schutzer.

I did not intend to have been reduced to writing. If the court wishes me to, I will.

I think if you don't do it, then you come the morning of the trial and for the first time make elbow to your colleague and then we are going to have a recess while he is reviewing and determining what he is going to do about. I think to expedite the trial. That's the reason we have this.

How many exhibits do you? Is there any volume of exhibits?

If the exhibits are marked this juncture, we can at least expedite the trial of the case without taking any ruling on whether they are admissible or not, let's mark them from 1 to 50 if that's how many are, or whatever you have.

Now have these all been displayed to your colleagues before today?

He has had an opportunity to review and inspect them.

Let us mark them for identification.

I don't intend to submit all of them for evidence, but they are numbered.

Let me have them in the order they are marked.

Exhibit S - 1 for identification, photo, the front of an apartment with a car;
S - 2 for identification, photo, apartment, crowd of people in front.
S - 3 for identification, photo of hallway.
S - 4 for identification, photo, door.
S - 5 for identification, photo, room, playpen.
S - 6 for identification, photo, kitchen.
S - 7 for identification, photo, baseboard.
S - 8 for identification, photo, playpen.
S - 9 for identification, photo, sofa.
S - 10 for identification, photo, hallway with toys.
S - 11 for identification, photo, bathroom.
S - 12 for identification, photo, bathroom with body in tub.
S - 13 for identification, photo, bathroom wall with bloodstains.
S - 14 for identification, photo, tub with body.
S - 15 for identification, photo, body in tub.
S - 16 for identification, photo, body on slab with wound.
S - 17 for identification, photo, body on slab, left arm.
S - 18, photo, body on slab, full-length.
S - 19 photo, body, gash on neck.
S - 20, photo, tub without body.
S - 21 photo, knife with ruler.
S - 22 photo, right hand, male
S - 23, photo, right arm, male
S - 24, photo, lower torso, male
S - 25 lower torso, male, right side
S - 26 photo, male, defendant

Tina Ann Healey 149

S - 27, photo, car, Chevy, 398FDI
S - 28, photo, left side, car.

All right. Anything else at this juncture, prosecutor?

No, sir.

Thank you. Now tell me this, gentlemen. How many witnesses do you contemplate calling, prosecutor?

12 to 14, sir.

Mr. Schutzer?

Your Honor, at this time six or seven. All right. How long do you think it will take, prosecutor?

Eight days, sir.

Mr. Schutzer?

Your Honor, I think about seven or eight days.

All right. Gentlemen, I would appreciate very much if you, Mr. prosecutor, can put together all materials that you're going to have for your adversary, make them available for inspection. If there are any other problems arise, please communicate with the court.

I hate, you asked prosecution to prepare in order on the findings the determination of the court; it is necessary to prepare in order on the discovery issue?

That's the most important part of it that you are going to make your discovery on or before October 29, 1976, at which time you will deliver or permit Mr. Schuster to inspect it and that's the way it's done. As of that date if you don't do it you will be out of time. All right, thank you, gentlemen.

(End of hearing.)

Bonus Material Part II

Essex County Courthouse
Newark, NJ

November 15, 1976

The State of New Jersey v. Stephen Moore

Before: Hon. Ralph Fusco

Disclaimer: The following transcripts are official documents of which I, the author, am in rightful possession. The format of these transcripts has been modified to provide the audience with a clearer format than the original one; however, the actual content, including typos, spelling, punctuation, and more, has not been edited and will not be edited.

Opening Statements

Good morning ladies and gentlemen. Sorry for your inconvenience. All right, gentlemen. Prosecutor, do you leave the polling of the Jury? Yes, Your Honor. All right. We have two more who we are waiting for. Good morning. We will wait the other juror. Good morning Jury was sworn in whenever you are ready. Prosecutor Judge Fusco, Mr. Schutzer, Mr. Foreman, ladies and gentlemen of the Jury my name is Dennis Mautone. As you told, I am the assistant prosecutor in Essex County. I am charged with the responsibility of presenting a case to you, a case that is brought before you by indictment 4406 of the '75 term. This indictment is the spark, the catalyst to bring us all here to decide the issues based on the testimony we will hear come from the witness stand, and from whatever evidence will be introduced in this case. By this indictment Stephen C Moore is charged by the grand jury state of New Jersey 1976 in the town of Belleville, that he did willfully, feloniously and of malice aforethought kill and murder Donna Litchfield, and count to of the indictment the grand jurors charge that Stephen dictate and place and in the jurisdiction set forth in the first date in his possession a dangerous knife during the commission of that unlawful killing in New Jersey.

Ladies and gentlemen, all unlawful killings are considered to be murder in the $2^{nd\circ}$. There are certain proofs that will be used from the witness stand which may either elevate the crime to murder in the $1^{st\circ}$, in those proofs will be necessary in order to find of murder in the $1^{st\circ}$. We all have a very important function in the determination of this case. Mr.

Schutzer is here to ensure the defendant proper legal representation. Your Honor, Judge Fusco, is charged with the responsibility of making certain legal judgments, rulings, during the pendency of these proceedings, and with charging you as to the law that you are to apply to the case, or to the facts of the case that you here testify to. My responsibility as the assistant prosecutor in charge of this case is to present it to you as clearly and consistently as I can. I will do everything in my power to do. Responsibility ladies and gentlemen, if that responsibility of that fact. You will be asked to listen to the testimony that comes from the stands. Will be asked to sift through the evidence that is produced in this case, you will be asked to come to a fair and just conclusion based on the law as a judge tells you, and as applied to the facts that you here. Now when making these determinations you will be asked to go into the Jury. Do not, and for you, do not leave your common sense, your reasonableness, your everyday experiences, without. Bring them in there with you. It will be very important, very useful in determining the true issues in this case. I want to outline for you very briefly with the state intends to prove in this case, so that you will have, or to assist you in following the testimony as it comes forth. States case essentially will revolve around July 13 and July 14, 1976. July 13, 1976 we will show you that Stephen Moore, the defendant in this case united with the victim, Litchfield, at the home of her sister in Bloomfield that during the visit Donna told Stephen she did not want to see him anymore.

You will hear how Stephen reacted to that rejection, and what that defendant did, and how he left that house, and how he proceeded to Surf City, New Jersey. He went to the house of his friends that O'Dell's and he spent the evening with them. And how the next morning with his plan developing and knowing what he intended to do, Mr. Moore took a knife from the service station of his friend Mr. O'Dell. And with that knife in his possession he proceeded to North Jersey and aware of his intention to take the life of Donna Litchfield he went to the bank in Montclair, New Jersey, and withdrew the sum of $$1000.00

He then proceeded to the last place he'd seen the victim, but she was not there. He was informed that she had gone to her own apartment in Belleville, and then he proceeded to that apartment and knowing his intention he entered the apartment and he was met by the victim. A friend of hers, Valerie Iacobacci, will testify, and you will hear how there were three children in the apartment and that Mr. Moore was engaged in a conversation with the victim, and the victim was cleaning the apartment, and he went into the bathroom and you will hear how the victim exited the bathroom, went into the bathroom, continued cleaning, when Mr. Moore then affected the purpose he going to Belleville. He killed Donna Litchfield. Donna Litchfield fought for her life, ladies and gentlemen, but to no avail. Mr. Moore then left the bathroom and went into the kitchen, washed the blood from his person, and left the apartment with his getaway many and hands. He proceeded to Surf City, New Jersey. The police officers arrived, gathered as much information as they could, and were able to contact the Surf City police information he received in Mr. Moore was in Surf City, New Jersey.

Testimony that you will hear testify to, in evidence you will see produced the lead you to a conclusion, ladies and gentlemen, the Mr. Moore on July 14, 1976, intended and planned the murder of Donna Litchfield, he did in fact murder her.

In the testimony comes in, I will ask you to evaluate a when you go into the Jury event. Usually common sense, is your reasonableness, your everyday experiences will have no trouble rendering a fair and just verdict. This allying was very brief. You will hear the testimony, you will be asked to evaluate. I will speak to you again at the conclusion of the case. Keep an open mind and listen to all the testimony. That's all the state asked. Evaluate here evaluate a fairly based on the law. Thank you very much, ladies and gentlemen.

Thank you, prosecutor.

Mr. Schutzer, whenever you're ready.

Thank you, sir. Ladies and gentlemen of the jury, it's been sad that the trial by jury is a tool which we use in our society to extract the maximum amount of truth from conflicting sources of the story. Now you have just heard a story from the prosecutor asked what the state intends to prove to you people. The problem is that there is more here than meets the. The problem is that there is a whole iceberg. There is ninth of an iceberg beneath the tip which the prosecutor has just indicated to you. He has just indicated a very credible story about a seemingly normal if there is such thing, crime. My point is this, ladies and gentlemen. What the prosecutors told you, what I am telling you now, are what we intend to prove, but we don't know. We weren't there.

With due respect to Mr. Mautone, he wasn't there, I wasn't there, you people and bad. We are going to have to describe this case, or you are going to have to decide this case based upon what you hear from the witness stand, based upon the evidence which is presented. You are going to have to decide this case we call credible, believable testimony, credible, believable evidence, ladies and gentlemen. The fact that Mr. Moore sits there accused of this crime doesn't indicate that he is guilty in the matter but the prosecutor says. Doesn't indicate anything more that he is being charged with this crime. It doesn't indicate he planned to murder, that he killed Donna Litchfield. It doesn't indicate anything at all, and I ask you ladies and gentlemen to consider that. there also must be a degree of mental in other words, as it's been put in the past, and must not only be an evil doing parent, that evil meaning mind. Ladies and gentlemen, Mr. Mautone is going to indicate to you that because Mr. Moore, my client was there at the scene of the crime, that because certain tax he may have committed were in fact committed by hand, that this indicated Mr. Moore knew what he was doing, that this indicated that Mr. Moore knew what he was doing was wrong. Well, I'm going to submit to you people frankly that is not the case. Appearances deceive. Every single day we hear that people who really don't know what they are doing. This is not just a defense which sprung up in order to give you an excuse to acquit a man.

This is very serious business, because I am indicating to you that Mr. Moore may not have known what he was doing on July 13 and 14th and even before that. The prosecutor's case centers on July 13 and 14th. Ladies and gentlemen, I'm going to ask you to consider long before that, because Mr. Moore appears to have done certain things on the 14th and 13th I'm going to ask you not to consider that so much as to consider the whole picture.

Ladies and gentlemen, when we talk about insanity, and that's what we are talking about there are all kinds of insanity, all kinds of mental illness, emotional disturbance, doctors can hardly define them, but what we are talking about in this particular case is the fact that whatever Stephen Moore may have done on July 13 and 14th he really didn't know, and why is that, because he was acting under the doctors call for lack of better word, and it's a technical term, he was acting under delusions, hallucinations.

This is not a joke. It is a very serious crime, and I'm not attempting to lessen what happened to poor Donna Litchfield by saying to you, well, he didn't know what was happening. The point is that Stephen Moore didn't know what he was doing. The point is that he didn't know what he was doing was wrong, as the law defines it. He acted under certain premises, which you people and I and the judge, which we normally don't act under. He acted under a whole different set of rules. What were the delusions to see the more? Suppose I were to give you a compass, anyone of you, and I were to say, you are a great navigator, you know your way around, here is a compass, I want you to go do Northeast, but what you don't know if that the compass is off by 10° to 15°, and so you take the compass, being a perfectly good navigator, knowing full well what you have to do, and you take it and you proceed along a course thinking that where you are going is do Northeast, but you are not going do Northeast, who are really going east, and you may find that you are off by about 30 miles. Ladies and gentlemen this is what happened to Stephen Moore. He started off from a false compass reading. He got information that you and I don't have to. He started out from what we call false premise.

Everything he did after that may have looked normal, may have appeared like he was sane, but he wasn't. He was traveling in a completely different direction. The same thing if we were going to play games solitaire, only the deck is smudged, so that the suit and the denominations I mixed up, and we sit there and Mr. Moore is going to play games solitaire, and he knows the rules and he knows the sanctions and he proceeds to play it in a rational manner, but what he doesn't realize is that he is making mistakes.

This is the only way I can describe it to you, ladies and gentlemen this is what happened to Mr. Moore, and this is not a joke. Mr. Moore was playing with a partially smudged deck. He was making mistakes. He was proceeding from false premises.

Now I indicated to you earlier that whatever evidence in this case is going to come from the witness stand I am going to allow you people to see evidence there is to present in this case. I am not going to go into it because I think you are going to see for yourselves how sick Mr. Moore was on July 14, and I think you are going to see for yourselves how sick he still is. We are not talking about sick being somebody who has a hoarse throat or a cough or a rash. This is a disease of the mind Mr. Moore suffers from. Can happen to anyone of us. You will find that how it happened to Mr. Moore, how it developed, what it is, and how it manifests itself, but we don't have any observable physical criteria to observe the disease, we don't have the coughing, the hoarseness, or the rash.

We have what you are going to say when the defense presents its case, the testimony of his friends and relatives as to behavior which he has had in the past. You are going to see how bizarre some of the behavior wise and you are going to hear from doctors, ladies and gentlemen, doctors who are used to observing certain criteria just like x-rays or blood tests, who are used to observing a particular person in a particular manner, in order to detect mental illness.

You're going to hear from those doctors how sick Mr. Moore was on July 14, and how sick he is today, and you're going to hear why Mr. Moore cannot possibly have been responsible as to the law for conviction of a crime, for the commission of the act which the state charges. But because the tests employed are not objective, and because they are not like x-rays and blood tests and not like, I am going to ask you people not to disregard that, that the defendant may still be sick, that he is in fact sick mentally.

I am going to ask you people to consider throughout this trial, the reason I demonstrated for you, with the examples I did, I'm going to ask you people to consider at every stage of the trial, the delusions, the false premises Mr. Moore may have labored under, that we are going to prove to your satisfaction heated labor under on July 14. We are going to ask you to consider whether under our laws as the judge will charge you, ladies and gentlemen, Mr. Moore can be considered legally responsible for having committed this crime. Now we are not going to deny his presence at the scene, we are not going to deny that he removed money; we are not going to deny he did any of the things that Mr. Mautone he did. The point is this. Because a person is insane, and you will see that from the testimony of the doctors, because a person is insane doesn't he is not intelligent, he can't act rationally, it doesn't mean he can't function in a normal way, apparently, physically, observably.

The point is that he is not normal; he is not really functioning in a normal way. The point is this, ladies and gentlemen. Mr. Moore's delusions, is false premises, his hallucinations, made him the way he did. I intelligence can be put to the service of our delusions, and you will see that. You will see that insanity does not preclude intelligence. You will see that insanity does not mean a person is incapable of planning something. I can plan to walk from here to there, and that's a plan, and it's a premeditated plan, but by walking from here to there based upon a delusion, based upon a false premise, the result is going to be I am doing something that I really have no control over. I am doing something that I totally don't have a cognitive understanding of. I'm doing something I don't really know the consequences of.

Now you are going to see a lot of evidence in this particular case, and some of it is going to be extremely pleasant for most of us. Many of them are going to be photographs, I imagine. This particular crime is an ugly crime. The defendant is not denying that. I'm here to say to you, well, it doesn't mean a thing! Life is important. It is very important, ladies and gentlemen, but I'm going to ask you in fairness not to allow your sympathies for the victim, and we will have sympathy; I have sympathy; I'm going to ask you not to allow your sympathy for the victim, not to allow your stomach when you look at pictures or when you hear the testimony about this case, to override your eyes and your ears, your intelligence, your common sense, not override the function which you people have, to decide fairly, to get at what I originally spoke to you about, to get at the truth.

We are here to get at the truth, not to convict a man, not to get a man off. We are here to find out what happened, and to deal with it in the most appropriate manner. I'm asking you, ladies and gentlemen, again, in fairness to the state, not for sympathy for Stephen Moore because he is sick, for Stephen Moore, no, I'm asking you to consider this in a rational light. Consider the proofs that the state presents, and that the defendant will present, as you must, without any passion, without any prejudiced, without any sympathy or motion, and it's going to be a very, very difficult job, perhaps even more difficult than Mr. Mautone's job and my job. It's going to be very difficult to sit there and say, well, I know this was a brutal crime, I know that it was gory, and I know I went and wanted to happen to me or somebody in my family, but still sit there and say that I have a duty. The law imposes upon me a duty when I was sworn in the jury box to decide fairly, to decide upon the facts, the evidence, the credible evidence presented from the jury box.

It's going to be very difficult. It's going to be particularly difficult in view of the fact, as I indicated to you before, that none of us really know what went on that day. None of us ever know for sure what went on in Stephen Moore's mind.

We can only estimate to some degree of reasonable certainty, reasonable medical certainty, that Stephen Moore was now playing with a full deck in his mind, and I think that when all of the evidence is in, including the case, I think when you hear the testimony of his friends, and his relatives, and the doctors, you are going to find that there is a preponderance of evidence, a greater amount of evidence that shows that although Mr. Moore looked sane and acted sane that he was not sane.

So ladies and gentlemen, I'm going to ask you to consider all of these things as you listen to the testimony in this case, I'm going to ask you not to listen to your stomach or with your heart, but with your eyes and your ears and your minds. And I'm going to ask you to try to be fair. I realize that this case, as in every case is extremely important, because we are not just dealing with Donna Litchfield's life; unfortunately she is not here, they are also dealing now with another life, life matter who it is, is important and that's one of the primary values of our society life.

State of New Jersey versus Stephen C Moore

November 16th, 1976 Essex County Courthouse Newark, New Jersey

The jury enters the courtroom. Good morning ladies and gentlemen. Forgive me for the unnecessary wait. Prosecutor, do you waive the polling of the Jury?

Yes, I do, Your Honor.

Mr. Schutzer- Sir, do you waive the polling of the Jury?

Yes, I do, Your Honor.

Thank you. All right, call your witness, prosecutor.

Valerie Iacobacci Testimony

Thank you, good morning, Sir. I call Valerie Iacobacci.

Ms. Iacobacci, where do you live?

East Passaic Ave., Bloomfield.

Do you know a man named Stephen Moore?

Yes.

When did you first make acquaintance with this individual?

About a year ago.

Would you tell me how he first met Stephen Moore, please?

My girlfriend went to junk her van.

Excuse me, what is your girlfriends name?

My girlfriend Jay, and the man she wanted to sell it to told her to go to the junkyard where he was working, and that's how I met him.

And did Mr. Moore and this girl subsequently strike up a relationship?

Yes.

At a later time, did you know a Donna Litchfield?

Yes.

At a later time, did Donna Litchfield meet Stephen Moore, to your knowledge?

I introduced him to her.

Do you recall when approximately this was?

Maybe last November.

Now could you describe, if you can, the relationship that existed between Stephen Moore and Donna Litchfield?

Well, I know that Donna really loved Steve. She really wanted to marry, but...

I am talking about the period between November and July 14. Would you describe to us just briefly what type of relationship they had?

A boyfriend girlfriend relationship.

Did Mr. Moore ever spend any time Donna her apartment?

Yes.

Did he ever spend the night with her?

Yes.

And did you have occasion during this period, at least from November until July 14, 1976, to have discussions with Stephen Moore?

Some, yes.

And did he ever frighten you in any way?

No.

Would you describe his mannerisms for us, please.

He was all right. He was just, to me he was very inconsiderate, that's all.

What do you mean by inconsiderate?

He would tell Donna he would be there a certain time, and he wouldn't be there.

How did he treat Donna? Let me rephrase the question. I will withdraw the question.

Prior— did you see Donna on July 14, 1976?

Yes.

Where did you see Donna?

I picked her up at her mother's house and I took her to her apartment.

It was after 1230. Maybe about 1 o'clock. When you went to the apartment, what, if anything happened?

Well, we made the kids lunch in she got a phone call. She made a phone call to her sister, to tell her where she was, and then she got a phone call back from her sister, saying that Stephen had come to the house, to her mother's house, and then—

Your Honor, I'm going to object to this as being hearsay.

How about it, prosecutor?

I will withdraw that, Your Honor.

I'm going to ask it be stricken.

I will allow the answer to stand. Your objection is overruled.

Go ahead, Prosecutor.

Now how long after the initial phone call did, or, use me, let me withdraw that. Did Stephen Moore ever arrive at the apartment that day?

Yes.

Approximately how long after the initial phone call, the first phone call, did he arrive?

About 45 minutes.

What was Donna doing when Stephen arrived?

We were just talking.

And did you see Stephen when he got to the apartment?

Yes. What did he say, if anything, when he entered the apartment?

He didn't say anything. He just said hello Donna, and he like nodded to me.

Did he seem upset?

No.

Bothered in any way?

No.

Was there anything about his appearance—

I'm going to object to that. It calls for a conclusion.

I will allow it; your objection is overruled.

Was there anything about his appearance that frightened you that day?

No.

After Stephen said hello and nodded to you, what happened?

Well, Donna asked him if he wanted something to eat, and he said no, but he would take something to drink, and so he did. Do you want me to go on?

Just continue on to what happened after that?

And then she said to him, if you want to talk to me, come into the bathroom.

Do you know what, if anything, she was doing in the bathroom?

She was going to clean it.

Did Stephen have that drink?

Yes.

Do you know what it was that he drank?

I think it was juice. I am not sure.

Now when Donna initially went to the bathroom, did Mr. Moore go in with her?

Yes.

And did Donna or Mr. Moore ever out of the bathroom?

Donna came back out and she got paper towels.

How long after they first went into the bathroom, did they come out?? Did Donna come?

About a few minutes, maybe five minutes at the most.

And did she say anything when she came out of the bathroom?

She said, I don't believe this mess.

What did she do after she got paper towels? She went back into the bathroom.

Now when Donna went back into the bathroom the second time, was there anything that drew your attention to the bathroom?

She started screaming.

Did you hear her scream?

Oh, yes.

What did you do when you heard the scream?

I went into the living room see what happened. I didn't know if it was the kids or Donna, or what. I didn't know it was the kids or Donna, or what.

How many kids were there?

Three. Two of mine; One was Donna's.

How old are these children? 5 1/2, three, and .2.

Now you say you heard a scream anyway into the living room to see the children. Were the children doing anything?

They were standing by the couch.

Where was the noise coming from?

The bathroom.

Now did you go to the bathroom?

No, I didn't go into the bathroom.

Did you look into the bathroom?

I saw in the bathroom.

When you looked into the bathroom, what, if anything, did you see?

I saw Donna in the bathtub, and Stephen hitting her.

What was she doing?

Fighting with him.

And what was Stephen doing?

He was hitting her.

And you saw this, what did you do?

I took my kids and took them out of the apartment.

Why, because they would get in the way if I did anything else.

Excuse me?

They could have gotten in the way, if I went to try to do anything.

What do you do with your children when you took them? I locked them in my car.

After locking the children in the car, did you do anything else?

I went back into the apartment.

What did you do when you return to the apartment?

I picked up the phone, and I have the police.

Did the police answer the phone?

Yes.

What, if anything did you say when the police officer answered the phone?

I told him I thought I had the wrong number, or something like that.

Why did you say that?

168 The Man Who Murdered My Mother

I didn't hear anything else, all I heard was water, the water running, and I didn't know if they made up for what they did.

What did you do after you told the police, you have the wrong number? I hung up the phone, went to the bathroom door. When the bathroom door open or closed?

It was closed.

How did it open when you first went into the living room?

Yes.

What do you do when you approached the closed bathroom door?

I knocked on the door.

Did anything happen?

Nobody answered a first.

Then what did you do?

I knocked again, Stephen asked, who is? And I said, who do you think it is? And he opened the door, and he said," Donna is dead".

What did he say?

"Donna is dead"

He said," Donna is dead", what did you do when you heard that?

I told him I had to go, I turned around and walked away.

Did you leave the apartment?

Yes.

Where did you go when you left the apartment?

I got in my car and I went down her street, made a last, and I went down another street, and I went to a gas station.

What did you do when you got to the gas station?

I told the man to call the police.

Subsequently where you take into the police station?

Yes.

Did they ask you questions?

Yes.

Did they ask you the name of the man you saw on the apartment?

Yes.

Did you tell them?

Yes.

What name did you get them?

Stephen Moore.

Do you see that man here in the courtroom today?

Yes.

Can you point out him out, please.

He is over there. (Indicating Mr. Moore for the record.)

Miss Iacobacci, I'm going to show you several photos and ask you if you can tell us what they are or what they show. This is the first photo marked S - 1 for identification. That is Donna's apartment. Well, the apartment door.

And can you tell me what this is a photo of please. Well, this is the stairway going down into her apartment. I'm going to show you what has been marked S - 5 For identification, and was what that shows.

That's her front door, into her apartment.

And doesn't show the interior of the apartment?

Yes.

From there and tell us where the kitchen is located?

To the right.

Your Honor, we have a marker of some sort?

Certainly.

Would you please put a K on the air, indicating if you may, the entrance to the kitchen, into an arrow in the direction in which the kitchen would be. On that photograph, can you see the door to the bathroom?

No, not the door.

I'm going to show you what has been marked s-6 for identification, and ask if you could tell us what that is a photo of.

Donna's kitchen.

When you left back kitchen, was it in the same condition as it is in the photograph, no.

Can you tell us what, if anything, was different?

Well, the curtains, whatever they were, they are not there, and that's blood- it wasn't there.

Where the towels on the floor?

I don't think so, but I really don't know the towels were.

I'm going to show you what is the marked S-10 for identification can you please tell us what this is a photograph of?

Her hallway, going into her living room, to her bedroom.

S-11, please.

That's her bathroom.

S-8

it's her living room.

Thank you very much. Now, when you left the apartment and drove- or when you heard the screen and left from the kitchen, was there any water, or reddish water, on the kitchen floor, or anywhere around the kitchen floor?

No.

In all the time that you have known Stephen Moore, have you ever been afraid of him?

No.

Did he ever do anything to make you fear him?

No.

Or think he was abnormal?

No.

I have no further questions of this witness.

All right. This is a good time to take a recess. Ladies and gentlemen, 320. You may leave the courtroom if you would like to do please don't discuss the case with anyone.

Thank you.

(Court recessed)

The witness returned to the stand.

The jury entered the courtroom.

Anything else in this witness, Mr. prosecutor?

No, Your Honor.

All right, Mr. Schuzter.

Cross-examination by Mr. Schuzter:

Mrs. Iacobacci, when you heard Steve and Donna in the bathroom, you didn't hear them arguing, did you?

No.

You didn't really hear anything that was said, did you?

No, nothing said.

Okay, all you heard was screaming.

Yes.

Okay. Now going back just a little bit before that, when you indicated for that Don come out of the bathroom and on paper towels and said, I don't believe this mess, were you referring to what?

Well, her bathroom and a bunch of tiles in it.

The titles, okay. Do you remember talking with Donna earlier that day in her apartment about Stephen?

Yes.

All right. And do you remember Donna talking about getting married to Stephen?

Yes.

Okay. In other words, she wasn't to your knowledge contemplating breaking up with him, was she?

No, that's not true. She was, but– can I explain?

No. I am just–

Why can't the witness explain answer?

I am asking the question, attempting to ask one question were one at a time, at least.

You asked her if she had a reason, and you cut her off. If you want to withdraw the question, I will permit you to. I will withdraw the question.

Withdraw the question. put the next one.

She indicated to you she wanted to marry Stephen in a couple of months? Yes.

She was happy when she received a telephone call from her sister wasn't she?

Yes.

She was happy Stephen was coming over, right?

Yes.

She liked Steve, right?

Yes.

And you have had an opportunity to observe Stephen and Valerie, I mean Donna together quite often, isn't that so? Yes.

In other words, had gone out with them together?

Mostly at her apartment.

Okay. And during all the time that you observed Donna and Stephen together, you never thought that Donna was in danger, did you?

No.

And you never saw anything that indicated that Stephen was violent, did you, to your knowledge?

I never saw anything other than— can I explain? Well, I can't explain?

Let me ask you this.

Can the witness explain?

You can pick it up on the redirect, go ahead.

If you can possibly state, based upon your observations, would it be fair to say that Stephen's personality as a whole to you, if you can recall, was violent?

His personality as a whole?

Your Honor, I don't understand without would be based on.

I will allow the question.

You said— could you repeat that again?

Let me try and explain this better. When you say that Stephen's nature was to be violent as a whole? His nature as a whole, as a person, despite any, perhaps, incidents that might have happened, but as a whole would you say he was a violent person to your knowledge?

No, it wasn't violent

In you observed the incident in the bathroom pretty closely, or you observed it, is that correct?

Yes.

Now based on your observations and based upon what you know about the and what you knew of them together and based upon what you know Donna's feelings for Steve, would you say that what was going on in the bathroom on July 14 was consistent with Stephen's personality?

Your Honor, I object.

I will allow the question.

Was consistent?

Would you say that was something you expected from Stephen Moore?

No, not expected.

Okay. Thank you.

Redirect examination by Mr. Mautone:

You were asked if Stephen wanted to marry Donna, correct, by counsel, defense counsel?

Right.

You wanted to explain; would you please explain what you wanted to explain then.

She didn't want to marry him. She didn't care for him, but he was always doing things laced with income over like I said, on time, and he would always take off places, you know, he would go away for months or something. She got aggravated with that, even though her dealings were different than what she was going to do. I don't know how to explain it that well.

And as part of that aggravation, did you know she told that she did not want to see him anymore?

Yes, she did say that.

Part of the conversation that morning, she had also indicated to you she didn't want to see Stephen anymore, she had told him that?

She had told him that, right.

You are asked how Stephen treat Donna in a general way. Well do you know any specific incidents where Stephen hit Donna?

Yes.

Your Honor, I am going to object as being irrelevant at this time.

I will allow it. You open the door on your cross-examination.

Where did Stephen hit Donna? You mean where, physically?

Yes, where physically.

In the eye.

Was there any damage as a result of that?

She had a black eye.

When Stephen came into the apartment that day, did you see a knife on him?

Objection, Your Honor

I will allow the question.

No, I did not.

Did you see any weapons of any type in his hands?

No.

Where honest person anywhere? No.

Mrs. Iacobacci, did anyone ever entered the apartment, Donna Litchfield's apartment, other then by the front door? Yes.

How else would you get into the apartment?

Through her window.

Do you know of anyone personally that went through the window?

Well, I did.

Who else?

Steve did.

Anyone else?

Donna did.

How can you get through that window? What do you mean, how can you get through the window?

Where's the window located, where does it exit out of or out into?

From her kitchen into her parking lot.

Do you have to climb up to get in through the window?

No.

Just step right into the apartment?

Right.

Did you use that, did you use that method of getting in and out yourself?

Yes. If I parked in the back. Whenever I parked in the back.

After Stephen open the bathroom door, and said that Donna was dead, did he say anything else to you?

No.

When you got a chance to look into the bathroom, at that time, the second time, when Stephen opened the door, did you see Donna?

I saw her legs.

Where were her legs?

Hanging out of the tub.

Where was her body?

In the bathtub.

Did you observe the water?

Yes.

Was it clear? No, it was like a dingy gray color.

It was when you saw that you left the apartment?

Right.

As soon as you got to the gas station, you called the police?

No; I told the man to.

The man called the police?

uh huh

When did you tell the man?

I don't know. I don't know.

Were you nervous?

Yes.

Did you indicate that there was trouble somewhere?

I told my girlfriend was dead, I think my: I'm not sure what I said.

Did you tell him the address?

Yes, I did tell him the address.

Do you know of any other incidents when Stephen and Donna had arguments?

I am going to object. I don't believe that's relevant to this particular crime.

I will allow it.

They had arguments, but I do remember one time spit in her face. I don't remember why, though.

So he didn't always treat her very gentlemanly?

No.

Object to the question.

I will allow it.

I no further questions, Your Honor.

Mr. Schutzer?

May I recross?

Certainly.

Thank you, sir.

Re-cross examination by Mr. Schuszter:

Mrs. Iacobacci, referring back to the incident you discussed a moment ago, when Stephen hit Donna in the eye.

Yes.

Were you present?

No, I wasn't there.

How do you find out about that?

Because I called her up crying and I asked her what was wrong. And she didn't answer me right away, and I knew that you been there, and I said, did he hit you, because that's the first question I always ask, and she said yeah. And I said, I will be right there.

You weren't there, so you really don't know what happened?

No, I don't know what happened. I didn't see it.

You only know— I am sorry— the question I am asking you is this, is that you don't know for sure what happened except for what Donna told you, isn't that so?

Donna is not going to lie to me.

I didn't say that. I am sorry if I'm getting that impression, but you were there, and what about the other incident when you claim that he had arguing; were you present during any of those incidents?

Yeah. I know he spit in her face, I was there.

Do you regard that as being a little unusual, perhaps?

I think it's disgusting.

Is it something that you would do? The witness is continuing.

Pardon?

The witness was attempting to continue.

Your Honor, I'm sorry, I believe the witness had finished. I apologize if she had not.

I was going to say it wasn't unusual, but it was disgusting.

Thank you.

Is it something that you have ever seen anyone else do? Yes.

I object

Sustain the objection.

During those arguments, did you ever hear what was said?

I might have.

Did you perhaps ever hear Stephen tell Donna that maybe he thought she was reading his mind?

No.

Did you ever hear him say that he thought she was a witch?

No.

Did you ever hear him say perhaps he thought she was trying to poison him?

No.

Did you ever hear them say he thought she might be an FBI agent or CIA agent, or someone was out to kill him?

No.

You were present during all of the arguments they may have had, were you?

No.

How does she know if they had more arguments that she was present at?

I will allow the question and answer stands.

Is fair to say there might have been other arguments when these things were said, when you were not present?

I will object.

I will sustain the objection.

Why did Don indicate she wanted to break it off with Steve? What reason did she get to you if any that she wanted to break it off with Steve?

He treated her rotten; even though she did care for him, he treated her rotten.

Did she ever say to you, I want to break it off with Steve because he is crazy?

No.

How often did Steve climb in through the window?

I don't know how many times he climbed in the window. I know one time that he climbed in the window.

Did you discuss this case with anyone prior to you coming here today?

Yes I discussed it.

With whom?

With the prosecutor.

And did you discuss the questions that may be asked of you or the answers that you might give, perhaps?

He asked me questions and I told my answers.

Did he stay to you, perhaps, what questions he may ask you?

Yes.

When Stephen open the bathroom door, after you had not, and he said, Don is said, he said it just like that?

Donna is dead.

Matter-of-factly, in other words?

Yes.

He was calm?

Calm. I don't know, like he was in a rush, or something but not like— what you mean by rush?

Well, late he had, I don't know, how you look like when you have to go somewhere?

I don't know if he had to go somewhere, but you asked me how you looked.

Will want me to think that he looked like he had to go somewhere?

Because that's the kind of look he had.

What was the look, if you can describe it?

Just looked, I don't know; how can you describe the look?

He just stood there. Did he come after you?

No, he didn't.

Did he try to get past you to rush out of the apartment?

No.

Did you leave first?

Yes.

Did you have any idea how long Steve and Steve there?

I have no idea.

Yet he looked like he was in a hurry to get out of the apartment, is that correct? Seems to me he did.

How was his facial expression, was a relaxed, or was agitated, if you can recall?

I don't know.

You don't know?

I don't know. He was wet.

He was wet?

 wet.

Aside from that, what the space look like? Was it— I'm trying to help you. Was it contorted, was it—

Your Honor, I will object. Question has been asked and answered. She doesn't know.

I will allow the answer to stand.

He was just wet. That's all I know, he was wet.

So in other words— and you can correct me if I'm wrong— what you are saying is that you really didn't notice what his face looked like.

Well, I stared straight in the face. All I know is he was wet.

I am asking you a little bit more than that. I'm asking you if you can, and it is not funny, but I'm asking you if you can tell me what his face looks like in terms of attitude.

I'm going to object. We have been over this. The witness indicates—

I will allow the question. Can you answer it? If you can't, say so.

I don't think I can answer that.

At the time that you were standing there, and Stephen open the door, would it be fair to say that you were a little upset?

Yes. I was a little upset.

Would it be fair to say you were near hysterical?

No.

Would it be fair to say that you were near hysterical, taking the children out of the apartment and bringing them into the car, driving, later on, down to the police station?

Your Honor, this is a pretty extensive period of time now.

How about it, Mr. Schuster.

Well, let me ask you this. Was there any time during the period the first knew that something was wrong, until the period of time that you went and called the police at the gas station, then you were hysterical, if you can recall?

After I left the apartment.

After you left the apartment?

Yes.

But not in the apartment?

No

You had no reason to fear Stephen, in other words?

No. I mean, he was hitting her, but I didn't know what was going on. I didn't–

I am talking about when he– let's go back a little. When he opened the door and you were standing there, and you saw the legs dangling over the tub, and Stephen indicated to you that Donna is dead, were you afraid then?

I don't know.

Did you exit the apartment quickly?

I walked out of the apartment, and ran up the stairs.

Is it your testimony, and correct me if I am wrong, that you said, I had to go somewhere?

I had to go.

And you quickly exited, as quickly as you could. Would it be fair to say you do so because you were frightened? Half way.

That is like being a little pregnant.

I object.

Why don't you ask questions, Mr. Schutzer?

I'm sorry.

You have no right. When you want to testify subject yourself to cross-examination. I think it's unfair to make comments of the witness. Your question, sir.

So at the time you left, you are somewhat frightened, is that so?

I didn't think she was dead. Yes, I was somewhat frightened.

You something was very wrong, when you saw her legs dangling over the tub.

Yes, I did.

Your primary object at the time was to get out of the apartment, isn't that correct?

Yes. Your primary object in exiting was to get to a phone and call the police as quickly as possible, is that correct?

Right.

As you indicate that you didn't know whether she was dead, you do recall telling somebody after that quick, quick get me the police because my girlfriend has been murdered, I think she has been murdered. You don't recall saying any of that?

I must have, I don't know.

You don't remember what you said? Is it possible that you were not looking–

Your Honor, I don't wish to interrupt, but we are dealing with possibilities when we have a witness on the stand

I will rephrase the question.

Do you think that the time that you looked at Stephen in the face, you might have been a little too frightened to see exactly what his face looked like?

No.

You were calm?

I wasn't calm. I was nervous, but I was not frightened.

All right. Thank you. I no further questions.

Prosecutor?

Yes, I have some, Your Honor.

Redirect by Mr. Mautone:

Mr. Schutzer asked you did you discuss this case with anybody and you indicated that you disgusted with myself. Did I tell you what to say, or did I ask you questions concerning the crime?

You asked me questions.

Did I ever once tell you that I don't want you to say something or tell you something to say other than the truth?

No.

You are asked on a redirect, that you don't know whether or not Stevens dropped Donna in the face; other than a phone call did you ever see Donna's face after Stephen hit her in the eye?

Yes.

How shortly after the phone call did you see her face?

About 15 minutes.

What did you do after you got the phone call, after Donner calls you, Brian, what happened?

Oh, I called her.

All right. After you called her, what did you do?

I went to her apartment.

Did you see her face?

Yes.

Did you see any marks or damage on her face?

Yes it was all black and blue.

Now, did Stephen Moore have or will you and talk to you yourself on the phone or in person?

Yes.

How often was that?

Once every couple days, or whatever; like that.

Any time during these conversations, did he ever give you any indication or any reason to fear for any particular purpose?

No.

Your Honor, I'm going to object, only because this is already been gone into indirect.

I will allow it. You opened the door on your recross, Mr. Schuster. Go-ahead.

Did you ever any time during these conversations, come to the conclusion that Stephen Moore was crazy?

No.

Who introduced Stephen Moore to Donna Litchfield?

I did.

How long have you known Stephen Moore before you introduce him to Donna Litchfield?

Maybe two or three months, something like that.

You had no reason to fear Stephen Moore think that he was crazy when you introduce him to Donna.

I would have introduced him as I thought he was crazy.

Stephen first opened the door to the bathroom, said Donna was dead, what did you see first, Stephen or Donna?

I think Stephen.

So when you first saw Stephen's face and when you looked at Stephen and saw he was wet, and when Stephen said Donna is dead you had not yet seen Donna in the bathtub, did you?

When you open the door— can I—

Go ahead.

When he opened the door he was wet, so I could see beyond him, to, so I think it was after I saw Donna, that's when he said Donna was dead.

Excuse me?

I think after I saw Donna, that's when he said," Donna is dead". But I didn't see Donna before he opened the door.

Now you had never seen any knife?

No.

And when you looked at the water, you thought it was a grayish color?

Yes.

And you were very nervous at this time?

Yes.

And then you left the apartment?

Right.

I have no further questions, Your Honor.

I have a few just a few short questions, sir.

Mrs. Iacobacci, do you recall my asking you a question whether you discussed the case with anyone prior to this appearance here in court today, and you said that you discussed it with the prosecutor and all that? Did you discuss it at any time with me?

Yes.

Did I ask you some questions out in the hall?

Yes.

And at that time did you answer some questions and refuse to answer other questions?

Yes.

I am going to object. That's her right.

I am going to allow it. Go ahead.

Did I indicate to you at the time that I began to ask you these questions and prior to asking you these questions, then you had the right not to answer any of?

You told me I had the right not to answer.

And I indicated to you that I would abide by that. Right.

And you chose not to answer certain of my questions, is that correct? Right.

When the door was opened and you looked at Stephen, and Stephen said, Donna is dead, what it more or less you testify that you saw beyond Stephen actually to the tub, and is in it a fact that you actually saw Donna in the tub and Stephen almost simultaneously, or within a few seconds of each other?

Yes. But it was Stephen and then Donna in the tub.

How much time elapsed between the time you first saw Stephen and you saw Donna in the tub? Would you say it was five seconds?

Yes.

When did you introduce Stephen to Donna?

Around November, I guess.

November 1974?

No. This is 1976.

This was July 1976— 1975 that would have been right?

1975.

And you had occasion to have telephone conversations Stephen is that correct?

Yes.

During all of that time, as you have previously indicated, you have no reason to be frightened of him, is that so?

Right.

And isn't it so that as you have testified you never would have introduced Stephen to Donna I thought he was crazy? That's right. And had he manifested to you anything that would have appeared crazy in the normal sense, right?

Right.

So that this particular incident must have come in an extremely great surprise to you?

Your Honor, I will object.

I will sustain the objection.

Again, did you feel this was consistent with Stephen Morris past behavior and his conversations with you?

I will object.

I will sustain the objection.

Was this the type of act, given your past experience with Stephen Moore, conversations, your exposure to him, with this type of act that you would have expected from Stephen Moore?

Your Honor, I object. Who can expect murder from anyone.

Listing the objection.

I'm going to object to that comment by the prosecutor.

I sustain the objection to the question. Put your next one, sir.

Thank you.

Did you ever think that Stephen Moore would ever do this to Donna Litchfield?

Your Honor—

Sustain the objection.

All right. I have no further questions.

Mr. prosecutor?

I have nothing further.

Rodney O'Dell Testimony

Your Honor, the state will call Mr. Rodney O'Dell

(The following took place at the sidebar.)

Your Honor.

Yes Mr. Schutzer.

I have reason to believe from discussing this testimony with Mr. O'Dell that Mr. Mautone is going to attempt to elicit from him information concerning conversations between Mr. O'Dell and Dr. Latimer acting as my agent prior to bringing this before the jury I would request the court make a ruling as to whether it's relevant and as to whether it might in fact be more prejudicial and probative in this matter.

What do you say prosecutor?

I fully intend to interview and question Mr. O'Dell has regards to his conversations with Dr. Latimer and Mr. Schutzer. If the court wishes to hear outside the presence of the jury, I have no objection. Dr. Latimer interviewed Mr. O'Dell as an agent for the defense, as part of the discussion Dr. Latimer told Mr. O'Dell it would be better if you did not tell the prosecutor certain parts of their conversation. He was then told to contact Mr. Schutzer before he talked to me. Dr. Latimer was speaking from the standpoint of the psychiatric defense, point certain information regarding Stephen is confidential, and should not be revealed until the proper time when I was ready to reveal it to the state, with respect to that I do not believe that that particular juncture of the case it's going to be probative or evidential.

In the preparation, and I believe the defense has attempted to influence Mr. O'Dell, and will continually tends to influence Mr. O'Dell, and that any delay would be prejudicial to the State, and for close the state inquiring into an area which in my opinion very probated at the approach taken by both Dr. Latimer and Mr. Schulze, in preparing the defense. Your Honor I would ask for recess now in order to have Mr. O'Dell brought down to my office to have a formal statement taken from him. I would object. What is the purpose? It is necessary because of his relationship with the defendant, it would be necessary to connect him to the statements as he has told me. I don't have them committed to writing, only two witnesses to them, as, again, he has contacted the defense, and talked to the defense.

This is my problem. Let's say Dr. Latimer never testifies. How is this man's testimony evidential now?

The knife that was used was Mr. O'Dell's knife.

Ok, I will limit it to that, but the discussion with Dr. Latimer, has nothing to do with this case at this juncture.

For the record Your Honor, I would like to note the prosecutor I take an extremely dim view of this particular statement by Mr. Mautone. The defense has not attempted to influence anyone. Mr. O'Dell- it's known to Mr. Mautone and the state Mr. O'Dell is a friend of my client for 10 years on one hand; and on the other hand, I was contacted by Mr. O'Dell; I did not contact him, and Mr. O'Dell told me, that he was under the impression he was possibly been harassed.

That's a misstatement.

One at a time, gentlemen.

On the other hand, Your Honor, I don't believe that particularly relevant at this point, because it may be a matter at all a rebuttal. At this particular juncture, attempting to prove homicide; carries no evidence whatever I have introduced side opening to the insanity defense; as far as Mr. O'Dell, and he has done, his testimony has not become less and less striking. That's an extremely unfair characterization by the prosecutor. I take a dim view of that professionally, and I want it on the record.

Your Honor, I want to record to reflect some further action may be taken at the conclusion of this case if we are talking about it in the profession of views to be taken.

Prosecutor, I will not be threatened.

One at a time.

I will hear you both. You both have an opportunity, you both insist on talking together. Go ahead, Mr. prosecutor. You are in the midst of making a statement. When he is finished, I will hear you, Mr. Schutzer. Conclude.

Because the delicacy of the situation, I believe the defense of insanity has been posed brought before the jury. Dr. Latimer will be a witness, I see no value in precluding me from inquiring of this witness if he was contacted by the defense, if any discussions were had between them. At this juncture, if this court is going to preclude me from inquiring at this witness if he was contacted by the defense, if any discussions were had between them. At this juncture, the court is going to preclude me from going into that, now, I would ask for the reasons, to take Mr. Dell down to my office and take a formal statement.

Your Honor, Mr. O'Dell, first of all, is not a state's witness, he is also a defense witness, subpoenaed by the defense. His name appeared on the defense witness list long before Mr. Mautone placed him on a state's witness list. I'm not making any objection to his testifying here.

The problem is that if he is going to be called as a state's witness any matter Mr. Mautone may bring up with respect to a conversation with Dr. Latimer will be so irrelevant as to be misleading.

I will. The objection is overruled.

End of sidebar discussion

Direct Examination by Mr. Mautone:

Mr. O'Dell, do you know a man by the name of Stephen Moore?

I do.

For how long have you known him?

Approximately 10 years.

Can you describe your relationship with him please?

He was a friend of mine.

Turn your attention, July 13, 1976, you have an opportunity that day to see Mr. Moore?

I'm not familiar with July 13. I believe So.

Are you familiar with the Donna Litchfield?

I am.

Are you familiar with the date that occurred?

I am.

John your attention to the date prior to the death of Donna Litchfield, did you have occasion to see Stephen Moore?

I did.

Where?

At my house.

Approximately what time did he arrive at your house? 5 to 7 in the evening.

5 o'clock to 7 o'clock? Somewhere in that time period.

Sir, do you own and operate a business?

I do.

What type of business is it?

It's a gas station and service station, two different.

Where's that relation to your house?

I live above it.

Did Mr. Moore spend the night with you?

He did.

At your house?

Yes, sir.

Can you describe his mood that evening?

Depressed, despondent.

A gas station, to keep certain implemented tools used in the trade?

Yes.

And one of them is a knife?

Yes.

Can you describe the nature keeping a gas station I kept a gas station?

It is a hunting type of thing, with a laminated handle, with a sever on.

You identified that night if you saw it?

Yes, I could.

S-42 for identification, a plastic container, in which is contained a knife.

Mr. O'Dell, could you tell us where that nice I'm sorry I'm going to show you what is markedS-42 for identification, this plastic bag, and ask you if you can tell us what is contained inside that bag.

It is the knife that came from my gas station.

Where was this knife kept at your gas station?

On the wall behind the workbench at the back of the station.

Was Stephen Moore and gas station on the day of July 14th, the date Donna Litchfield died?

Yes, he was.

Did you at any time during that day see him in the area in which the knife was kept?

I did.

Did Stephen Moore eventually leave your gas station Surf City?

Yes, he did.

Would you tell us approximately what time he left, if you know?

Between 1030 and 1130 in the morning.

After Mr. Moore left your gas station did you have occasion to go look for your knife?

No, I didn't.

At any time after he left your gas station did you go look for your knife?

Yes, I did.

When?

I believe it was the day of the 15th.

The day after Miss Litchfield's death?

I believe it was the day after.

Were you able to find your knife?

No.

Did anyone actually contact you regarding this knife?

Yes.

Who?

The Belleville police department

Do they bring the knife down to you?

They did.

Did they ask you if you can identify it?

Yes they did.

Were you able to?

Yes, I was.

How were you able to identify this knife as being yours, sir?

Well, it's the color of the handle, the characteristics, the way it's made, and also the fact that the way the blade is ground. I used to sharpen it on the grinding wheel.

Mr. O'Dell, I'm going to show you what is marked S - 31 in identification, and ask you if you could tell us who is depicted in those photographs.

Stephen and Donna.

Your Honor.

Mr. Schutzer?

Yes, I've the same objection I noted earlier to this, and I believe it was excluded.

How about it, prosecutor?

I would move any testimony regarding that be stricken. I will see you at the sidebar, gentlemen.

(The following took place at the sidebar)

As far as I'm concerned, I believe this is getting to the back door what the prosecutor cannot get in through the front door. Now I told the court before I had not had access to this picture when he brought it up and had the victims sister testify. As far as I am concerned, Your Honor excluded that from the evidence. I'm going to make the same objection to that now, as I possibly can, because as far as I'm concerned, this is an indication of the underhanded techniques used by the state to prove its case.

Prosecutor… This photograph, as I explained to the court when the original motion was made to exclude it, I received it that day.

When did you receive it? The day was attempted to be admitted. I believe yesterday. Monday. Where did you receive it from?

The Belleville Police Department.

I sustained the objection. They are supposed to give it to you the day they get it.

(End of sidebar discussion.)

Mr. O'Dell, subsequent to your identifying that knife, did you talk with anyone from the defense about this case?

Just recently, within the last two weeks.

Who was that, sir?

Dr. Latimer, and attorney Schutzer.

Could you tell us what you told Dr. Latimer, please, sir?

Dr. Latimer asked me if..

I'm going to object to what Dr. Latimer asked him. Anything Dr. Latimer said would be hearsay, and inadmissible at this time.

How about it, prosecutor?

If you asked him what he said, I will allow this, not with Dr. Latimer said.

Would you tell us what you told Dr. Latimer, please?

I told him that Stephen had been troubled by something over the past few months, that I wasn't certain what it was, that he just had it bit himself.

Did you tell him anything else?

I answer the questions that he asked, specific questions he asked me.

Do you recall I discussion about chess?

He brought that up.

Did you respond to that? I didn't. There wasn't any response to the need to do that.

Did he ask anything about Stephen, his ability to play chess?

No. He alluded to it as if I knew what he was speaking about.

Mr. O'Dell, did you tell Dr. Latimer anything about Stephen Moore's ability to play chess?

I didn't tell him anything about his ability to play chess, no, not me.

Mr. O'Dell, did you tell Dr. Latimer anything about Stephen Moore's ability to handle business affairs?

No, I didn't.

Mr. O'Dell, did you tell Dr. Latimer anything about Stephen Moore's fear of the Mafia?

I believe I did.

Do you recall having a conversation with me this morning?

I did. I do.

Do you recall indicating to me conversations you had concerning chest praying, with Dr. Latimer?

I do.

What did you indicate to me this morning, sir?

That he didn't want me to speak to you prior to the trial about those matters.

Again, I'm going to object; that's also hearsay, and I will move to have it be stricken.

I will allow it to stand.

Dr. Latimer did not want you to talk to me about the conversations you had with him prior to the trial?

He did not want me to talk to you about Stephen's paranoia concerning the Mafia, nor his ability to play chess, nor his business acumen.

Excuse me, he did not want you to talk to me about what?

Dr. Latimer indicated it would be detrimental to the defense's case if I were to speak to you concerning Stephen Moore's paranoia regarding the Mafia, his business acumen or his ability to play chess.

So he indicated to you it will be better for the defense if you not tell me about the certain items?

Yes.

That was in an interview you had with Dr. Latimer?

That's right.

Did he suggest you anything prior to talking to me?

He suggested I contact attorney Schutzer.

Did you contact him?

I did.

Did you had this discussion with Mr. Schutzer regarding your conversation with Dr. Latimer, wherein he said it would be detrimental if you told me about Mr. Moore's business abilities, abilities to play chess, or his fear of the Mafia?

I don't believe I discussed those with attorney Schutzer. I spoke to him regarding whether or not I was under an obligation to speak to you or an obligation not to speak to you. I didn't know what my legal position was that point.

Did he suggest what you should do?

He suggested that the less I said the better it would be best for the defense's case, but that whether or not I spoke to you with entirely up to me.

He told you whatever you said to me would be entirely up to you, the less he said to me the better it would be for the defense?

I'm going to object.

I'm going to sustain the objection.

Were there other discussions between Dr. Latimer and Mr. Schutzer indicating you should limit the information that you gave to me?

Following those instances?

Yes, or prior to those instances, sir.

I don't believe so. Not that I recall.

You don't recall those two specific instances?

I don't.

I've no further questions of this witness, Your Honor.

Mr. Schutzer?

Cross-examination by Mr. Schutzer:

Mr. Dell, you indicated that Mr. Moore was staying at your house the night before?

That's correct.

You indicated you know him for about 10 years, is that correct?

Yes.

Would you say that at the time, around the time of this incident, the 13th, and the 14th, that Stephen was staying with you because he had no other place to stay at that time?

I would imagine he had other places to stay. He just probably preferred to stay with me.

Would you say he regarded your home as a second home?

To a large extent, yes.

Now with respect to the knife that you testified concerning, did you notice that knife was missing before the Belleville police contacted you concerning it?

Before the Belleville police contacted me, yes, I noticed it before.

When did you notice it before then?

Well it was brought to my attention that the knife possibly was mine and I went to look to see if the knife was there. I couldn't find it.

Prior to that, when was the last time that you had really looked for that knife?

I had not been working in the gas station for a number of weeks. I had been in the other store.

So that prior to July 14 and 15th, you may have misplaced the knife?

Well, I wouldn't have misplaced the knife because I wasn't working there.

Where there other people working in the station? So it might have been replaced or taken by someone else? You don't know what may have happened, or when it was taken, if it were taken, do you.

No, I don't. Not exactly, no.

You indicated in a conversation with Dr. Latimer who as you know is a defense psychiatrist in this case, you indicated to him that you know that Stephen had been troubled by something for, oh, the past couple of months, and know that he has been bothered by something, you didn't know what it was, that he had not been himself?

That's true.

You noticed a visible change in him?

Yes.

Would you be able to describe for me at this time what that visible change was, if you could? He was afraid of something? That somebody was out to get him, but it wasn't exactly clear who it was.

It wasn't clear to you, in other words?

No. He wouldn't specify exactly. You couldn't pin him down as to who it was.

But you know he was afraid of somebody or something, isn't that so?

Right. That's the feeling I had, yes.

Would you say he was very afraid?

Yes, I would.

Would you say it bordered on maybe panic, from what you could observe?

I did, yes I would.

Did he do anything strange during that period of time that led you to believe he was really panic stricken at the time?

He did.

What did he do?

He used to, and go without notice at all kinds of weird hours. He would arise to stay the night we would go to bed and find him pacing back and forth get up in the morning and he would be gone, apparently left sometime during the night.

So that his comings and goings really were erratic, yes. I mean, he never said he was coming, never said he was leaving, just came and went. On one occasion about 2 o'clock in the morning, I was awakened to find out he climbed up the roof that leads up to the sundeck.

The roof of your house?

Yes, the roof of my house only covers part of the building. The other part of the building there is a doorway from my apartment, leaving out onto a sundeck, over the garage. The roof is actually the roof of the garage pays, and he had to climb up onto the top of the garage roof, came into the doorway.

Is or any other way to get up where he came in?

Through the window.

With their door there, or whatever?

There is a door there.

There is. So he could have conveniently gone through the door to get through where he was going?

If the court please, the man is now a defense witness. I would like to be able to cross-examine him as well to all the testimony coming—

The door is open. You open the door. Go ahead.

Now, he would come in through the window, but there were other means of access getting into where he was going. He didn't come in through the window. I am sorry. He climbed onto the roof of the garage, came through the door.

Did he ever come through Windows to your knowledge?

Not through mine, to somebody else's. I was told about.

I will ask it to be stricken.

I will allow it to stand.

Will anyone else notice these things in your presence? Oh, yes.

Who would that be?

Well mainly my wife.

And what is her name?

Jean O'Dell.

You have known Stephen Moore quite a long time, 10 years you indicated, is that so?

That's true.

And during that period of time that you had known him, you have had occasion to observe him, isn't that so?

That's true.

And you have had occasion to see him with other people?

That's true.

During that period of time, you have had the opportunity to hear what others would say that him, is that so?

That's right.

And you've had the opportunity to discuss him yourself, isn't that so?

That's true.

Based upon your friendship with him and your observations and the discussions which you had, in your knowledge of his behavior in the past, would you be able to tell me whether the incident on July 14, 1976, was consistent with his character as you knew it?

I will sustain the objection.

Your Honor, I object.

Sustain the objection.

Would you indicate for me what type of person Stephen was, what type character you observed him to have during all the. That you knew him?

I considered him to be a lot of fun to have around, he was always pleasant, never aggressive or a problem or anything of that nature.

Did you ever hear anybody say anything about him being violent?

No.

Did you ever hear anybody ever--

I object to the hearsay question.

This is a cross examination.

Sustain the objection.

Did you know Stephen to be one of your own knowledge of generous or gentle person?

That was my belief, yes.

Do you have any instances that you might be able to get the jury and the court that you might be able to use to illustrate his generosity or his gentility?

Well he was, you know, he used to do a lot of favors for people, just out of the clear blue sky. For instance, I moved to Vermont on one occasion a number of years back, and I had an and MGDT at that time in various stages of disassembly.

An automobile?

Yes, classic fine car, and just one day Stephen showed up with that car some 300 miles on the flatbed trailer, just to bring it to me so it wouldn't get left in Jersey City while I was somewhere out of state. I know of other things that don't relate to me but….

Well to your knowledge and in your presence have you ever seen him strike anyone?

No, never.

By the way, Mr. O'Dell, were you subpoenaed to testify as a defense witness?

Yes, I was.

And was it before or after Mr. Mautone and the police spoke to you that you were contacted by Dr. Latimer?

I object. I don't see the relevancy of the question.

I will sustain the objection.

We contacted by Dr. Latimer, which is by telephone, did you–

Is that a question or statement, sir?

I will allow the question.

Did you indicate to Dr. Latimer any apprehensions you had about testifying in general?

I don't believe so. Not until after he, you know, suggested that there were certain things he would prefer I couldn't say. At that point I had no apprehensions at all.

Based upon what he told you, did you get the impression did he actually tell you not to discuss the case?

No, he didn't but he asked me to speak to you and I did get the impression since I was going to be subpoenaed as a defense witness there may be legal reasons why you should talk to the prosecutor.

So later on you spoke to me, isn't that so?

That's correct.

Did you call me or did I call you?

I called you and you return my call, I believe.

Right. I returned your call. Did you ask me whether you should testify? Whether you should talk to the state?

I believe I did, yes, that's why was calling you.

And do you recall asking me whether I felt it was illegal impediment to you talking to the state?

That's correct.

What did I reply?

That there wasn't.

I told you, as well, I felt at this point it would not be in the best interest of my client to give too much information, isn't that so?

That's correct.

And at the time I did so, did I indicated to you that it was because the defense was going to be in Saturday and some of the material would be confidential?

Your Honor, I object.

I sustain the objection to suggesting answers to the witness.

I am asking the questions—

I am sustaining the objection. It is not a question.

Your Honor, may I note for the record the fact that the door was opened by the prosecutor?

I sustain the objection. You are suggesting the answers. You can ask him what you said, but don't tell what you said.

I am sorry, sir.

What did I say to you, if you can recall?

Well, it was, he said to me that there is going to be a defense of insanity, and it would not be beneficial to the defense to have, for me to give the prosecutor certain information at this time.

And did I say eventually that the information would come out anyway? Yes.

Your Honor, I object to that.

Sustain the objection.

And did I ever in any way prohibit you from speaking to the prosecutor?

Your Honor, I object.

I sustain the objection.

Did you to your knowledge or anyone in your family receive a telephone call concerning your testimony or your wife's testimony in this matter?

I believe I received a telephone call you are referring to.

I didn't hear the answer to that. I believe I know the telephone call you are referring to.

And was the substance of that call to your knowledge, if you know, your own personal knowledge.

Whether it was told to you to cooperate fully with the state, yes.

Did Latimer indicate to you he was operating as a defense agent?

Yes, he did.

I object to that question.

I will allow that question.

Did Dr. Latimer indicate to you that because the defense with insanity there may be certain privileged matters?

I get to that question, Your Honor.

Sustain the objection.

And did I fact have a conversation with you prior to your testimony here today?

Yes, you did.

During that period of time, did I indicate to you that you should not cooperate with the state?

No, you did not.

Did I indicate to you that you should withhold information?

No, you didn't.

Your Honor, I had no further questions.

Mr. prosecutor?

Mr. O'Dell, do you have knowledge of the phone call received by your wife for Mr. Schutzer?

Yes, I do.

Do you know where the phone call was made from?

From your office.

And I also talk to your wife on the phone conversation?

I believe so.

Was your wife upset about that phone conversation?

To some extent.

Why, sir?

Because she believed that Schutzer was saying over the phone was not–

Sir?

To put in her words, she believed that he was putting words in her mouth; in other words, he was saying things over the phone that she wasn't saying.

His responses to her on the phone were not responsive to her questions to him?

That was her feelings, yes.

She got the feeling, then, what Mr. Schutzer was saying was for my benefit, not hers?

That is correct.

I'm going to object to the prosecutor putting words into the witnesses' mouth.

I will allow it. Your objection is overruled. I will allow you, sir.

All right, let's take a short recess, please.

3 o'clock, please and thank you.

(Court recessed)

Mr. Schutzer?

Yes, Your Honor. May I be heard outside the presence of this witness, prosecutor, any objection? Not knowing what Mr. Schutzer is about to present in this case, which I don't think anything that is either on the record or before the court in any other matter would indicate.

As to whether or not the defense counsel or Dr. Latimer has been besmirched by proceedings going on in this courtroom, they were not besmirched by anything other than their own actions, and I believe they are accountable for them in the preparation of this defense.

As was directed to the court, Mr. O'Dell is a close friend of Mr. Moore. Mr. O'Dell was contacted by the defense, and it was requested that he delete certain bits of information from the prosecution.

Your Honor-

He spoke to defense counsel. I would ask Mr. Schutzer allow me to finish, as I allowed him the same courtesy.

I apologize.

He was approached by defense counsel and he testified that defense counsel indicated to him, not the state indicated to him or nothing that the state did, but that the defense in the preparation of their case indicated to Mr. O'Dell that it would be in the interests of the defense that he give the state the minimal amount of information necessary, the implication thereby is not to volunteer anything that might in any way impeach the defense of insanity.

There is nothing brought on by the state. It is part of the defense's presentation preparation of the case. I think it's relevant to the case, and the methods in which they approach the defense is not something the state should have to pay for.

Mr. Schutzer?

Your Honor, again, I reiterate my position.

Don't reiterate; say something new. I have heard your position twice.

It is highly relevant to this procedure and in fact a big Mr. Mautone with due respect, has misinterpreted and by his questioning of the witness was misinterpreting, misleading the jury with respect to certain matters, I'm not going to go into these matters at this time. I believe there may be a possibility of a threat being carried out.

I would like to ask where is the body? I want to see the body.

Pardon?

If I'm being charged, alleged homicide, the countries turning communist, I was in California, came back. They all got arrested in the same car for drunken driving. I will read it to you. I have a letter right here from them.

Mr. Moore if you have something to say you want to talk to me, you have to talk a little louder, so this young lady here can hear you. I'm telling a few people to drop you a line. I wrote letters to Pres. Ford, got no answer from him. Speak slower, Mr. Moore. This young lady can't understand you.

I wrote a letter to Pres. Ford, legalizing marijuana, kind of stupid getting busted for a little grass and a car. I couldn't see people getting hit in $8 million for campaign funds to go on television saying, hey, I will be president of the United States, this is what I can do for you people. Do you know what I mean? So anyway, getting back to my girlfriends, I could help a lot of people, I could be consistent with Jimmy Carter, he already went down, but I don't know if my father and mother alive, I tried to call them from the hospital in the jail next-door here, nothing accomplished, and here I have a letter saying my friends in California visited to the country being communists. I don't know.

It's a stupid game. I don't understand it. I would like to see these people who got arrested in California for drunken driving. That's stupid, one person driving the car at a time, David D'Alessio, Phil Narris, this is kind of serious thing, Dave, 20 years old, girlfriend, two kids sporting, she is working, too, it's new game, in the jury paid five dollars a day. I can't see wasting all this time. I realize all you government people, get $20,000 a year, I'm the working man, I'm not trying to be wise to you, sir, but I got equipment everywhere, when the country is being turned communist, a girl waiting in Belleville, when she gets divorced we will get married, so here I am sitting in jail, alleged homicide and Surf City, so where is the body, that's all I ask, bring the body in, laid on the table, the knife, gun, who was the witnesses?

Supposedly I killed this body. Let's get it over with, bring the body now I'm serious. To the cops shooter had offered something, anybody heard the body at the girl when she was sleeping, trying to free me, put me up for 20 years, is there a plan trying to kidnap me? The Kansas City Star went out of business, the world Tribune, a fight between the paper companies is this one little United States.

This is pretty serious. I don't half to go into heavy science. I'm being wise, I know the ethics of man, the ethics of life I know, so I should get a job, I ask for a job to get food, a couple little pies, some cigarettes, matches it's crazy. I get a small income, I can't collect unemployment, I make $5000 a year, pay 800 a year taxes on it, made a gross last year on top of that $2000. Serious. Who given on the I managed, I didn't complain, and the country is going communists. It serious $8 million for campaign funds so where is Pres. Ford? He should be right in this courtroom don't you think so? He is running the United States. Is he dead? Was he assassinated what is going on you the relevance of the works for shafts?

Request the other witnesses also be out of the courtroom?

Of course not.

During this exchange.

No, sir.

Again, Your Honor—

Anything this man has to say the other witnesses can rebut.

I deny your application to withdraw any of the witnesses from the courtroom at this time.

With respect to my application, hold it. Mr. Moore, do you have anything else?

Yes. I got letters from Jersey City. My friend lives in Little Falls, why is he writing from Jersey City? I try to make phone calls. I can't make phone calls that appear. They got in a hospital. I don't understand what is going on. Give me medicine in my food. It's no game. I'm trying to be wise. Just bring the body in? Get it over with. Where is the body? If there is no body, then it is kidnapping, false charges, over and done. So bring the body in tomorrow. She is in the ground, take her up, that is all there is to it.

It serious. Makes sense. Do you have to talk to your superior?

That's the president of the United States.

Do you have anything else, Mr. Moore?

Mr. Schutzer wants to be heard.

I'm not trying to say I'm crazy, but you have to bring the body in. Say this person instead. There are magicians. I don't know if the person is dead or not.

When you're finished, Mr. Schutzer wants to be heard.

I am not in the Mafia. Go ahead.

Are you finished?

I am not actually finished, but I might continue tomorrow if the case goes on and on. I am not going to stop. When I finished, put in jail for 100 years.

Mr. Schutzer?

With respect to the application I'm making to the court, I am respectfully asking the court the witnesses sitting here to be removed.

On what ground Mr. Schutzer??

On the ground it will be prejudicial should those witnesses be recalled. I am making an application for no one but the court and the prosecutor at this point.

No. Your application is— I don't run anything in and camera, sir. There isn't anybody who hasn't a right to hear what about you, sir. Since when are lawyers favored suitors, sir? You are suggesting an ethical conduct on the part of the prosecutor, suggesting the prosecutor is threatening criminal action. I haven't heard any such threats. I run a public courtroom, and anybody has a right to be here, and the only time witnesses have not right to be here as if they are going to part somebody else's testimony, not rebut testimony.

I will hear you on the prosecutor's answer to make a ruling on the mistrial.

Your Honor, I'm not inputting unethical conduct to the prosecutor. I mentioned at sidebar I thought his method unfair because of the matter previously ruled upon. I have the impression that because I did back the prosecutor had taken it upon himself to get revenge upon me playing quote, unquote, with the big boys.

Now, Your Honor, again, if there are any charges of ethics here, they are being directed at me. I resent Ben as a professional man, resent Ben because I think more importantly the question is Mr. Moore's innocent of the charge and he is being seriously shortchanged in the matter is allowed to go before the jury the way it is.

Yes, sir?

No, there isn't, sir.

Prosecutor, else? Your Honor, I do nothing as a matter of revenge, simply do my job, and my job is to present the state's case, and that's what I'm doing.

Your Honor, respectfully that is exactly what I was doing, perhaps I don't to make out the same way Mr. Mautone does, and perhaps I don't do my job as he would like to do it, but, Your Honor, I did my job in the best manner I know how, as well. Perhaps I don't have the experience Mr. Mautone has perhaps I had the expertise he does, but I'm doing my job and do matter which I regard being consistent with good professional ethics.

The mistrial is denied.

Bring in the Jury

Mr. O'Dell resumes best stand.

Examination continues by Mr. Schutzer:

When did Stephen return if at all to your home and Surf City on July 14?

About 5 o'clock.

Did you ask him where he been?

Yes, I did.

And did he reply to you?

Yes, he did.

What was his reply?

Up north.

Now when he replied to you, do you recall if he had any emotion in his voice?

That was all he said, and then he walked out. I didn't notice any particular emotion in his voice.

Did he appear quiet to you?

Yes.

He testified on direct Betty was kind of moody the last couple of months, despondent?

Yes.

When he returned, he appeared respect?

I only saw him for about two minutes myself.

Do you happen to remember what he was wearing?

Plaid shirt was large black and white checked, or something. At any rate it was a checked final. It was a final shirt and had a striped on the left-hand sleeve from the elbow almost all the way down I remember that. It was the middle of July, and it was unusual for him to wear something like that.

Stephen generally a heavy smoker?

Not that heavy.

On this particular day, you noticed a lot of cigarette butts?

Yes.

And when he said to you that he had been up north, was it said in a matter-of-fact manner?

I thought so at the time.

Nothing unusual?

I didn't notice anything unusual at the time, no.

Do you know where he went after he came back and you say you saw him for two minutes? Do you know where he went after he came back to Surf City? Did he go and where? In other words, before the police picked him up?

He must've gone someplace to buy the lemonade. Maybe at the pizzeria at the street. That's the only place around that sells the lemonade that I know of. I also saw him coming across the street from directly across street that was what he was doing with their I have no idea.

Did you notice whether Stephen was in a hurry back, or did he look like he was very?

I would say he definitely was now in a hurry.

Definitely was not?

He definitely was not. He just sat there.

Just sat there?

Yes, he was sitting there drinking lemonade. Well, see you have to understand I have a gas station, and an adjoining plant store. I was in the plant store. He spent most of his time in the office at the gas station. I happen to know he sat there because I was told that's where he spent most of his time sitting.

I would object to all the testimony about his attitude where he was sitting.

I will allow it.

Mr. prosecutor?

Mr. O'Dell, Stephen was not a heavy smoker?

It depends what you consider a heavy smoker.

What do you consider a heavy smoker, sir?

I would say three packs a day.

At that rate, Stephen return to your store, you noticed a large number cigarette butts in the ashtray where he was sitting?

Yes, I noticed that after he was arrested.

After he was arrested. So there were an unusually large number cigarette butts in the ashtray?

Yes.

So he was smoking particularly heavy on that day or about that time.

Yes.

Now you say when he came back he was wearing a plaid shirt with a cut on the arm?

Well, it wasn't a cut. It appeared to be the same was—

I am side. I want to show you what has been marked as - 26 for identification, and ask you if you could tell us what that is.

That's the shirt he was wearing. That's Stephen Moore.

That's the shirt he was wearing when he returned to Surf City?

That's right.

Was that the shirt he was wearing when he left that morning?

No it is not.

Do you recall that?

Yes, I do.

Do you recall what kind of shirt he was wearing when he left that morning?

I believe it was a light blue, faded blue T-shirt.

That it had a collar and buttons?

It may have, not full buttons.

When you refer to a T-shirt, and undershirt?

Jersey, pullover type shirt.

Now, sir, on one occasion Mr. Moore entered her home through I believe it's like a patio door on the top of the garage?

Yeah you could call it that.

Was that early or late evening?

About 2 o'clock in the morning.

Do you have locks on your doors, sir?

I do.

Were you awake when Mr. Moore entered the house?

No.

Were your doors locked?

Downstairs, yes.

Was the upstairs patio door open?

No.

Was it opened?

It was unlocked.

Unlocked?

It was not open, it was unlocked.

So that was the only means of entry into your house that was unlocked?

That's correct.

I have no further questions.

Mr. Schutzer?

Yes, Your Honor.

Mr. O'Dell, to your knowledge, did Stephen travel a lot? Did he travel throughout the country?

Yes.

Recently, I referring to?

In a few months even before that July 14. Yes.

You were aware that?

Yes.

Answer your knowledge did he often carry clothing in his car?

Yes.

So he largely lived out of his car from time to time. More or less lived out of his car. So it would be unusual for him to go away in the morning and come back with different clothes on, what it?

Not necessarily.

But it is unusual for him to be wearing a flannel shirt in July?

I will object

I will allow the question.

I thought so at the time, that's why I remarked on it.

Mr. O'Dell, you indicated that you had not seen the knife in the gas station for several weeks prior to July 13?

I personally don't recall when I saw the knife last before July 13.

What is the last time you saw Stephen Moore before July 13? Before July 13?

Yes, sir. Quite a number of weeks. I don't remember the exact date. It was over a month.

Over a month. And that knife was one of the tools used in the gas station?

That's correct.

Do you know if Stephen Moore loved Donna Litchfield?

I object, Your Honor.

I will sustain the objection.

Did Stephen Moore ever talk to you about his love for Donna Litchfield?

I object

I will sustain the objection.

Tell him to define the word love. There is a dictionary here. Mr. Moore please keep your comments to yourself.

Mr. Dell, use the time Mr. Moore would just disappear. He said he would be a house and you would wake up and he would be gone. Did it seem unusual to you that a single youth in 1976 with no family obligations, with no job, with financial income, with friends in California, and a sister in Texas we decided to go on a vacation across country?

I'm going to object.

I will allow it. Your objection is overruled. Mr. shoots her, you opened the door. This witness testified he disappeared. I will allow the explanation. He called it a disappearance.

That he would go on vacation would be unusual, no.

That would go on a trip across the country for a period of time sound or seem unusual to you?

That in itself, no unusual no.

What makes it unusual?

The fact that neither his parents nor his girlfriend nor me or anybody that new where he was or where he had gone.

When was this trip, sir?

Pardon?

Approximately June. The month of June, I believe

Do you know of any time Stephen Moore went to Florida?

Sometime prior to March. January or February, I believe.

Your Honor, the ID heard in the sidebar moment?

Certainly

The fact that Mr. Moore decided to go on a vacation, travel around the country, to you seemed unusual because he didn't contact anyone, his parents or the like?

Right.

And went with this vacation?

I believe it was approximately the month of June. The month of June and the first two weeks of July. He returned just about 12 July.

Stephen Moore ever tell you he went to Missouri?

I don't believe so.

If you went to Missouri he would have told you, wouldn't he?

Objection.

I will allow the question.

If he went to Missouri he didn't tell me about it.

Well that would have been unusual?

I can't tell whether Stephen would have told me about it or not.

I think the prosecutor is arguing with the witness.

I don't think so. I think that the witness is volunteering answers to questions that haven't been asked. But the questions, prosecutor.

Mr. Moore never mentioned to you he was in Missouri?

No, he didn't, not to my knowledge.

Did you ever hear from anyone else he had been in Missouri?

I object.

I will allow the question.

No.

Did Mr. Moore go away during the month of May?

Whenever he disappeared. I don't exactly recall when not commenced. It may have been in May. He may have gone the later part of May and returned early June.

The later part of May, early June?

He may have. I don't recall. I just know he was gone for a long time.

It wasn't the beginning of May, though, was it?

It may have been.

It may have been. So you don't know when he went away?

Not exactly know.

But he was gone for a month?

At least.

Returning July 12 or 13th?

Yes.

So that if he left the first day of May he would have been gone the month of May, the month of June, two weeks of the month of July?

That's right.

I'm going to object to the conclusory nature of the question.

I will allow the question.

Do you recall him having left for two entire months?

I recall that he was gone, and I didn't know where he was for a long time.

You said it was about a month?

I believe it was at least a month.

I said a month to six weeks.

A month to six weeks, not 10 weeks?

It may have been 10 weeks. As I said, I don't know exactly when he left.

Isn't it true Mr. Moore did like to go on dictations to Florida, to Vermont, different parts of the country, sir to your knowledge?

To my knowledge, yes.

Now Mr. Moore indicated to you when he all of a sudden stopped working that he was afraid of, I believe your word was the family?

That's right.

Now, what do you interpret that to mean?

I interpreted it to mean that he was afraid of the mob.

Why did you get to the mob?

Well, because I asked him if that's what he meant, and he didn't deny it.

But he didn't confirm? No. He wouldn't confirm exactly who it was.

So it was your conclusion?

I believe it probably was.

It's your own conclusion based on the fact that Mr. Moore told you that he had a business contract with the man in the job, or wrecking business, that the business contracts with not being beneficial; and that he pulled out?

That's right.

And that there was some animosity between himself and the man under which, or with whom he answered this arrangement?

Right.

That he subsequently got another job in another wrecking business operation, correct?

Correct.

And that several accidents occurred during this period?

Correct.

And when you heard the word family, you interpreted it to mean the Mafia. Isn't it more reasonable to assume—

I'm going to object what is more reasonable to assume.

I haven't heard the question, sir.

Is the word family, when used in talking about his fears in relationship to the accident that occurred at a junkyard, without being referring to the owner of the first junkyard and his relatives, the owner of the second junkyard and his relatives?

I object.

That's true. I asked him about that. I will allow the question.

It is more logical to assume that is what family meant?

That's true. I asked him if that's what- that's why I included he met the Mafia because I asked him if that's what he meant by the family, and-

I believe on direct examination-

He indicated it was more than just a family involved. The specific family involved with the junkyard, yes.

Now you say he indicated it was more than that specific family?

Yes.

On direct examination indicated he had not indicated to you what he meant by that. You simply assumed it was the mob.

He never used the term Mafia but use the term family. I asked him if he met the family directly related to your, and he indicated it was a larger entity that.

Larger family?

Yes.

Sir, all of a sudden Mr. Moore became unemployed, is that your testimony was?

That's right.

You don't know of your own knowledge whether he was fired where he quit?

He told me he quit.

Do you remember the date that he became unemployed?

I do not.

Do you know a girl by the name of Jay or Betty?

No, I don't.

Do you know any of Stephen's girlfriends prior to Donna?

Yes.

Did he ever mention a Betty Switzer to you?

No, he didn't.

A girl by the name of Jay?

No.

To your knowledge, did he ever visit Pennsylvania?

Not to my knowledge.

Now the incidents of Mr. Moore coming in through the window, what happened on one occasion?

Came through the door.

It was the door?

It was the door on the second floor.

Stephen stayed your house on many occasions, did he not?

That's right.

You saw Stephen and Donna your house?

That's right

Was this prior to subsequent to the time that he indicated to you that one of his girlfriends, and I believe on direct examination you did use the plural, one of his girlfriends sisters had put a curse on him.

Subsequent.

So after he told you about the voodoo and the curse, then you saw Donna your house?

That's right.

Do you know a girl Valerie?

No.

Can you give us the specific names of any of the girls that Stephen Moore knew?

Jean– I don't know her last name.

Do you know where she lives?

Patterson, I believe

Any other names?

Just a girl he used to go with when he was about 18. She is out in Oregon, I believe her name is Sharon Beliss.

I am talking about in the last year, year and a half.

No.

But you know he had gone out with other girls.

The only girls I know of he went out with in the last year was a girl named Jean and Donna.

Did he ever mention any other girls to you?

Not to my knowledge, no.

Did he talked much about girls?

No.

No good.

Excuse me Mr. Moore?

I said no good.

So it's possible there are other girls you don't know?

Possible.

What is possible I would object to.

Your Honor, I have no further questions

Mr. Schutzer?

At this time I don't, but I would ask the court to reserve the right to call Mr. O'Dell.

No question about it. You can call him whenever you see fit. Thank you, Mr. O'Dell. Call your next witness.

Jean O'Dell Testimony

Next witness Jean O'Dell.

Jean O'Dell has been sworn in.

Direct examination by Mr. Schuzter:

Mrs. O'Dell, I don't ask you to keep your voice up all right please. Are you related in any way to Rodney O'Dell?

He is my husband.

And are you acquainted with Stephen Moore?

Yes, I am.

And how are you acquainted with Stephen Moore?

He was a friend of our family, my husband's family, for 10 years.

During the period of time, have you had occasion to see Stephen Moore?

Yes.

Where did you see him primarily?

Wherever we live he used to come and visit us.

Can you tell us how often that was?

Every couple of months.

Every couple of months he would come to you. And during the period of time that you saw, you had occasion to observe behavior?

Yes.

And you had occasion to talk to him and in turn haven't talked to you?

Yes.

And during that period of time that you had occasion to observe him, did you ever notice anything of an unusual nature or what you would regard as being unusual about Stephen Moore's behavior?

It would depend on what you are talking about.

Well, if you can remember the first instance you might have, it in that you saw anything unusual about that you might have remember?

We started to notice a difference in him around last February.

February this year, 1976?

Yes.

What kind of difference, if you can possibly tell the jury, did you notice Stephen Moore?

He was very distant, very depressed, occasionally irrational. He would change his mind often.

He changed his mind often, changed his mood?

I don't believe the witness said mood, defense counsel has reiterated.

Put your next question, Mr. Schuster. I will allow it.

Mrs. O'Dell, you have to speak louder. The jurors are having difficulty hearing you.

Now Mrs. O'Dell, you indicated Mr. Moore acted in an irrational matter. Can you get an instance what you would regard as being irrational?

Once he came over, of the latter, over our balcony, 18 in a side door at 2 o'clock in the morning.

At 2 o'clock in the morning. And as a result of his doing that, did you and your husband do anything?

We got up fast.

Were you awakened?

 yes.

Had he ever done that before?

No.

And how I have a client is that?

15 to 20 feet.

Were you aware of whether or not even more was employed or not?

Not that time. Not for February on.

Not from February on. Prior to February, were you aware as to whether he was employed or not?

He was self-employed.

Self-employed. Did he work— how many jobs you work if you recall?

I have known him to work up to three jobs in a day.

Three jobs in a day. That's three different jobs or three different tasks?

Three different jobs.

Three different jobs. And would you say he was industrious?

Yes. Definitely.

And when was this? During the period prior to February 1976 correct?

Yes.

Would you say he was hard-working?

Yes.

And did there come a time when Mr. Moore was now working, he was not doing anything?

Yes.

What was that period of time?

It was after December of last year.

He just— he sold his appointment and he would— well, he thought he would go back to school, but he didn't.

Did he ever give you anything or do anything for you?

I object, your honor I don't see the relevancy to his generosity.

I will allow it. Go ahead

He gave everything he owned away.

He everything he owned away?

Yes.

As far as I know he gave my husband and his brother a wrecker.

What is a wrecker?

A tow truck.

Do you have any idea as to the approximate value of that wrecker?

I object. I don't see the relevancy.

I will allow it

Around $3000.

A $3000 wrecker was given to you and your husband. Stephen say why he was giving it to you?

He said he didn't think he would have any use for it.

Just be to your husband, and did he have for anything in return?

No.

Did you have occasion to talk with Stephen following December and January and February 1976?

Yes.

During those periods of time, did you have any difficulties talking with him?

Yes.

Would you describe for us what policy you had talking with him, what, if anything he did, or you did?

Well, like he would— you would be talking to him and he wouldn't listen. He would just start talking about something else.

Could you be more specific? When you get some ideas out to perhaps— was he staring into space or—

I object to the leading nature of the questions.

I will allow it.

He would jump around, you know— you couldn't-he would say he was going to go back to school and he wanted to build a hospital and then the next minute he was going to take off for California, where a vacation. He couldn't you couldn't predict anything. We went to Vermont to go skiing, and my son broke his leg, and Steve said he had a premonition that this was going to happen, and he thought he could predict the future.
--

He said to you, he felt that predict the future?

Yes.

I object to the repetition by the defense counsel.

Just put the next question, Mr. Schutzer.

Did he ever indicate anyone predicts the future aside from himself?

Not that I know of.

Did he ever indicate whether anyone can read his mind?

He thought that somebody had control of his mind for a while. Somebody had a lock of his hair.

Somebody had a lock of his hair. Did he indicate to you who he thought had a lock of his hair?

It was somebody's sister. I don't know who the person was.

Somebody sister. Now, Mrs. O'Dell did you know Donna Lee Litchfield?

I met her twice.

You met her twice. And where was that?

At my home. What was the occasion for you meeting her?

Steve brought her down to visit.

And did you have occasion any time that Stephen and Donna visiting your home, to have any discussions with Donna Litchfield?

Not in my home. Just general conversations about children, but she would call me up.

Donna called me up when Steve left for California and we didn't know where he was at the time, and she had called me up to find out if I had seen or heard from him, and she told me that she thought he thought people were after him.

She told you this?

Yes. That he would come in her bedroom window.

This is hearsay. There is no foundation for this.

I will allow it. That he was afraid her apartment was bogged and they had to have the top running and a stereo blasting or else he wouldn't talk.

Was this the only way she felt that she said Stephen felt safe when he talked?

Yes.

Judge, I object to the leading nature of the question.

I will allow it.

Yes.

When the time was running and the music was blasting?

Either that, or he would have to write a note.

Write a note you explain that? Instead of having a conversation verbally, he would write a note. Whose idea was that?

Steve's. He thought the apartment was bugged.

Did he express, did I ever say to you whether Stephen had done anything unusual?

You me anymore peculiar behavior?

Yes.

Just that she didn't know what– he was unpredictable. He was very unpredictable.

He was very unpredictable. And did she ever indicate to you whether he had ever done anything bizarre in her presence or perhaps unusual in her presence?

She wasn't afraid of him, she just thought he was unpredictable and didn't always control his mind.

He couldn't what?

Have control of his mind.

Have control of his mind. And did Donna ever indicate to you anything about Steve coming in through windows?

Yes.

What did she say to you?

She said he didn't frequently.

She said he didn't frequently?

He would calm in the bedroom window.

Did she indicate to you whether that was unusual or disturbing to her? Yes. What did she say?

Well, it would scare her, because it would be frequently and it would happen at night.

We are talking about one specific window Donna Litchfield department. I object to the common defense counsel made, putting it in the plural.

Did she ever really whether she thought that was crazy or not?

I will object to that.

I will sustain the objection.

Were you aware as to whether Donna and Stephen wanted to get married?

She told me he wanted to marry her and move away.

And did she give you or did she in fact want to marry him at that point?

She didn't intend to marry him, as far as I know.

Why was that? She ever tell you why?

She was afraid they would find themselves far away from where she was normally living, and he might take off for some other place. She was not going to leave where she was living she did not have intentions of marrying him.

Did she ever say she wouldn't marry him because she thought he was crazy?

I don't remember her saying that, those exact words.

Now have to your conversations, and your observations of Stephen Moore, were you able to form an opinion in your mind as to whether he was able to make a connection with reality?

Not always.

Not always. Why is that?

He was really sure that his father was being blackmailed a one point.

Is that what he told you?

Yes.

Did he say anything else we with respect to that?

His father finally convinced him he wasn't.

Did you ever fear he might be, that he might be killed?

Yes.

Did he express that fear to you?

Yes.

Did he ever talk to you about death?

Yes.

And what, if you can recall, did he say about death?

I remember saying he thought he was going to be dead within six months.

Did he give a reason for that?

No.

He just felt he would be dead in six months.

Do you know whether he used drugs to your knowledge?

He didn't use them, no.

Do you know whether he smokes cigarettes heavily?

Yes.

Did you have occasion to go on a trip with Steve to go anywhere?

We went skiing in Vermont.

Who was that?

My husband, my family, my children, my husband and I.

How many children do you have?

Four.

All of you went up to Vermont and Stephen went with you?

Yes.

When you went up there, did anything unusual happened?

Well, he would get up and leave, like he predicted, he predicted my son was going to break his life. He got very upset because we didn't have insurance, and my son broke his leg and it was like he thought he knew this was going to happen.

Stephen told you he thought he predicted her son would break his leg?

Yes

Did Stephen ever really to you any incidents with respect to car accidents?

He had two accidents.

Your Honor, again I'm going to defense counsel to please not leave as much as he is. Go ahead I will out a question.

I believe he has had two accidents in December, and he thought somebody had rigged it, the Mafia had rigged it.

Do you ever discussed the Mafia and any other occasions with you?

No.

Now does your husband have another brother?

Yes, he has two brothers.

What are the names of the brothers?

Jeffrey O'Dell and Cole O'Dell.

Now with respect to Jeffrey O'Dell, did Stephen over express any concern to you about him?

Jeff got married in February and Stephen was very upset about it. He thought that he has chosen the wrong girl, and that she was only after his money, which he doesn't have.

In did he overexpress to you any fears with respect to Jeff's wife?

He was afraid she was going to hurt him. If she ever hurt him, he would kill her.

It all the time you now and Stephen Moore, have you ever known him to be a violent person?

No. No; I had never seen argue or fight with anybody.

Never seen argue or fight with anybody. Now you said that you have noticed a significant, was it a significant change that you noticed in Stephen from about December or February on?

Yes. I called the father up. Steve's birthday is May 15. I called father of a couple days before that we thought Stephen needed help. We thought he was going to harm himself.

Did he ever talk about harming himself?

No. It was just a fear we had.

Based upon other conversations you have had with him?

Yes, I am sorry.

Did you ever discuss witchcraft with you or voodoo?

Well, he thought about somebody having a lock of his hair, and having control over. That's the only kind of witchcraft I remember talking about.

Who do you say had a lock of his hair?

Somebody sister. I don't know if Donna's sister or somebody else. I don't know.

When did he send that to you?

It was sometime in February or March.

To your knowledge, with Stephen Moore seeing Donna Litchfield about time?

Yes.

Now, Mrs. O'Dell you ample opportunity, having you to view Stephen Moore's behavior, to talk with him, to listen to what he said to you to see all the things that you have described?

Yes

It all. Time that you observed that, and because of that observation, because those conversations, because of what you know about Steven's personality, the a you would be able to come to as to whether he was sane or insane?

Your Honor, I'm going to object.

I will sustain the objection

I believe he wasn't normal.

You believe he was not normal. When we discussed the Mafia and a curse on, the lock of hair, the people following him, and things like that, did he ever appear afraid to you, if you can recall?

He didn't appear to be a free while he was in our home. I felt he felt safe in our home while he was there.

In other words, you would say your home was a haven for him. Without be a fair assumption?

Well I know I didn't think it was about, or anything like that. He didn't that way with us. He seemed to relax more, but he was completely withdrawn.

So what be a fair assumption to say that Stephen Moore felt her home was a haven?

I guess so.

I have no further questions, Your Honor, of this witness.

All right. Thank you. Ladies and gentlemen, I'm going to excuse you now to return tomorrow morning at 9 o'clock.

Mrs. Rutherford Moore Testimony

Call your next witness, prosecutor.

The defense calls Mrs. Rutherford Moore.

All right, Mrs. Moore.

Direct examination by Mr. Schutzer:

Mrs. Moore I'm going to ask you to keep your voice up so that all the jurors can hear you.

Mrs. Moore, Stephen Moore your son?

Yes, he is.

To your knowledge, Mrs. Moore, has Stephen ever had any problems during his life?

I object.

Of an unusual nature.

I will allow it.

No; just the usual problems of not always doing well in school, which many people have.

And it's even ever have any problems in school that were perhaps more unusual than other people?

Your Honor—

She answered he never had any problems except not doing well in school. Put the next question.

I am pursuing that.

Oh, no; I will sustain the objection.

Yes.

Did Stephen ever attend a public school?

Yes, he did. Elementary school.

Elementary school?

Yes.

Did there come a time Stephen ever attended any other schools?

Yes. He went away to school, he went where there would be smaller classes and she would get more individual attention.

And what was the need for more individual attention, if you recall, if you know?

In order to get more help with courses that he wasn't doing well in, supervised study hall, that sort of thing.

And what schools, if you can recall, did you send him to?

He went to Indian mound school in Connecticut, and graduated from there, in eighth grade, went for seventh and eighth grade; went to storm King school in New York State for freshman year, and then he went to school in Freiburg, in Maine for sophomore year. He then went to a day school in New York for the next three years, and graduated from high school there, commuted from home.

Do you recall the name of the school in New York?

The Stevenson school.

Do you know the full name?

Robert Louis Stevenson school.

Is that a school for emotionally disturbed youngsters?

I object to the leading nature.

I will allow it.

It was a school for students who are not doing their best in school, for whatever emotional reasons or simply educational reasons, lack of confidence, mainly.

And was a you are feeling that Stephen had a learning disability?

He had problems with English courses, courses dealing with verbal things. He did better in mathematics, that sort of thing.

In other words, he had difficulty with courses?

Expressing himself, and felt ill at ease that way.

Was your feeling as his mother that these difficulties were emotionally based?

Your Honor—

Sustain the objection. You are leading the witness, sir.

Why did you send him to the Robert Louis Stevenson school?

He wanted to go there. A friend of his, the roommate, the brother of his roommate at storm King was going there, and he told him about it, and he wrote for a catalog and told us he would like to very much, go.

And to your knowledge did any of the members of that school ever contact you with respect to Stephen having any problem?

The policy of the school was to deal—

Your Honor, I will object to that. I believe that's hearsay.

I will allow the question. The answer to proceed— go ahead. She is not answering what they were told, she is answering whether she was contacted. Go ahead, Mrs. Moore.

The school had a policy of dealing directly with the students. They did not want to contact the parents. You went for an interview before the student was accepted and after that they did not want you to visit the school until graduation.

I see. And did there come a time when anyone did contact you concerning Stephen school problems?

We heard from Mr. Douglas, who was a psychologist, the students that vent there were referred to psychologist who discussed with them any school problems that they might have, and then one would hear from them. You were not encouraged to meet them, because they felt the student would talk to them more freely to the person if they did not feel what they said was being repeated to the parents.

And do you know the full name of Mr. Douglas, by the way?

Just Peter Douglas. That's all I know

And Mr. Douglas contacted you concerning Stephen?

A few times, yes.

Did he ever discuss Stephen's problems with you, if any?

What I remember mainly, he said that he seemed to have a lot–

I object, Your Honor.

I sustain the objection, what Mr. Douglas said. Put the next question.

Now, Mrs. Moore, I'm going to ask you another question, let me ask you this, and all the time that Stephen has been your son has he been gainfully employed?

Yes. Ever since he was 15 or 16 he has worked and earned all his own spending money.

Did he ever receive any money from you and your husband?

He received funds for his education, but he earned his own spending money for his own needs, and when he was very interested in working on cars and earned all his money to buy the car parts and whatever he wanted for that.

On the average, how many jobs did Stephen ever holds at one time? If you can remember.

He occasionally held two jobs at once, one day time, one working evening hours. He worked long hours, always.

So that aside from education funds, he never received any money, spending money, or anything, from you and your husband?

No. He was going to school in New York, he worked as a messenger, for the post office, worked for a direct mailing company, the kind that gets list of people who send out mail, and he worked for them one summer.

So he worked for all his own money?

Yes.

Did he have a trust fund of any type?

There was one that was to help with his education it was set up because a relative had lost both of his sons. They both died while they were single, so he had no descendants and he was set up not just for Stephen but for other great nieces and nephews, simply because of the tragedy in his own family.

So, in other words, you are saying it was an education fund?

Yes. Basically to help with that.

And aside from that fund for education, and aside from whatever fund you and your husband gave Stephen for education, he earned most of his own money?

Yes. Here and all his own spending money. He did not ask for money.

What type of boy has Stephen been for most of his life?

Your Honor, I'm going to object to the vague nature.

I will allow it.

He has been hard-working. He has been helpful and generous to friends.

Would you say that Stephen was a violent person?

No. We never saw any evidence of this. I never heard of any evidence of it, either.

Now did there come a time when you began to notice something significant about Stephen was changing?

We noticed around March that he apparently was now working anymore. He had had his own business for the last three or four years, and he spoke about perhaps giving that up, perhaps going back to school. He did not seem too busy, as he had always been before, which concerned us, because it was a change from the way he had behaved before. He also seemed somewhat depressed and quiet. He would simply sit without saying anything, which was very unusual for him.

How long would you sit and not say anything? Can you recall an instance where that happened?

In May. Early in May he came by to leave some things in our garage, a few tools, some of his old tools, if your car parts, and I was in the back yard raking leaves, and he just got out of his truck that he had his things and, and he just sat on the back steps and just sort of stared, and ordinarily he would have, if he had seen I was doing something, he would've offered to help, and he just sat there, which bothered me, and so I finally said, well, Steve, maybe you could help me rake a little bit, and he said all right and so he got up and rates for a few minutes, and I went on inside, and I looked out, and he had gone back to just sitting on the steps again, and he just seemed to sit there and stare, which I'd never seen him do before. Because usually even if the neighbors were outside and he saw the lady getting out of her car with groceries, he would run over to help her take them in the house, and this was just most unusual for him to behave like this so finally I said well if you have things in the trunk that you want to unload, I think you better get them out before it gets to be evening, so then he did and he got the things out of the trunk.

How long of the. Would you say he was sitting and staring if you can recall?

Well, it was an hour and a half or something like that. I had never seen him like this before.

For an hour and a half he sat there and just stared into space?

Well, he just looked at the ground.

He had never done that before to your knowledge?

I don't remember his having done that before.

So that you began to notice a change, then from February or March on in Stephen, he had given up his business or whatever jobs he had?

Yes, he had, and sold his equipment that he had. And then he said that he wanted, that he thought he would travel and see something of the country that he had not seen. He had been working steadily for the last for five years without really taking much of a vacation, as far as we knew.

Did you regard that is unusual, that your son should suddenly pick up and want to travel?

No. The fact that–

I will object.

I will allow it. Go ahead

Well, he spoke in terms of travel for a few weeks and then come back. I did not see anything unusual about that.

Did you hear from him?

Well the thing that was strange, he came by, it was Mother's Day, brought something, and then he said he would be back in a few days, and we heard nothing more from him until I think it was about two weeks later, and he called and I said, well, where are you Steve? And he said that he was out west, that he had gotten a real pass and that he was traveling on that you can go anywhere you want for a certain period of time, and I said, well, will you be back in a few weeks? And he said yes, he would, so then we heard nothing more until about two weeks later. He called and he said that he had run out of money, and I said well what about Eurail pass, and he said it expired and he couldn't use that anymore, and I said well where are you, and he said you really don't want to know? And I said yes, that I really would need to know in order to send him any money, and he said well, he was in Montana, and I said well I will try to get in touch with Western Union and find out how I can send you money.

But this was the Memorial Day weekend, it was Saturday afternoon, and I said I don't know what places will be open, but I said what is your number? And I found out and he said I will call you back in a little while and I said well it may take me a few minutes I will have to call and find out where we could go to, I knew the Montclair Western Union office was closed, and I said I would have to find out where we could send his money, so I waited there in the house, this was maybe 4 o'clock or so Saturday afternoon and we waited all afternoon and evening, and I heard nothing more from him, which concerned me but I thought well perhaps he found some kind of temporary job in order to earn a little bit, because he never called asking for money before. This was very unusual.

This was the first time he had called asking for money?

Yes. And he had been in Montana when he was about 15. He had gone out with a couple of friends, and a new he knew the area.

But surprised you he was calling from all these places?

Yes, it did, and he didn't- I never-I heard nothing more from him until about a week later. He came back home and he looked all worn out, and I said," did you hitchhike"? And he said yes, and he seemed to be exhausted, and he went to the shower and went to sleep.

And he came back, did he still look moody and depressed to you?

Yes, he-

Your Honor, I don't recall the witness ever saying that. That's a leading question formulating an answer.

I am inclined to agree.

I am sorry. I will withdraw the question, Your Honor.

Would you please tell me how he looked when he came back, Mrs. Moore?

He looked exhausted. His eyes were bloodshot and he looked- I never seen him look really that worn out. He slept until the next day. Then- he left his motorcycle in our garage, and he spent the afternoon working on his motorcycle, because he wanted to travel more, and take that with him. This was his main reason, I gathered, that he had come home, was to get the motorcycle, which had been broken, and that's why he couldn't take it when he left before.

All right. Did you ever know of Stephens – whether he had any girlfriends?

Very little about girlfriends. He had never volunteered much, and I didn't ask.

Calling your attention to around February or March of this year, did he happened to mention a particular girlfriend to you at any time?

Not that early, no.

When if at all did he mention it to you?

Later. Perhaps the end of April, early in May, he mentioned he had a girlfriend.

What was the name?

He just mentioned Donna. That's all. He didn't mention any other name.

Just Donna. Now did he ever have any conversations with you concerning this Donna?

The only time was when he- this was early in May, also. He came in and seemed quiet. He said," my girlfriend thinks I am crazy," and this seemed a strange thing for him to say, and he said"I feel as if I had a devil inside me that made me say things because I don't want to say things that would hurt people," and that's all he said, but it seemed a strange thing for him to say.

He mentioned the word devil inside him?

Yes. He said he felt as though he had a devil inside him, that was making him say things.

How did he appear when he said that to you, if you can—

He seemed depressed. He sat down and just sort of, he didn't want to say any more than that.

In other words, now was all of this behavior that you described consistent to what you knew to be your son's behavior in the past?

No, because he had been busy. We really hadn't seen him that much because he worked such long hours, and he had never talked like this before about anybody.

Did Stephen ever mention to you whether anyone was after him?

He said that he had had a car accident in Newark, and he thought that this was, that somebody had deliberately tried to run into him. He also said that there had been an accident in the junkyard where he had worked, some equipment there had been an accident with some equipment and he thought perhaps this was not an accident way it had seemed to be, maybe somebody had made a fall or something. I didn't really understand too much about that.

When he discussed that, did he have any appearance of fear on his face to your knowledge?

I'm going to object.

I am inclined to sustain the objection. You are suggesting answers.

All right, Your Honor. I am sorry. I will withdraw that question.

Mrs. Moore, did Stephen ever express any fear for his life to you?

I don't remember that he expressed fear.

Did you ever receive any correspondence from Stephen that might lead you to believe that he was in fear of his life? We had a letter from him saying what he would like in case something happened to him, he would like any funds that he might have two go to his sisters, and any tools or any car equipment to go to the O'Dell brothers, the three O'Dell Brothers.

By the way, was your husband, being Dr. Moore, was he being blackmailed?

Oh, no. No. There would be no reason for that.

Did you ever know Stephen to be in trouble with the police?

No. I think when he was 13 or 14 he turned in a false fire alarm with two or three boys. That's all I know about.

Other than that, you never knew him to be a robber, did you?

Oh, no. No.

Your Honor, I object. I'm going to asked to come to sidebar.

I would like to ask this be marked.

Certainly, let me have it.

And the contents.

D - 103 for identification, letter and envelope.

The following took place at the sidebar

Prosecutor?

I would like to see the original before we comment, but I believe this is a copy of—

I showed him the original this morning.

Go ahead.

I was given this this morning, in violation of the discovery rules. I knew nothing about it. I was not apprised of its existence until this morning. I'm going to ask it be excluded.

If I may reply to that, Your Honor, I knew nothing about the existence— I was not provided myself all of the discovery.

Oh, no, no. Let's talk about this.

Wait a minute.

Mr. Schutzer, let's limit ourselves to the objection the state is making. That's all I want to hear. Go ahead.

I did not receive this until this week.

What day this week?

When I spoke with Mrs. Moore this last week.

And you have had it in your possession or that time?

No, Your Honor, I did not anticipate calling Mrs. Moore?

When did you have this letter in your possession?

This week, Your Honor.

Yesterday. What time? Last night.

My problem is the fact that now the state is attempting to turn against me the same thing I've been attempting to do against them. Your Honor I didn't receive— I had a discovery request out since August, to see the clothing of the deceased, the knife, the lab report concerning all of the materials in the possession of the prosecutor's office; I didn't receive the report from the lab yesterday until I was in court. Now, when I received that report I did not make objection to it because I received it only yesterday. I read it, and looked through it. I did not object to it. With respect to the clothing which I asked to see, with respect to the knife I requested to see, I had no objection, it was provided to me; I had an opportunity to see it, an opportunity to view it, making objection during that period of time. I felt there was nothing to bar its exclusion by the state. You will note, your honor, that the exclusion, that the reason for the motion to exclude it have nothing to do that I only received those things where knowledge receipt of them the other day. The prosecutor suddenly said he didn't see it. He had an opportunity to read it, he had an opportunity to go through it, and he had an opportunity to do anything. It is not that long of a letter. I'm sure the prosecutor is capable of reading and understanding the circumstances, Your Honor, I think it's perfectly admissible.

Prosecutor, why are you prejudiced by reason of the fact that you just received it today?

Your Honor, I have no opportunity to inquire into the method that this might have been transmitted. It's got a postmark may second. I just see it now. There is a wealth of evidence in this case. There were cards, envelopes…

How are you prejudiced by this fact that you just saw this today?

Well sir how I my prejudiced I have not had the opportunity to prepare myself in any way.

You will have Friday, Saturday and Sunday to do so. Your objection is overruled.

End of sidebar discussion.

Mrs. Moore, I'm going to show you what has been marked D - 103 for identification, am I going to ask you if you recognize this.

Yes.

And can you tell me what it is?

Well it's a letter saying that if anything happened to him that I leave all my possessions to my two sisters, tools should go to Jeff and Rodney O'Dell.

And when did you receive this letter Mrs. Moore?

It was early in May. It was postmarked 7 May, from the Newark.

Did that letter strike you as unusual?

Yes, it upset me very much. I didn't expect anything like that when I opened the envelope.

what was your reaction to that letter?

I thought that he must feel perhaps he was in danger of some kind.

Your Honor, I'm going to object to the impression.

I sustain the objection to the reaction of Mrs. Moore. Put the next question.

Do you recognize the handwriting?

Yes.

Who's is it?

Stephen's.

Is that his signature?

Yes. His handwriting on his signature.

The handwriting on the envelope, whose is that?

His, also.

Did this letter come in the mail?

Yes, he came in the mail.

And what address it come to?

Our address in Montclair.

Is the address on the envelope your address to Montclair?

Yes.

Your Honor, I'm going to ask this be admitted into evidence.

Did Stephen ever indicate to you whether he wanted to marry his present girlfriend?

No, he did not.

Did Stephen ever indicate to you that he was angry with his present girlfriend?

No.

Your Honor, the questions are very leading impressions. I have no objection but- picking and trying to guide the witness into a position I object to...

I am inclined to agree with counsel. Why don't you ask her what Mr. Moore said to his mother without suggesting?

Aside from what you already testified to did your son ever speak about his present girlfriend, Donna, to you in any other-

No.

On any other occasions?

No.

Have you ever known your son to be aggressive?

No. Just the usual amount of any boy who wants to work and-

Have you ever known him to fight with anybody?

No. I had never seen him fight with anybody.

I will object.

I will allow it.

Have you ever known him to use a knife or a gun?

Oh, oh—

I will object to this, Your Honor.

No.

I will allow it.

Have you ever seen him lose his temper?

Not really. Nothing serious at all.

Everybody has arguments, I guess, but I never saw him really lose his temper.

The last time— was it the last time you heard from Steve when he sent you that letter saying he thought something might happen to him?

No, because we had had the phone conversations I mentioned in May, then he came back early in June. It was the first week and in June that he came back a week after. As I said, he called from Montana, and said that he needed money, but apparently hitchhiked home.

In the next time you heard from Steve was when?

Well, he had left with the motorcycle the Monday of the first weekend in June. He called a week later, and I asked him whether he was at the shore he said no, that he was on the other side, and I said where do you mean, and he said California.

Mrs. Moore, based upon your opportunities to observe your son and listen to him and talk to him, during the last couple of months before July of this year, did it seem to your son, did it seem to you like your son was on the run?

I object to the leading nature of the question.

I will sustain the objection.

Did it seem to you that your son might be afraid of something?

I object again to the leading nature of the question.

I think this is repetitious. I will sustain the objection.

I will withdraw it. I have no further questions. Thank you very much, Mrs. Moore.

Does the prosecutor have any questions?

Yes, Your Honor.

Cross-examination by Mr. Mautone

Mrs. Moore, he went to the Robert Louis Stevenson school simply for education reasons?

Yes.

He was having difficulties in English and that type of subject?

Yes. Aha. Huh

And it was his idea to go there?

Yes; we had never heard of the school. A friend of his told him about it.

A friend of his had gone, and he wanted to go with this friend?

Yes.

Now, this trust fund you indicated was set up just for his education; did it ends after his education ended, or is it still continuing?

No. It would continue.

So he is receiving income from the trust fund?

Yes. It is not a great amount, and he had always worked to earn his own funds.

What is the amount?

I'm going to asked the prosecutor if he will allow the witness to finish her answer.

Mrs. Moore, had you finished your answer?

I am sorry if I interrupted.

You asked the amount of it?

Yes.

It's between $3,000 and $4,000 a year.

For how many years has this been going on?

For how many years had he received the $3,000 or $4,000 a year?

It had been for perhaps seven or eight years. It was to be used for education.

When was the last year he went to school?

I imagine around 19- I'm trying to think. He finished at Stevenson in 1969. He went to Franklin Institute for a year after that. That would've been around 1970, 1971 I would imagine.

For at least five years he had been working very industriously?

That's right. He has had his own trucking business.

His own business?

Yes.

Receiving the money from the trust fund?

That's right.

Know when he came to visit you or when he came to visit you in May, what were you doing?

I was raking leaves in the backyard.

And he just sat and watched you raking leaves?

Yes; which was unusual because ordinarily he would've helped me.

In the month of May you were raking leaves?

The backyard. The front yard we do in the fall, but this is just in the back. I was clearing up what I had not gone around to doing the last fall. That's all.

And he indicated to you I believe you said on direct that he had been working very hard for years and then maybe he would like to take a trip around the country?

Yes.

You didn't see anything unusual in that, did you?

No, I did not.

And when did he leave on this trip?

He left in early May.

And he took the train?

Yes. He started out on the train. Then he started flying.

And the motorcycle was left in your garage? Yes, because there was something wrong with it, apparently.

When did he lay the motorcycle up in your garage?

Early in May I imagine, before he left. He left on the last time I'd seen him, he came by on Mother's Day, and–

Do you remember the date?

It was at that Sunday, whatever mothers– the eighth or ninth, something like that, of May.

You said in the early part of May 1976 he was in New Jersey?

Yes.

No, I believe you are asked did he tell you much about his girlfriends, and you said he never talked much about anything.

I said he had not talked about his girlfriends.

He never told you much about his girlfriends at all?

No. And I did not ask.

Did you speak to anyone from the defense before coming here and testifying, Mrs. Moore?

From the defense?

Did you talk to Mr. Schutzer or any of his representatives?

Mr. Schutzer, yes.

Did you speak to Dr. Latimer?

Yes.

Do you love your son, Mrs. Moore?

Of course.

I'm going to object to that question.

How are you objecting to that?

I don't see how that's relevant.

I will allow it.

I think the prosecutor is trying to infer something that's not so.

I will allow it. Anything else, Mr. prosecutor?

No.

Mr. Schutzer?

Yes, Your Honor

Mrs. Moore, with respect to the trust fund, I think you indicated that you can correct me if I am wrong, was that fun entirely for Stephen?

Oh, no.

Out of that three to $4000, who else had access to the fund? No one would have had.

No one would have had access to it?

No.

It was a trust fund?

It was a trust fund. It was set up to help with education of great nieces and nephews of the person who set it up, because his one son drowned and the other was killed in a plane crash.

The other nieces and nephews, how many did they number?

I object.

Sustain the objection.

Did your son have an apartment, Mrs. Moore?

Yes.

Where was that?

In Bloomfield.

At what address if you recall?

On Grove Street. He had it for five years.

He had it for five years. Did there come a time when to your knowledge he gave it up?

He gave it up in May.

In May of this year?

Yes.

And do you recall whether Stephen ever told his father that someone was after him? Were you ever present during those conversations?

No.

Did Stephen ever indicate to you whether he wished to hurt anybody?

I object, Your Honor.

I sustain the objection.

I have no further questions.

Mr. prosecutor?

No further questions.

Thank you, Mrs. Moore. Watch your step getting down.

Closing Statements

Good morning ladies and gentlemen. First of all, I want to thank you all are sitting on this case and being jurors. I know that you all were summoned here is jurors. The point is you gave the case your attention, you gave the case your unbiased attention, gave of your time, came away from your homes, your families and your jobs.

Most importantly is being here to give Stephen Moore his day in court, and that's important.

Mr. Schutzer, if you would like to begin.

Thank you, Your Honor.

Ladies and gentlemen the crime is murder, is no denying the crime is murder.

Where's the body? Where's the proof? How can you say it's murder case? Mr. Moore please refrain from speaking.

Because the penalty is great in the crime the most serious crime penal system, there is the greatest need for you people to be very, very cautious in assessing, in weighing all of the evidence in this case. As I indicated to you at the onset, we are not going to deny Stephen Moore was present at the scene of the crime. Now ladies and gentlemen, we are not going to deny Stephen Moore kill Donna Litchfield. The point is that murder in terms of the way the law defines murder in our society is not what Stephen

Moore committed. He killed Donna Litchfield, he didn't murder her.

Murder is the unlawful taking of a life without justifiable excuse, without any mitigating circumstances, premeditation, and as I indicated to you at the onset ladies and gentlemen, that means that there has to be more than just a simple physical act of committing murder or any other crime. There has to be the mental element, there has to be, the evil doing hands, the knife going into Donna Litchfield's body, and the evil meaning mind. In this case there was an excuse, there was justification which the law recognizes in which the judge will charge, and the judge will charge you as to the law and accept the law.

We all feel pretty outraged I think, about what happens to Donna Litchfield. I think you people look at these pictures and I hesitate to look at them if you look at the pictures and imagine the agony and suffering which Donna Litchfield went through, I think you can along with me the revulsion that you feel when you look at the pictures, and when you think about what one can do to another.

The ladies and gentlemen, is this the work of somebody who knew what he was doing? When you look at these pictures, you sit there and say, "He killed her like any hitman." He killed her, sure. She rejected him, so he killed her. No, ladies and gentlemen you look at these pictures, and you think kind of madman would stab a girl 69 times, what kinds of energy had to be built up in a person, what kind of a frenzy that a person have to be able to go in were able to do that?

How do you know she was stabbed 69 times? Mr. Moore, please refrain from speaking.

The answer, ladies and gentlemen, from within Stephen Moore himself. Usually, as I indicated to you at the onset, if you get a disease and the disease comes from without in most cases, a germ a splinter, a tumor, anything like that, which is easily manifested. You can take an x-ray or blood test or something like that, but in this case which Stephen Moore suffered from was not something from without. The disease was Stephen Moore. This was part of his very makeup. The disease was in his mind as much as we might like to sit here and say, well, I diagnosed this or I diagnosed that, we can't to a certainty.

Ladies and gentlemen, there are certain ways that we can diagnose disease, and I think it's obvious at this point with the amount of evidence, the type of evidence here, the ways of examining a person to determine the existence of a mental disease such as his will to his ability to rationally and premeditatedly plan a crime, are present. We have objective psychological test, we have the subjective analysis of doctors, psychiatrists.

Now you have seen them all, you have had an opportunity to look at them. Say one thing, ladies and gentlemen, and I don't really want to dignify it by saying too much about it, there was some talk in this case, and some testimony in this case, some attempts in this case on the part of the State to place in question the conduct of myself; the conduct of Dr. Latimer,

I'm going to object at this point; I normally would not t object during the summation, but the testimony came from the defense witnesses, there was nothing the State did to elicit it except asked the question.

I will allow the comment. You may rebut in your closing argument.

There was the money from whatever source, and I believe one of the witnesses only ageist witness but also a state's witness at one time. There was testimony concerning the conduct of either myself or Dr. Latimer. Now ladies and gentlemen, I'm going to ask for one thing about that. My conduct is not at issue here, Dr. Latimer's conduct is not at issue here. The judge's conduct, Mr. Mautone's conduct, with due respect, is not an issue here the conduct of my client, Stephen Moore, is at issue here.

Mr. Moore is on trial, no one else. There is an old saying when you have a weak case, where you have no facts that you hammer personalities, and ladies and gentlemen, when you are a grasping at straws, that's what you do.

I ask you to consider the conduct of the issue, the only issue indicate is whether Stephen Moore given the legal definition of murder in this state, and given the legal excuse and the definitions as described to that of insanity in this state, is responsible legally for having killed Donna Litchfield.

Again, there is no question physically the committed, but if somebody injects some sort of serum into my arm and I can't control myself, and in a spasm I go and I strike one of you with a knife in my hand and I just happen to have a knife in my, it was something I couldn't control, it was something that made me, I committed the physical act, I may have even killed one of you if I have the knife in my hand, and it suddenly goes awry.

The mere fact that I kill you is not murder. There is an additional factor. Did I intend to kill you?

Did I premeditate and plan to kill you? Did I have control over my actions? Did I have control over my mind, and my body, as you and I as normal people do, and I say to you that Stephen Moore did not.

Ladies and gentlemen, the judge is going you that you are the sole judges of the facts in this case. The facts are very clear, despite all of the attempts to cloud the issues, and throw in red herrings, despite all of the attempts at obscuring everything from the major issue in this case, I think he can be very, very clear to you people the type of disease that Mr. Moore was laboring under at the time he killed Donna Litchfield.

Mr. Mautone at the beginning of this case indicated to you that you had to be fair to the State as well as the defense, and I ask that you be fair to the State, I ask that you consider your civic duty, you to look at the facts. I ask you to look at the credible evidence. It was said in the opening statement is not the greater number of witnesses who testify here, it is whether you believe them, whether they are credible.

You people are going to determine credibility of the witnesses. You are going to determine the weight to be given to the evidence that has been admitted into this case, and you are ultimately going to determine whether Stephen Moore's conduct was something he could control or something he could not control.

You are going to determine whether Stephen Moore knew that he was doing something that was not right or he did not know he was not doing something right. The evidence is long, it's lengthy, it's a long trial. I don't want to go into a great deal of it, as I think it would consume a lot more time than is necessary. People are not stupid. You can see when someone is insane. You can see when issues are being clouded. So what about the testimony?

The major thing I think I would like to ask you to do, remember that appearances are very deceiving. The State contends that Mr. Moore was sane, rational, intended to commit the murder of Donna Litchfield.

The state contends the Mr. Moore knew the Nature and quality of his acts. That was brought out a great deal. The other part of the standard is whether he knew what he was doing was right or wrong. Now ladies and gentlemen, I am going to be a member of an army, and I am going to be told as part of my mission to go into enemy territory, this is information given to me now which I have in my mind, and I am told to blow up a bridge, then when I'm finished blowing up the bridge, and that acts in is not an immoral thing. The act in and of itself is wrong to do in peace. But in my mind I know it's war time, and in my mind I know I am told to do my duty, it's right to blow up the bridge, so I blow up the bridge. And what do I do, stick around, we to get shot by the enemy? I may run, I may walk, but I get out of there and my getting out of there doesn't make what I did any less right in my mind.

Stephen Moore labored under delusions, and false premises. The evidence is very clear that Mr. Moore misconceived reality. Now if Mr. Moore was capable in the illegal definition of insanity being able to distinguish between what was right and what was wrong, if Mr. Moore was as sane at the state contends he was, why then did not the state present one single solitary witness on rebuttal to refute the proof that the defense offered that Mr. Moore was not insane, was not sane.

Who are the witnesses that the state put on to show that Mr. Moore was saying at the time of the crime?

How do you know there was a crime, Schutzer? Mr. Moore please refrain from speaking.

Joan Campbell, a girl probably never had any experience with the police who admits that when she gave the statement the words were not all hers. She saw a white male walking. It aroused her suspicions. Are these the ordinary terms of a 16-year-old girl? And what did she see? She saw a wet man walking fast out of the house, head down, getting into a car and driving away.

Mary Ann Norton, the bank teller, never met Stephen Moore before, probably sees hundreds of people a day in the course of her business, and when questioned as to whether she could tell whether Mr. Moore looked normal or abnormal she said he looked fine to me.

Sgt. Strain from the Surf City police, who said, he appeared normal, I spent 3 ½ hours within. How can Sgt. Strain as a short-term observer of Mr. Moore, make a diagnosis as to whether this man was suffering from any kind of a disease? He could have been suffering from syphilis and it might not have showed, unless you pulled his pants down.

That's my point, ladies and gentlemen. I indicated to you at the outset we are going to try to show you that something beyond the tip of the iceberg. The state has consistently throughout this case attempted to keep you about the water line, has attempted consistently to show you just the tip of the iceberg. The state didn't present anybody that went below the surface. The one witness the state presented, the one witness who could determine the issue is Sanity, Dr. Kern. With due respect to Dr. Kern, he is a fine gentleman, excellent doctor, for whom I have the greatest respect. Dr. Kern didn't know Stephen Moore prior to the day he examined, and he examined him three months after the crime, three months.

Dr. Latimer saw Stephen three days after the crime. Dr. Schlesinger less than a week after the commission of the crime. Now we are told, was very important to know the facts surrounding the crime in order to make a diagnosis. That simply isn't true. The object here was to get an objective examination. Dr. Latimer used sound medical procedure, he used what he was trained to do, the method he was trained to use, get history.

Did the state present to you one witness who knew Stephen Moore for more than a fleeting moment, who said to you he appeared normal? He was normal, he acted normal, I know 10 years ago as he always acted normal.

Did the state sat that?

I object.

I will sustain the objection.

It is not the state's burden.

Continue on the facts of the case, Mr. Schutzer.

One word about that, ladies and gentlemen. I apologize for my overzealousness in this case. As I indicated to you before, the crime is murder. With due respect to Mr. Mautone, the tensions in this case have run very, very high. He has been edgy and I have been edgy, but ladies and gentlemen, I ask you not to consider the actions of either one of us, I ask you not to consider the judge's actions. These are things we do because we are lawyers, judges, because we are trained to do that. We have certain obligations as lawyers, certain rules of evidence we must comply with. Don't hold it against the state's case, don't hold it against the defense because of the overzealousness of the Council. This is our job.

The most telling testimony in this case, was that Dr. Kern, the state psychiatrist who admits on cross examination that a psychosis or evidence of psychosis once established is presumed to continue, that an underlying illness is presumed to continue. He had evidence of underlying psychosis. He had evidence that Stephen was delusional. He had evidence that he really didn't know reality half of the time, evidence from friends reports that were furnished to him from schools, and friends who knew him for years.

Let me digress for a moment. Valerie Iacobacci was the one witness the state presented who knew Stephen Moore a reasonably greater period of time than the other witnesses who testified. The problem I have with Valerie was not that I couldn't understand her situation, I think any of us feel bitter after having seen our best friend murdered. That's the point. When she testified on direct examination she was very upset, very tearful, very cooperative, when asked questions, and I think again, you are recollection governs, not mine, but if you recall, and I ask you to consider that when I cross examines her the tears disappeared. She seemed a little bit more strong, she seems to be almost belligerent. Did it seem that way to you?

Again, no one blames her. Frankly it strains credibility and defies logic to assume that anyone confronted with a situation that poor Valerie was confronted with, when Stephen Moore opened that door, and she saw the legs of that girl hanging over the tub, it's inconceivable to imagine that her fear didn't overshadow her eyesight so damn much that she literally didn't know what she saw when she looked at Stephen Moore's face, and when was the last time she saw him? He had been traveling. She said, I was half afraid, I was a little afraid when I opened the door. Later on I was hysterical when I made the call.

Ask yourselves, ladies and gentlemen, ask yourselves if you are Valerie and the door opened and you saw what she saw would you be able to Stephen looked normal, he appeared normal, he appeared as he always did. I would be running for my life, and that's what she did, I wouldn't look to carefully behind me, either.

So getting back to Dr. Kern, the one witness who is able to make a reasonably coherent evaluation as to whether Stephen Moore was saying were not insane. His testimony is perhaps the most significant, maybe more significant than Dr. Latimer. He admits by virtue of accepted authority that once evidence of psychosis is established it continues. There may be appearance of remission, the periods of remission are not returns to normalcy, the periods of remission are maybe a lessening of symptoms, so that they are not readily apparent to people who observe as short-term, but he admits it continues. He admits with all the materials that were submitted to him by the state, by the defense, with all the statements of the O'Dells, Billy Miller, Brian McWalters, on and on, he admits that these definitely show evidence of psychosis, of an underlying illness.

He says that he agrees with Dr. Latimers's conclusion on July 17, he agrees with Dr.Schlesinger's conclusions on July 25, and makes the same conclusions when he sees him on October 17, so we have three points, point a, point b and point C.

Point A- is as much as a year before this incident, when the defense documented evidence of the normalcy, evidence of psychosis. Now is presumed to continue, and then comes points B, the time of the murder, July 14, 1976, all of a sudden Stephen Moore's delusions subside to the point where he becomes capable of distinguishing between right and wrong. All of a sudden the illness which the doctors described as being severe when he saw him, all of a sudden they on this seems to subside to the point where he appears so rational, so lucid, that he stabbed a girl 69 times, and even taking Dr. Roy's testimony, what kind of energy does it take to stab a person one time with a knife like you saw? What type of energy?

Then you come to point C. Point C one now., he is very psychotic. Paranoid schizophrenia, the whole thing, so the state asks you to believe Stephen Moore was characterized by a sanity sandwich.

Point A, evidence of psychosis, Point B, no evidence of psychosis, kills girlfriend, 69 times with a knife, Point C, returns to psychosis again. The lucid interval, the sane interval was in the middle like a sandwich. The state asks you to believe that. Mr. Mautone said it. Use your common sense. Use your logic. Use your everyday experiences. You have seen Mr. Moore sitting in court day after day. Now, ladies and gentlemen, there was ample testimony to the fact that Mr. Moore has never to the knowledge of the doctors who examined him, and they are all in agreement, he has never faked his condition. He has never faked his madness.

Dr. Douglas, who upon examination testifies that as far back as 10 or 12 years ago, when the kid was an adolescent, he was already exhibiting a character disorder which the Dr., Mr. Douglas, characterized as a walking time bomb. He was unable to express his emotions. You are not dealing with a kid who was violent, a kid who you would expect anything, and if he was rejected by his girlfriend, who said, I don't want to see you anymore, he would stab **her**. You are not dealing with that type of person. You are not dealing with that at all. You are dealing with the kind of a kid who was, as Mr. Miller described him, a beautiful person, nonviolent, broke up fights, did things for other people, was very generous. Even Mr. Douglas who saw him as much as 10 years ago, who saw him as a walking time bomb, said this is not the kind of kid he expected to work out frustrations, anxieties, in a violent manner, but he said it might come spilling out that way one day.

Now if you get the testimony of all these people, all these people who say that this kid was nonviolent, he was not that kind of a kid who would do this kind of thing, and he stabbed his girlfriend 69 times, something is wrong somewhere in the interim between the time Mr. Douglas saw him and the doctors of this case saw him, something happened. Maybe we will never know what, the science of psychiatry being an inexact science. We may never be able to determine for sure what caused this.

One thing is for sure, that to a high degree of medical certainty and even despite the denials of Dr. Kern, this man was insane. He was not able to distinguish between right and wrong, he was not able to say like you and I that if I kill Valerie, or if I kill Donna, or if I kill Jeff O'Dell's wife, where if I kill anybody that it's wrong to do so, because in my mind it's right, and why is that right?

This killing started some time Stephen Moore's past. What happened? There are normal people who have childhoods in which they are rejected, there are normal people who have rich parents who don't give them much love and attention. Something, though, somehow happens to an abnormal degree, which made this kid so damned frustrated that these feelings of rejection smoldered in him. There was no way he could let it out in a violent manner, because he wasn't that type of kid, so he went on for years and years. At some point he may have developed an interest in the occult. He saw that there were books, books taken from his home, E.S.P., Evil, Journeys Outside the mind. Take those books, and the preoccupation which

Mr. Moore may have had that type of subject, take that and fit it into the paranoid delusional system, which was described to you, in which you will have with you in the jury room as a drawing. Take that and it into the general scheme of Mr. Moore's delusions, the delusions that they, somebody, Donna, was after him.

First it was Momma, then the C.I.A., and then the F.B.I, later on it was the mob, the Mafia, and eventually it was Donna. Again, I'm not saying it was right Mr. Moore killed. What I am is that in his mind it was justified and in the eyes of the law as the judge will charge it to you it was justified. He looked upon Donna for some unknown reason as a threat to his masculinity, as a threat to his being, as a threat to his existence as a man, as a human being, as a person.

We don't really know what happened July 14, 1976, but re-live, if you will, which may, what might have gone on his mind. The kids feel that people are after him. Afraid of being bugged, of being heard. He writes notes between people so no one will hear. He gets a number from a friend so that he can make sure his phone is not being tapped, he is constantly traveling all over the country. Says that he to escape someone or something and then Donna rejects him. Donna may very well have thought he was crazy, so she rejects. The stress and that rejection, there is testimony Stephen Moore loved Donna, stress from that rejection may have been so take that it made the delusions which he already had maybe worse. He thought Donna was bewitching him, trying control his mind, trying to control his thoughts. He may have gone into the bathroom and we will never know what happened.

We can say with some fair degree of probability whatever Donna may have done, whatever, how little, it may have been nothing more than picking up a bar of soap, but to Stephen Moore, with his mind in that delusional state, Donna was something else, thinking she was in imposter, thinking she was a witch, someone who was going to kill him, he went into a panic. In most cases when we go into a panic the adrenaline in our bodies goes crazy. Mother have been known to pick up cars when their babies were trapped underneath. The energy generated by that panic created a frenzy so powerful it resulted in the act that we have before us, resulted in the killing of Donna Litchfield, and it was uncontroverted in this case. The killing was brutal.

Killing in war is something society sanctions. Killing is often brutal, too. How many times have the bodies come home mangled, how many times have men come back in basket? How many times have men done things to each other, human beings done things to each other that are unspeakable because they thought they were doing what was right. It is no different than what Stephen Moore thought. He was in a war. To him he thought he was in a war, when he responded to Dr. Latimer questions about whether it was all right to kill. He said, yes, it would be all right in a war. He was in a war. He was in a war against those people who were after him to kill him. To Stephen Moore, not to you or I, Stephen Moore, and in the eyes of the law Stephen Moore killed out of self-defense, psychological self-defense. He was so distorted in his mind as not to be able to appreciate the difference between what was right and what was wrong, and there was testimony that a person could go into remission and he can become more acute, but one thing that was undisputed was that stress in almost all instances would bring on the acute paranoid episode.

It's undisputed that the stress, as Dr. Kern testified would very well result in one of two ways of reacting to it. A person who perceives themselves as the victim, the person who perceives himself as cornered, would attack, and the attack might very well be with a great deal of rage. This is an awful lot to try to comprehend, and a lot of psychological testimony. I don't think the lawyers or law students get as much education in the law of psychiatry, the field of psychiatry and laws you people have. I ask that you bring whatever knowledge you have learned in this courtroom, both from the state psychiatrist and from the defense psychiatrist, into the jury room with you and apply it to the facts as you have seen, apply it to the evidence which was presented.

A person is presumed sane unless in past history it is presented to show him not saying. It is not an oversimplification. I ask you to weigh the evidence very carefully, remembering the crime of murder carries the most serious penalty in our society. Now unfortunately, or fortunately as the case may be, I had the disadvantage of speaking to you first. Mr. Mautone under the procedural rules of our system, has what I consider to be the advantage of speaking to you last. When he says is going to be fresher in your minds. What he says is going to be able to rebut a great deal of what I say. It's going to sound reasonable and logical to you. He is going to raise a great many points, will raise doubts in your mind as to what I'm saying to you now, you are not stupid, and I ask you not to allow yourselves to continue to be misled as to the issue of this case.

Your Honor, I'm going to object to this.

I will allow the comments, Mr. prosecutor, you may answer them.

So I'm going to ask you, ladies and gentlemen, to consider when the prosecutor, as is his right, speaks to you, and he may very well make some telling points, persuasive points, and I will not be permitted to get up again, maybe that's better because I talk so much, but I will not be able to get up and replied to anything he says, so I ask you people to remember carefully everything you have seen and heard in this case. I am not going to ask you for a verdict, I am going to ask you to consider the evidence, and to apply what you know to be the principles of justice in the case, apply the law and the judge will give it to you then to render the verdict that you consider to be just and fair. I ask you to consider, that Stephen Moore in the eyes of the law is not guilty, he is sick, and we have ways of dealing with that, and I assure you there will be ways of dealing with it, and I thank you for your time and your patience, for listening to all of this.

Thank you, Mr. Schutzer.

Go ahead, Mr. Prosecutor.

Thank you, Your Honor.

Ladies and gentlemen, when you came into this courtroom, you were asked several questions of me. One of the questions was, would you be able to fairly and unbiasedly separate a mental problem that either see or perceive, from the legal definition of insanity in the state of New Jersey, and would you be able to base your opinion and your judgment on the facts you heard testified to, and you all responded yes. There are several points at which I disagree with the defense, but that's not for me to do. You heard the testimony. I asked you to pay close attention to all of the evidence, to listen to all the testimony and to employ and use your common sense, because that's the most important tool you have in deciding this case. The question is not whether or not Stephen Moore from a disease of the mind, because ladies and gentlemen, that is a requirement just to get him into the box. Without a disease of the mind, he can't even be considered for the defense of insanity, and nobody refutes that. Nobody contests that.

The formula continues. It does not stop there, as the defense would have you believe. The basic, the most important element for is at the time of the commission of the crime did the defendant know the nature and quality of his act. Did he know that sticking a knife into the body of Donna Litchfield was going to produce suitable harm or death? That's all that means. It means no more.

And then we go on, you know that what he was doing was wrong. That's all that means. Did you know that society would not like him to do what he was doing, or that he simply should not do what he was doing, that it would be punishable, and these are the elements, these are the considerations that we get to. Now you are asked why didn't the state produce any witnesses. Well, ladies and gentlemen, Mr. Schutzer has it a little bit backwards. The State has the obligation of proving the crime. This state must show that certain acts, certain elements essential to the crime exist. That's our responsibility in every case, and that is the end of the state's responsibility unless the defense does something where takes further action that necessitates more.

In this case the defense is pleaded the defense of insanity. Do not, I beg you, confuse insanity with psychosis. We have had testimony as to the difference, and I believe even Dr. Latimer, reluctant as he was, admitted that they are not the same. They are simply not the same. A psychotic person can be responsible for his acts. He can know the nature and quality of his acts, just no man under a given set of circumstances may not be responsible. As Mr. Schutzer indicated, his arm is under the control of something else, he is not responsible for what the arm does, but a psychotic person also, can be responsible, and that is why the formula exists.

What normal person plans and premeditates the murder of another human being? It doesn't happen. It is not the normal run-of-the-mill thing. Dr. Schlesinger testified; the Boston strangler? Well, he knew what he was doing, therefore he is not insane under the law.

The only way that we can determine whether or not at the time of the commission of the act Stephen Moore knew the nature and quality of the act, he knew that what he was doing was wrong, is to examine what he in fact did. Dr. Kern tells us there is no possible way to know without looking at the acts the man performs. And I submit to you that Dr. Kern is the only, only credible, medical psychiatrist testimony we have heard, and we will talk about that a little later, because we are going through the case, and we are going to see what Stephen were dead, and we are going to be what that indicates based on our common sense, based on our own reasonableness, because again psychosis in is not enough.

Remember the formula, and let's apply some of the facts, let's apply all of the facts to the formula.

Stephen Moore loved Donna Litchfield. He visited her after his journey, which, by the way, the defense tries to construe at this wild ranting trip across the country, a man that worked for five or six years his mother testified that he was really getting worn down from work, why did you go on a trip? Good idea, you will say nobody knew where he was. His mother was getting cards from him, telephone calls she knew where he was.

What is so unusual about a single 26-year-old man with an independent source of income, deciding to travel across the country? Nothing. Absolutely nothing.

Mr. Moore returns, he needs his girlfriends, Donna Litchfield, there is testimony that Donna was getting fed up with Stephen not being around, not paying much attention to her, and she broke up with. I don't want to see you anymore. You don't treat me like a proper woman, just leave me alone, I don't want to see you anymore. Stephen is dejected. He goes to Sur City, he is depressed, and he is quiet that night, and he is thinking about Donna.

The important point, ladies and gentlemen, is he is thinking. He is planning, and he is plotting, this shows some cognitive process in and of itself. The next morning he wakes up, still quiet and depressed. What does he do? He goes to the old Dallas gas station and he gets the knife. Now Mr. Schutzer made a big to do about, well, you never saw the knife, it could have gone here, could have been there. The fact ladies and gentlemen, is that the knife was used for the operation of the gas station, that it was never needed, it was never missing. If It was missing, it would have been noticed. And Mr. Moore had not been near the gas station for some period of time. The only conclusion that can be drawn from that is that the knife was taken on 14 July, 1976, the day he deliberated, premeditated and planned the murder of Donna Lee Litchfield, knowingly, because he knew what he was going to do, he knew what he needed the knife for, he needed the knife to plunge into her body, and to cause her death.

He knew the nature and quality of the act that he had on his mind.

Just from the facts of what he was doing. He takes the knife and he drives to North Jersey. What does he do when he gets to North Jersey, ladies and gentlemen? Look at the evidence. Don't ignore it, because there is only three types of testimony, three possible ways of proving the case, one, eyewitness testimony, one is tangible evidence, and the other is circumstantial evidence. Circumstantial evidence is very important. We will talk about that as soon as we go over these documents.

And what happened at the bank? He arrives at the American National Bank, Mary nan Norton is there, here is her copy, and you will see, the tellers copy. When he is arrested, found to have the customer's copy of the withdrawal slip, and here is the signature card from the bank.

Now we are asked to believe that a man in a psychotic episode, a man out of touch with reality, is going to go into a bank, go up to a bank teller, and tell them I wanted thousand bucks cash, please. She sends him to a bank checker, who have to make sure everything is okay and that this guy isn't going to send a nut back to the cashier to say "give him 1000 bucks, it's all right."

Ladies and gentlemen, that's absurd. He knew he was doing. Rodney O'Dell said Stephen sometimes displayed periods of anxiety, sometimes was difficult, but it was quite obvious and there were other times when he knew exactly what he was doing. Rodney O'Dell, his friend. And I suggest to you, ladies and gentlemen, this day, Stephen Moore knew exactly what he was doing. He goes into the bank and takes out $1000. Why did he take out that thousand dollars, ladies and gentlemen? Pocket money? He took out that thousand dollars because he knew what he was going to do. He knew what that night he had with him was for, what he intended to do with it, and she was going to have to hot foot it back out across country, go pick up his Kawasaki in Arizona, wherever it was, and be gone.

He plans the crime, he planned his escape. Shows nothing more than cognitive process. He is thinking, and he knows what his intention is. He goes to the house where he last met Donna, her mother's house in Bloomfield. He rings the doorbell, Donna sister answers, is donna here? No, I think she's at her apartment. Okay, thank you. Are these the actions and the words of a man as the defense would make you believe who was operating under a psychotic rage, that had to kill Donna in this rage? He is not enraged, he is planning and plotting. He knows.

He leaves Bloomfield, with the knife, with his thousand dollars get away money, and he goes to Belleville. He arrived at the apartment in Belleville, he walked into the apartment. Now this girl who is supposed to be this fantastic threat to Stephen Moore's very existence, offers him something to eat and drink. Sits down in the kitchen, he says, oh, I will have something to drink. Is she a threat to his very existence? Is he panicked and enraged when he first sees her? No.

From the kitchen, Donna is cleaning her bathroom. The tiles are down; Valerie explained that to us, Donna had said if you want to talk to me, Steve, come into the bathroom, for at least five minutes before the girl comes out to get the more paper towels.

Now, ladies and gentlemen, the circumstantial evidence. For those of you who have children, if you walk into the kitchen and little Johnny is standing there and there's jam on his face and a jam on the kitchen table, open, is it necessary for you to see

Johnny had actually put his hand in an jar in order for you to know as a matter of fact that Johnny had gone jam jar? No. By what you see and buy what you know you can conclude it is a fact that Johnny had been in the jar.

Stephen Moore was in the bathroom with Donna Lee Litchfield five minutes. No psychotic rage bothering him then. But he had his knife with him, he was ready. He had his getaway money with him. He was ready. And isn't it fair and safe to conclude that he try Donna to go back out with him and she refused, and his crime went into process, and he kills Donna when she returns to not bathroom the second time, and Valerie heard the screams.

Now you are asked to look at these photographs and see how horrendous, how horrific, this crime is.

Well, ladies and gentlemen if this is a horrendous, horrific stabbing, and I don't know of any that is not, it is because Donna Lee Litchfield did not die easily. Not because of him, and his enraged state, but because of her, fighting for her life, fighting until the last drop of blood.

Look at the pictures. You will see them. Examine the wounds. Dr. Roy circled the wounds on the abdomen and chest the superficial wounds he had noted. Some don't even show. You will get a chance to see some of the autopsy photos that show the arms with the defense wounds. Defense wounds, Donna was fighting for her life, and that is why there are 69 stab wounds on this young girl, because she did not die easily. She refused to die easily.

Valerie here's the screams, and what is her initial reaction? She fears for the children. She runs out. First she thinks it's the kids, but that's not the kind of scream kids will make, fears for the children, and brings them out of the apartment, brings them to safety, and then she returns to the apartment, and starts to call the Belleville police but she didn't hear any more noise.

Now when she initially saw them in the bathroom, all she saw was Stephen coming down on her like this, and Donna fighting with her arms. She took a quick look and said, let me get these kids out of here. Stephen was killing Donna as she was bringing the children to the car. When Valerie returns, Donna was already dead. She assumes they had made up, and she canceled the phone call to the police. That assumption was wrong. You recall the door to the bathroom was open when Valerie looked, and she left the apartment when she returns, the bathroom door was closed. Again, reasonable assumption Mr. Moore saw that Valerie and the kids left the apartment, he knew it, he closed the door, and he was trying to clean up the mess from himself when the knock on the door came. "Who is it?" "It's me, who do you think it is?" He thought she had left, obviously surprised by the knock and the return of Valerie.

He opened the door, and what does he say? "Donna is dead." Did he not know the nature and the quality of his act? Did he not know that sticking that knife into Donna Lee Litchfield had caused her death? Yes, he did, he did by his own statement Valerie, Donna is dead. Same as saying, I know that the knife penetrated her body and caused her death.

Another thing, while we are talking about the photographs and the autopsy, Dr. Roy testified none of those wounds are post mortom. None of those wounds received by the victim happened after her death. Ladies and gentlemen, a crazy man reacting in a crazy rage? Once the victim stopped struggling is that going to stop him penetrating her with that knife? He knew exactly what he was doing. He knew exactly when he had killed Donna and he had to do nothing more and he knew it and he stopped. If he was insane, insane and psychotic are not the same, it he was insane, would he have stopped? Donna had been fighting with him, his rage would had built up; it is the rage defense would had expected you to believe, his rage would have increased, and he would have kept going, stabbing, but that's not what happened. He knew what his task was, his functioning was that day, and when he completed his act and he knew that Donna was dead, he had to know more to accomplish his purpose.

There is testimony further that Stephen Moore left that bathroom and went to the kitchen, there is testimony from various witnesses and they are some photographs that we will ask you to consider that have been put into evidence. Consider that Donna was in the tub cleaning the tub, filled up with water, stopped by her hair in the drain, and paper towels. You will be able to see how obvious that is from the police photographs and the knife was stuck underneath her body. He couldn't get it, you couldn't see down through the blood he water. So he left, he said let me get out of here, and he went to the kitchen. You will notice there are footprints in the bathroom, bloody footprints. You will notice there are areas of the kitchen floor showing radiators with blood spattered on them. By the way, is this our infamous window, infamous window that the defense would have you believe Stephen Moore climbed in and out of and that made him a psychotic? The window Valerie used to get in the apartment, the window that Donna used to get in the apartment because it was right by the parking lot and if you look you see the headlight of a car right by the window. Yet the defense initially tried to put in as some absurdity even more character, and traits. Observe the photograph more closely and you will see the circles where the firemen and police officers observed blood splatter. You will see the damp towel on the floor.

Stephen Moore went from the bathroom to the kitchen, and he started to wash the blood off of himself. Now Dr. Latimer says, and this has got to be the number one absurdity, he was cleaning his hands like a mechanic after he is done with his job. That's laughable, ladies and gentlemen, laughable he was getting the evidence of his guilt off of his body do what he did was wrong, and he knew he couldn't go walking around the streets bloodstained and strewn with blood, and he watched himself clean in that kitchen, and he did a very thorough job.

He walked out of the apartment and he went right past the firemen, hey you, did you call for help? He walked quickly toward his car with his head down, Joan Campbell testified. Now it's, the defense tries to imply there was hanky-panky with Joan Campbell because her statement was taken and in her statement it says white male. Ladies and gentlemen, not Barney Miller, where somebody sits there typing every word. Is a police officer trying to get the information down in a statement, and he is sitting there banging away like a little chicken, and she says, I saw a white guy come out of the apartment, and what does he use? He used white male. He used his language expressing her words. She saw the statement, that's exactly what I told the cop, there is nothing in there other than what is officer. Another little tricky ploy to try to make it look like the state is trying to create a diversion here.

The state is trying to show you the essential facts. Joan Campbell season come out of his car, come out of the apartment walked past the firemen, get into his car, and drive away. Dr. Latimer would have you believe driving 92 miles, taking $1000 get away money out of the bank, walking quickly to your car is not an indication that he tried to fool you. Watching the blood off himself is not an indication that he tried to hide what he had done. Ladies and gentlemen, that's an absurdity. He drives to Surf City, where he is seen by his friends sitting in the room, smoking an unusually large number of cigarettes. He was apprehensive, he knew what he did, he knew it was wrong, and he was sitting there apprehensively smoking those cigarettes.

The police came and arrested him. Well, he didn't try to escape, did he? Five guys from the Surf City police come in a small room, walk in, where is he going? If he tried to escape he would be crazy, but he didn't. He understood. He couldn't go anywhere. Sgt. Strain sees this man in the Surf City Police Department and reads him his Miranda warnings and they are read to him one by one. Then the sergeant says to Stephen Moore do you understand that you have the right to an attorney? His answer is yes. Cognitive thought process. He knows what is going on.

Do you want to make a statement without an attorney? No.

Do you understand these rights? Yes.

Sgt. Strain observed him for 3 ½ hours, and experienced police officer. And there was nothing to make him think that this man was an utterly absurd individual. There was testimony that there were times when Stephen Moore was perfectly all right. This was in fact one of those times. There was testimony that witnesses called by the defense who took the stand said they felt an obligation to the defendant. I ask you is that the type of witness that you want to guide you to reach an impartial verdict, a man that is helping to set up a defense? Ladies and gentlemen, the facts of this case proved the plan, premeditated and deliberate murder of Donna Lee Litchfield by Stephen Moore.

Dr. Latimer attempted to cloud those facts. Why? Because he ignored them. On cross-examination he is asked isn't it true that psychosis and insanity are not synonymous? And he is forced to say yes, forced to after I had to get psychology books were this out, look into them. He wouldn't tell us that of his own volition.

Psychosis and insanity are not the same, and that all of the respected authorities agree that you must know what happened at the time of the crime in order to determine whether or not the nature quality of the act, that you must know what happened at the time of the crime order to whether or not the man knew what he was doing was wrong. Yet in his exhaustive preparation of this defense neglected to do that one fundamental basic thing. What? Why? Because it did not, it did not sit well with his conclusion, ladies and gentlemen, he didn't know anything about this guy's background, when he didn't know anything about the facts of the crime, that the man did not know the nature and quality of his act and did not know that. He knew nothing, yet he made a conclusion within a high degree of medical certainty, which he himself finally had to admit was invalid.

What other invalid observation did he make? Well, the guy made a clang association. He said, "I didn't have a gun me." The doctor, read the sentence." Where had you gun?" Language barrier. Oh, yeah, I didn't think about that. What else did he think about? The defendant is portrayed as a very meek, mild mannered man around town. His friend, Mr. Miller testified that they were very close friends, very good friends. Mr. Miller thinks that everyone should carry clubs and bats in their car. Mr. Miller obviously likes to throw the hands when he goes into a bar. Would a meek, mild-mannered individual, at the defense has portrayed him, pal around with choose to be friends with, a violent, obviously aggressive individual such as Mr. Miller? The defense has told us not anymore than was absolutely necessary. They have told us nothing other than what we already know. Mr. Moore is a psychotic. That's not enough. The state has the burden of proving the case by all the evidence. The circumstantial evidence documentation.

While I am talking about that, consider the care that Mr. Moore took in cleansing the blood from his clothing. The clothes were picked up by the police in a wet condition in the back of his car, sent to the laboratory, and found to contain no blood. He did not only wash his hands and face, ladies and gentlemen, he washed all the blood out of these clothes. Does that sound like a man that did not know what he had done? There is no blood on his clothing, only a small portion on the shoelace of the sneakers. He was meticulous and cleaning the blood off of his clothing. He missed a small part of the shoelace of the sneakers, that is all.

Ladies and gentlemen, he knew, he knew. You will see the personal papers recovered from Mr. Moore. You will see the other items. Look at the evidence. The pictures are not pretty, but consider them with Dr. Roy's autopsy and one or two of the autopsy photos will show you that Donna Lee Litchfield fought for her life and that caused severe number of wounds, not any surge of energy which reasonably he would have had as soon as he walked into the apartment. Ladies and gentlemen, case is a case of planned, premeditated murder. All murders in the state of New Jersey are considered to be murder in the 2nd degree, unless and until such time the state presents evidence to you that either elevates it to murder in the 1ˢᵗ degree or reduces it to a homicide which does not apply to this case.

This is murder, knowing the nature and quality of the act, and what he had wrong. Mr. Moore played and plotted the murder of Donna Lee Litchfield. He is guilty of murder in the 1ˢᵗ degree, based on the facts as we have heard them testified to. Psychosis and insanity are not synonymous; deliberate, deliberate based on the facts you heard. Render a fair and impartial verdict, and evaluate because it's the defenses obligation to show by a preponderance of the credible evidence he did not know the nature and quality of his act at the time of the crime, ladies and gentlemen, Stephen Moore knew what he had done, keep in mind when he finally said," all right, I killed her you figured it out."

Don't leave any of the elements out, any of the facts. Examine them thoroughly, carefully, and you will have no trouble coming to a fair and just verdict, and that's all the state asks for. Thank you very much. Sorry for the time, Your Honor.

Thank you, prosecutor.

Verdict

The jury entered the courtroom with their verdict at 4 PM.

Mr. McTernan, would you please receive the verdict?

Members of the jury, have you agreed upon your verdict?

Yes, we have, sir.

Mr. Foreman, is your verdict unanimous?

Yes, it is.

Mr. Foreman, what is your verdict with regard to count one, willful deliberate and premeditated murder of Donna Litchfield?

Guilty.

Which degree of murder?

First degree.

With regard to count two, possession of a dangerous weapon, what is your verdict?

Guilty.

All right. Do you desire the jury to be polled?

Yes, Your Honor, I do.

On both counts, Schutzer or on each one separately?

On each separately, please.

Will you please pull the jury on the verdict of guilty of first-degree murder.

Members of the jury, the court has ordered the jury to be polled. As your name is called, each answer yes if this is your verdict, or not, if it is not your verdict.

With regard to count one- the jury was polled, each juror answered, yes.

Members of the jury, in the same manner you will be polled with regard to count two. If this is your verdict say yes, if no, say no. The Jury was polled, each juror answered, yes.

Ladies and gentlemen of the jury. I want to express my appreciation and thanks to you for your having sat beyond your usual tour of duty. I hope you have had an interesting and worthwhile experience. Are there any of you who have problems getting home, because the sheriff is standing by with vehicles if any of you have a problem. Will you gentlemen of the Sheriff staff please see to it that these jurors are escorted to their respective vehicles. I am going to excuse you now, wish you a happy Thanksgiving, and happy holidays for the end of the season. Thank you and good night.

The jury left the courtroom.

Will the exhibits please be returned to the parties who offered them.

Gentlemen, in view of the nature of the verdicts of the jury, at least so far as the sentence of the court is concerned, no presentence investigation is required. Will you please see to it that you have all the money you are entitled to, Mr. prosecutor.

Yes, I shall.

No presentence investigation report is necessary since the sentence is mandatory and the court's position is that the possession of a dangerous weapon at the time of the commission of the alleged offense with the homicide that was committed, and that there is no necessity for the court and the court will not impose a sentence as to that, so that I feel that it serves no purpose.

Now with respect to the courts sentencing, since no presentence investigation report is required under the law.

Prosecutor?

Your Honor, I would request the court to sentence immediately in that there is no presentence required, and the verdict of the jury is obvious.

Mr. Schutzer?

Your Honor, I would request that the court take some time to sentence Mr. Moore. I don't know whether the court has the right to do this, but I would ask that the court take some time to sentence him.

No time, get it over with, the verdict says guilty, how many years?

Mr. Moore, please refrain from speaking for a moment.

If the court is disposed toward a sentencing of Mr. Moore at this time, I would respectfully ask the court if a stay of a sentence pending appeal would be considered.

No appeal. I am going home.

Mr. Moore, please refrain from speaking.

This stay of appeal for what purpose, Mr. Schutzer?

Making an appeal.

Until sentence is imposed, you can't file a notice of appeal. So if you are considering filing a notice of appeal it might be more expeditious for you that the sentence is being imposed now rather than to delay it for several weeks or a month until my next sentence date.

All right. If the court is disposed to do that with the court's knowledge of my desire to appeal, perhaps sentence should be now and then I would ask the court upon the sentencing to consider my application.

What application are you making upon sentence?

When the court imposes sentence, I will make it at the proper time. Now is the court going to impose sentence?

Your Honor, I don't understand what Mr. Schutzer is saying. I would ask the court to impose sentence, the sentence is clear, it's mandatory under the law, I see no reason for delay.

Do you want to be heard on the sentence, Mr. Schutzer?

As I understand it, the sentence is life imprisonment, Your Honor. Do I have anything to say?

Well, the sentence with the life imprisonment, sentence on the alleged possession of a weapon, and I will give you the right of elocution as to the sentence the court should impose.

It is my understanding the court has merged the count of the possession of the weapon into the other count, into the count of first-degree murder. With that being the case, I would ask the court sentence the defendant alone on the first count.

Mr. Moore, do you want to say anything to me before I impose sentence?

Sentence me. Get it over with, judge. I tried everything I could, this is my lawyer, he did nothing for me, went through the whole proceedings.

Is there anything you want to say, Mr. Moore?

Nothing to say. I am asking with my two ears what did I do? I have no choice, I am innocence and you didn't bring in the body, I wanted the body in to see how it was killed and see what you are all talking about. Frankly, I don't know.

Your Honor.

Yes, Mr. Schutzer,

I am requesting something in line with what Dr. Latta mere has indicated to the court. I really would like to see for the time being Mr. Moore placed in Martland Medical Center and extensive neurological tests

Oh, no. The jury found him sane, Mr. Schutzer. This court isn't going to take action over the jury's verdict. That's a matter for the jury. And if he is sick the institution in Trenton, they know where to assign him. That's up to Mrs. Klein. They will settle that problem when he is in the institution that he is sent to thank you, gentlemen. A very well tried case.

End of hearing.

NOTE FROM THE AUTHOR

Word-of-mouth is crucial for any author to succeed. If you enjoyed the book, please leave a review online—anywhere you are able. Even if it's just a sentence or two. It would make all the difference and would be very much appreciated.

    Thanks!
    Tina

About the Author

Tina Ann Healey lives in Sparta, New Jersey with her husband and 2 children. Tina's passion is in advocating for the passing of Donna's Law, first in New Jersey, then nationwide. Donna's Law would remove the charge of Not Guilty by Reason of Insanity, making it more appropriately Guilty by Reason of Insanity.

Thank you so much for reading one of our **Biography / Memoirs**.

If you enjoyed our book, please check out our recommended title for your next great read!

Z.O.S. by Kay Merkel Boruff

"...dazzling in its specificity and intensity."

-C.W. Smith, author of *Understanding Women*

View other Black Rose Writing titles at
www.blackrosewriting.com/books and use promo code
PRINT to receive a **20% discount** when purchasing.

www.ingramcontent.com/pod-product-compliance
Lightning Source LLC
Chambersburg PA
CBHW052209090526
44584CB00016BA/1726